THE THREE WING

CLIFF EMENY'S STORY

TOM WOODS

WITH THE ASSISTANCE OF

JOAN EMENY

Zenith Publishing

National Library of New Zealand Cataloguing-in-Publication Data

Woods, Tom, 1931–
The Three Wings: the story of Cliff Emeny / Tom Woods
Includes bibliographical references.
ISBN 1-877365-11-4
1. Emeny, Cliff. 2.New Zealand. Royal New Zealand Air Force
–Biography. 3. Airmen – New Zealand –Biography.
4. World War, 1939-1945 – Medals. I. Title.
940.548193–dc22

ZENITH
PUBLISHING
Zenith Publishing
PO Box 752
49-55 Rimu Street extn
New Plymouth
New Zealand

www.zenithpublishing.co.nz

First Printed 2004

Cover by Shane Emeny

Contents

ACKNOWLEDGEMENTS

Many people have helped to make *The Three Wings* fly. It would never have started, of course, without the readiness of Cliff to share with me the turbulent years he lived through between 1939–1945. His wife Joan helped in so many ways. Whenever I saw her she would invariably have found another valuable paper or address or photograph that helped me to fill out the gaps in the story.

My thanks to Cliff's grandson Shane Emeny, who designed the cover of the book as a mark of the love and respect he had for his grandfather.

I felt very privileged, while writing the book, to have spoken by telephone or to have met personally several people who feature prominently in Cliff's story. First and foremost is Cliff's Canadian navigator Johnny Yanoto who shared with his pilot in so many life and death situations.

Secondly, to Ozzie Osboldstone (Wellington), Sylvia Heaven (née Edwards, Wellington) and Ian Walker (Auckland) my grateful thanks for sharing so readily with me your personal papers and your wartime memories.

Thirdly, my special thanks to Diana and Karnig Thomasian (United States) for their initial encouragement to me to get started and for the material they sent to me. Included in this material were some pencil sketches of the Rangoon Prison. Unfortunately I could not make contact (either by telephone or by letter) with the artist, George A Ratcliffe (46961661) 2nd Battalion KOYLI to ask his permission to include several of his brilliant and moving pencil sketches, which so graphically illustrate the dreadful conditions of the Rangoon POW prison.

I feel these sketches are not only works of art but are historically significant so I have taken the liberty of including several where appropriate.

The Tauranga Senior Net was a great help to me in learning the basic skills of the computer.

Finally, to my wife Patricia, who never doubted that one day I would complete what I had started and that eventually I would begin to understand and master the language and workings of my computer – thank you for everything!

Tom Woods
Tauranga
September 2004

PREFACE

One night a week for several months in the winter of 1999 I met Cliff Emeny to record the events of his early working life and his wartime experiences as he told them to me.

Cliff left school on his 13th birthday to make his own way in the world of the Depression of the 1930s. Within the next six years he had undergone training in the Territorial Army, studied by correspondence Aerodynamic Engineering and saved 450 pounds, enough to buy, if he had wished, a moderately priced house in Wellington. To cap it all off, in 1938 he worked his passage to the other side of the world. By his 19th birthday he had shown the initiative and determination that would stand him in such good stead in the years ahead.

He was just one of the millions of ordinary young men who became involved in what is now known as World War II. In this war civilians became as much part of the front line as the military. It became total warfare and this total warfare unleashed a horror and brutality and indifference to human life that resulted in the death of 50 million people – 20 million soldiers and 30 million civilians.

It is impossible for those born a generation or more after these events to visualise the scale of mobilisation and the subsequent deaths and suffering that followed. Even the numbers that perished in prisoner-of-war camps and the number that struggled to stay alive in these camps are beyond our capacity to comprehend. There were 300 000 Allied prisoners in Japanese camps alone.

Cliff Emeny was one of the millions of young men caught up in the horrors done in the name of war.

He heard the declaration of war while he was in London and a few weeks later he found himself serving as seaman-gunner on the *Wellington Star* making her maiden voyage to New Zealand. It was while serving on this ship that he saw ships torpedoed in the Atlantic and he himself first came under enemy fire.

So during the winter months of 1999, Cliff told me the story of the part he played in World War II. In this war he earned the right to wear the 'wings' of an air gunner, a radar observer and a pilot, and he saw action in the three disciplines he had qualified in. No other airman in any Air Force has to my knowledge, earned this distinction. What makes this achievement even more remarkable is the fact that he had qualified as a gunner in the pre-war Territorial Army and then in the opening months of the war served as a seaman-gunner. Within a few years he had served in the Army, the Merchant Navy and the Air Force.

I guess that his family must have heard many of the stories he told me. Perhaps they heard them more than once because he related them to me so fluently without the aid of notes or a diary. I am aware there are some stories his family heard that he didn't tell me. He told me more than once that the reason he was relating the account of his life was so his grandchildren would know what he did during the war and what his thoughts were of the utter senselessness of war. Appreciating what he had experienced, they would perhaps better understand their grandfather.

He was a natural raconteur. Sometimes I found myself laughing at what I heard while at other times I was moved to tears. Sometimes as he talked I became aware he was taking the 'Mickey' out of the stupidity that often confronted him in the RAF. Sometimes as he remembered a painful memory his voice broke and he would pause to regain his composure.

In March 1996 TV3 produced a documentary of his experiences as a Japanese prisoner of war in Rangoon. So barbarous was the treatment depicted in that re-enactment it seemed unbelievable to those of us watching over 50 years later. I found it even more moving when he personally told me the story.

His 80th birthday was celebrated with his family and friends at the RSA clubrooms in New Plymouth. It was a '40s evening' and we were asked to dress appropriately. Cliff came dressed in his old RAF uniform. It fitted him as if it had been tailor-made the week before. That evening he told us how when he took his old uniform out of its suitcase memories came flooding back. He then told us of an experience none of his family had heard before. It was the account of how in Canada he had visited the families of the members of 409 Squadron who had been killed. It was a very moving and touching account. Those who heard it could never again imagine that war was glamorous or a great adventure.

After he was shot down Cliff did not pilot a plane again until nearly 50 years later, when on his 64th birthday, his son Brett shouted him a solo flight in a glider and then it was all on again. With Brett as his instructor he soon regained his old flying skills.

Cliff delighted in flying Brett's two-seater Vampire Jet. (The Vampire was the next development of de Havilland after the Mosquito and Cliff felt very much at home in its wooden cockpit.) On Father's Day 2000, Cliff had his last flight with Brett. He took off from New Plymouth airport and flew around the mountain. Before landing he did a 'buzz and break' around the Control Tower at 400 mph, 50 feet above the ground. A month later he died.

It was the winter following his death that I began the work of transcribing the tapes. Then followed the longer and more difficult task of learning how to use a computer so I could type up the notes I had transcribed and arrange them in chronological order as faithfully as I could to the original. Some sections I was forced to rewrite because in his enthusiasm in telling the story, structure and grammar were forgotten. Throughout the writing of it I constantly reminded myself that this was Cliff's story, not mine. His humour, his sense of the ridiculous, his achievements, the pain and the agony were his.

The events he described to me had happened nearly 60 years before the telling but they were clearly etched on his mind and he told them as he remembered them.

PRE-WAR YEARS

I left school on my 13th birthday in 1933. On that day I got my first job working on a farm at Patiki in North Taranaki. It was hard work; milking and clearing out swamps with horse and bullock teams for five shillings a week, three meals a day and somewhere to sleep.

Early in 1937, when I was just 17, I enlisted in the Queen Alexandra's Mounted Rifles' Territorial Force. I gave my age as 19. Because I could ride, shoot and handle packhorses I was trained as a Vickers machine gunner. A packhorse carried the gun while another horse carried the ammunition.

The Army couldn't find a uniform small enough to fit me nor could they find a hat that would not slide down over my face. My sister Gladys took one look at me in my uniform, told me to

Mounted Rifles, Machine Gunner 1937/38.

Army School, Trentham.

take it off, and then she unstitched it, cut it up and re-sewed it and it was a good fit.

Eighteen months later I was invited to enrol in the army's 'Special Reserve Course' at Trentham Army School. This was a six-month course that ended at the time of the Munich Crisis. All those on the course were offered officer training in the New Zealand Army but when the authorities found out I was only 18 they deferred me for a further two years.

After leaving Trentham I went to Wellington to find myself a job. I called at the State Replacement Service and was given a six-week job at the Wellington Gentlemen's Club. This job was the greatest break that could ever have happened to me at 19. It introduced me to a world I had never experienced or even thought existed. It introduced me to a group of people that normally I would never have associated with.

I was paid 30 shillings a week and received one free meal a day at the club. More important than the pay and working conditions, however, I was taught something in that club I would never have learnt in any other job. I was taught the proper way of doing things: the proper way to set a table, to serve drinks, to dress, to speak to people. These six weeks were to prove invaluable to me in the years to come.

After the gentleman's club I found work at the Ngauranga Freezing Works. The work was hard but highly paid. The conditions were very different but I liked the men I was working with and they seemed to like me. By the end of the season I was earning nine pounds a week; that was three times the normal wage at that time and I could do any job on the chain. After work I enjoyed a three-course meal at the railway dining room, and would then, instead of catching a tram, walk along the wharves, up Willis Street and home to Brooklyn.

On my way home I would often see a group of men on the wharf. One evening I went over to see what they were doing.

Someone yelled, "That ginger-headed boy go with that gang" and suddenly I found that I had a job as a casual wharfie. I worked there a couple of nights a week. The work wasn't too hard and the pay, especially the overtime rates, was good.

Then I got a job at a café opposite the Majestic Theatre. I worked there on Wednesday and Friday evenings.

For the first time in my life I was earning big money so I could afford to buy good clothes. My cousin managed a mercer's shop and I quickly became one of his best customers. Every time I visited my cousin I bought a pair of socks, a shirt, a new suit and finally a second-hand dinner suit for six pounds.

By the age of 19 I had saved 450 pounds, enough to buy a house in Wellington in 1938. I had completed, by correspondence, a course in aerodynamics, was corresponding regularly with overseas pen pals and was leading a very active social life. Besides dancing I could play a good game of tennis and I enjoyed boating. I couldn't help thinking that in the six years since leaving school, the North Taranaki farm boy had come a long way.

The family had moved from Wellington to North Taranaki when I was four. My father had worked as a blacksmith in the coal-fired station at Evans Bay but he always wanted to try his hand at farming. Two years later, in 1926, we moved yet again to a leasehold farm at Te Kiri. It was some of the poorest land in Taranaki, high up on the southern slopes of the mountain. Stones, boulders, blackberry and bush covered most of the land with very little grass. Life on that farm was bleak and hard, with back-breaking work and the family was desperately poor. How different to the life I now lived six years later in Wellington.

One night I had my dinner as usual at the Railway Station dining room and then set off to walk around the wharf on my way home. I was passing a ship when two officers rushed down the gangplank and stood in front of me and asked, "Hey young fellow, how would you like a trip to England?" Two stewards had jumped ship and they were offering me a paid trip to England as a bathroom steward. It didn't take me long to make up my mind. They gave me 50 minutes to get back to the ship.

I ran to the gates of the wharf and hailed a taxi to take me to my 'digs'. I phoned the foreman of the freezing works to explain what was happening, packed my clothes in a suitcase, paid my rent, said goodbye to my landlady, grabbed another taxi and was back at the ship within an hour.

The world of 1938 was very different to that of today. You didn't need a passport – it was an open, free world. You could come and go as you pleased. I just got on the *Port Caroline* and sailed to England without a thought.

The *Port Caroline* was a ship of 9 000 tons. It carried 36 passengers and a cargo of wool. We ran into a terrible storm rounding Cape Horn and the deck cargo of wool was washed overboard. We re-coaled at Montevideo and then on to London.

When the ship reached London the captain asked me if he could make a deal with me. He told me that he had been a captain for 11 years and he could never enjoy an uninterrupted leave in London without having to return to the ship. All the crew, except the engineers, would be granted shore leave. He asked me if I would remain on board to look after the meals for the engineers. I was to cook their breakfast, prepare their lunch and spend the rest of the day as I liked, because in the evening the engineers always went into the city.

The captain made an agreement that if I would do this for him when the ship called in at Plymouth, Bristol, Liverpool and Glasgow, he would give me letters of introduction to youth groups and various people I could call in on when I was in these cities. I agreed and found the captain was as good as his word. His letters opened all kinds of social doors to me, a young New Zealander feeling his way on his first overseas experience.

My sister Gladys had taught me to dance and I discovered that in the world of the 1930s no matter where you were in the English-speaking world, there was always a dance where you could meet young people of your own age.

When the ship reached Glasgow and the crew was paid off the captain expressed his personal thanks to me by giving me a First Class Steward's Book that he signed and certified. At the time I didn't realise the value of this gift or its importance.

I bought a four-speed bike for a pound and found I could travel for two and sixpence a day. I could stay in a youth hostel for a shilling and buy a light meal for ninepence and a full meal for a shilling. When I got out of a city and saw a farmer working in his fields I would stop and talk to him. I would tell the farmer I had been brought up on a farm in New Zealand and this usually resulted in an invitation to look over his farm and to stay a day or two. When it came time to leave the farmer would usually send me off to meet some other farmer in another county so I criss-crossed England from one side to the other. I cycled through a rural pre-war England that was changed forever by the war.

Seven weeks after leaving Glasgow I arrived in London with 10 pounds in my pocket. Before leaving New Zealand I had arranged for my bank book to be sent to my young brother Dick who lived in Auckland. Dick had rheumatic fever when he was 14 and I had always taken it upon myself to look after him and then later find work for him. Unfortunately for me, just after I had left New Zealand the Government couldn't pay a five million pound loan back to the British Government. Exchange controls were imposed and private citizens could only send five pounds maximum out of the country at any one time.

When I went to the bank to withdraw some of the 450 pounds I had entrusted to Dick I found only five pounds left. Young Dick was musical, with a bright, outgoing personality. He had always longed to own a piano accordion so he went and bought the best there was with my money and then spent the rest on what he thought he needed. I never really begrudged his spending spree. He died of heart failure in 1942.

With 10 pounds to my name I went off to see the New Zealand High Commissioner about getting a job. I was ushered into Mr Jordan's office and over a cup of tea was told that there were three million other unemployed in England, all looking for work. After hearing how I had arrived in England, the High Commissioner suggested I make enquiries at the placement office on the wharf.

I walked down to the wharf, found the office and went in. The man behind the counter asked, "Show me your book." I showed him the book given to me by the captain of the *Port Caroline*.

"Hell," he said, "Where did you bloody well steal this? You are only 19. How long have you had this book? It takes 20 years to get a book like this."

I was quite indignant and replied, "Look, I'm not a steward but I worked my way from New Zealand to England on the *Port Caroline* and the captain gave it to me when he paid me off. He said I had earned it and he signed and certified it. He wouldn't have given it to me unless he thought I earned it."

"Well, I have never seen anyone your age with a book like this. But never mind. There is actually a ship right here looking for a chap like you who has got this book. You had better go down and see about it. It is a cruise ship that goes around the English, Irish and Scottish coasts on a three-week trip. The chief steward is a chap named Glover. He is a tough character but go and see if he will give you a job."

I made my way to the ship concerned. I was wearing my blue suit my cousin had sold me in Wellington. The ship was about 2 500 tons and carried 70 passengers. I found Mr Glover in the lounge and recognising him by the description given to me, walked up to him and asked, "Mr Glover?"

"Yep. Who are you?"

"Emeny is my name."

"Well you have a funny voice. Where do you come from?"

"New Zealand."

"Oh. Well what do you want?"

"Well I have come for this job you have."

"Right," he said, "Let me see your book." As soon as he saw it he asked, "And when did you bloody well go to sea? In your napkins?"

"No" I said, "not exactly."

"No" he snorted, "you'd be no good. Look at you in a suit. You look like an American millionaire spending your silly, damned father's money. You're a dandy. I'd be wasting my time with you."

"Well Mr Glover, I didn't come here to be insulted. I came here to apply for a job. If you took the time to find out about me I would be happy to tell you but if you go on insulting me you can keep your job and stuff it." And I turned and walked away. I got halfway across the lounge when he yelled,

"Hey! Hey! Come back here young fella. People don't talk to me like that. Tell me something about yourself."

Dressed in best suit, London 1939.

So I told him what I had done. He grunted a couple of times, shook his head, and asked me some more questions and then said, "All right, I'll take you on but I bet you I'll have to sack you at the first port we come to. I can't see how you will be any good. Bring your things down. We will be gone tomorrow."

By the time we had reached Glasgow he and I had become the best of mates and got on wonderfully well together. Perhaps it was because I was a good worker, got on well with the passengers and each time he got drunk at night I would put him to bed and take him a cup of tea first thing each morning.

Mr Glover lived in Glasgow and he took me to his home. Living next door was the Watson family. They were a tragic family. Mrs Watson was a widow with four boys and one girl. The father had been an engineer who had worked for 15 years in America to earn enough money for the family to move there too. He was granted American citizenship and in 1939 he came back to Glasgow to pack up his family and take them to America but he caught pneumonia and died. His widow was left to bring up her five children. Two of the boys were bakers, the eldest was a shipbuilder and in the Territorial Army. The youngest, Jimmy, was at school and his sister was a year or so older. I came to regard the Watson family as my home away from home. Jimmy and I still keep in touch to this day.

Again, as far as a job was concerned I had fallen on my feet. The cruise ship sailed from London to Bristol and across to Belfast and would spend a day at each place where the passengers would see the sights and enjoy themselves. Belfast then had a huge shipbuilding yard that was dominated by an aircraft carrier and cargo liner being built. Little did I know that a few months later I was to see this great cargo liner torpedoed in the Atlantic.

Chapter 2

DECLARATION OF WAR

The ship was in London on the outbreak of war and was immediately requisitioned by the Navy, so I was jobless again. I was walking down a street in London when I heard over a radio the Prime Minister make the Declaration of War.

The moment the Prime Minister finished his announcement the air raid sirens sounded and everyone rushed into the shelters expecting a massive bombing raid that would blow the world apart. Forty minutes later the all clear sounded and nothing had changed. That night there was a colossal thunderstorm over London that lasted for a couple of hours. With the noise of the thunder and the flashes of lightning it seemed an omen of the war to come.

I received notice from New Zealand House to make myself available to transfer to an English artillery regiment but no way was I going into the British Army. I had experienced enough of British regular force NCO instructors at Trentham to last a lifetime and I was not prepared to subject myself to that experience again.

In 1928 Kingsford Smith's Southern Cross had arrived in Wellington when I was eight. I was given a free ride in that famous aeroplane and the memory of that event had remained firmly in my mind so I decided to apply for the Air Force. I was told that the Air Force was so swamped with reservists and volunteers that it would take six months to clear the backlog and to come back then.

I decided to visit the Watson family in Glasgow. I hitched a ride on a truck and arrived there next morning. Two days later the eldest Watson boy left in the Expeditionary Force for France. Two days later the other two brothers announced that they were going to join the Navy. I had already decided that I wasn't going into the Army and as the Air Force didn't want me for another six months I decided I would join the Navy with them.

The three of us went off to the recruiting office together. The two brothers were bakers so they were put straight into catering. When the recruiting officer came to me and saw the record of my Territorial Army training he told me I would be placed as a gunner on a merchant ship. Each merchant ship needed three men trained in artillery. "We have a ship down there with a machine gun on board but no one knows how to use it. You will be given a 10-day conversion course training on naval guns and you will go on board that ship as a gunner/steward," I was told.

The ship was the *Wellington Star* and carried 55 passengers. It had diesel engines with a top speed of 28 knots and was on its maiden voyage. It was armed with a Vickers machine gun and one 6-inch and one 4-inch gun. When the guns were test fired the 4-inch fired all right but the 6-inch, mounted on the poop, split the poop wide open. The mounting was not strong enough to hold it when it was fired. The ship put into Liverpool to get the poop repaired and strengthened.

It took 10 days to repair the ship and we left without escort. It was known that the pocket battleship *Admiral Sheer*, a couple of German cruisers and an unknown number of submarines were in the Atlantic. At this early stage of the war no organised convoys had been formed. Several days out to sea the *Wellington Star* found herself sailing in company with three other ships. Two of them were barely visible on the horizon but the third ship was the cargo liner I had seen being built in the yards at

10

Belfast. About midday this ship seemed to veer away from the *Wellington Star* and we parted company. At two in the afternoon there was a tremendous flash and a loud explosion as the ship was torpedoed.

The *Wellington Star* turned and went as fast as it could go in the opposite direction. A quarter of an hour later a second explosion was seen. One of the ships on the horizon had been hit with a torpedo. The *Wellington Star* then headed out on the great circle journey up to Iceland and then south again. It took us three and a half weeks to cross the Atlantic as we zigzagged the whole way.

The Captain of the *Wellington Star* was a boozer and the first mate wasn't much better. The gossip amongst the crew was that they boozed their way across the Atlantic. The second mate, a fine man and a good officer, really ran the ship.

Seaman Gunner, 1939/40.

The ship had four or five crew members on each side of the ship on submarine lookout. The second mate decided he couldn't really spare men for lookout duties as well as all the general work and practising on the guns. With 40 adults on board, the mate suggested adult male passengers do submarine lookout on a rostered basis of two hours each. Despite the obvious danger to the ship from submarines, they refused to do it. They were

European Jewish refugees on their way to New Zealand. The mate's response was to withdraw all services from them. No crew member would wait on the tables, prepare the baths, or make the beds, no one would do anything for them. They could do it all because the crew was too busy defending the ship. Despite having seen two ships sunk the passengers seemed to think the war couldn't or wouldn't touch them.

We gradually got further and further across the Atlantic. One morning the lookout yelled he could see smoke. The ship turned away from it but it gradually got closer and closer. Without warning a great shell exploded in the sea about a mile behind us. It was the *Admiral Sheer*. The engineers wound the ship's speed up to its maximum 28 knots. The *Admiral Sheer*, that great pocket battleship, chased us all that night and all the next day. Our top lookout could just see her as a speck far off on the horizon. The next morning the battleship fired another shell that landed half a mile behind us but at midday she gave up and turned away. We had sent several signals to the Admiralty about what was happening and the Admiralty had replied telling us that several battleships were hurrying to our aid. We assumed that the Admiralty's messages were entirely fictitious – sent to bluff the Germans.

We went straight on towards the United States, made landfall at Florida and then next morning set out for Jamaica. It was on this leg of the voyage that I happened to look closely at one of the four big J locomotives carried as deck cargo. There on the front was the plate that read 'New Zealand Railways'. This was the first time I knew that I was returning to New Zealand.

When I was 16 I started corresponding with a Jamaican girl pen pal and we had continued to write regularly to each other. I let her know that I was arriving on the *Wellington Star* and asked if she could make contact with me while the ship was in Jamaica. She arrived at the ship the night we berthed. I invited her on board and took her to see the captain who gave me four days' leave. Floe and I spent four great days sightseeing together.

During the war she wrote to me regularly. She went to work in the New Zealand Embassy in Washington. There she met Walter Nash, the New Zealand Minister of Finance. Another young New Zealander was also corresponding with Floe. He worked in the dispatch department of Whitcombe and Tombs in Wellington. He owned a little dinghy and shot her a line about the boat he owned. The two of them started writing love letters to each other and decided they wanted to get married. Floe arranged through Walter Nash to get a free passage to New Zealand to marry this chap. She wrote and told me all about this when I was in Burma.

So we continued on and finally arrived in New Zealand. My great desire was to serve my country in the Air Force, but before I could do this I knew I had to make my peace with the Army.

Chapter 3

THE AIR FORCE

When the *Wellington Star* arrived back in New Zealand, the Army, who had been looking everywhere for me, met me off the ship. They decided I could have a few days' leave and I discovered that I had arrived home a few days before my eldest brother's wedding. The family had no idea I was back in New Zealand. I hired a private aeroplane to fly me from Wellington to the Hawera Aero Club and from there I phoned the family and asked for someone to pick me up. My brother was so excited that I was home for his wedding and we had a great family reunion and a great time.

After the wedding I returned to Wellington to make my peace with the Army. I was 19 at that time. I spoke to Major Weir, who was in charge of the regiment. He was very angry when I told him that I would not rejoin the Army as I was happy in the Merchant Navy, and if I couldn't stay in that service I would like to go into the Air Force.

"Look! You are going to do as you are bloody well told. You are a member of the New Zealand forces. We are going to put you straight into the Officers' Training Corp because you have already qualified for that. We want you right now!"

"No. I don't intend ever to serve in the Army," I replied.

"I tell you flatly. If you don't do as you are damned well told we will put you in jail," was his response.

"Well, Sir, you will not win that way. I'm already fighting in the war. I've already seen action. I've been out in the world since a boy of 13 and I've learnt to think for myself. I know what I want and I know where I am going."

So we argued each time we met. On the fifth occasion he really became exasperated and said, "Go into the bloody Air Force then. You are a bloody rebel and we don't want your type in the Army. The Air Force can have you!"

"Thank you Sir. Would you mind transferring me straight away?"

"Yes. Right. I'll do it right away."

I was given a week's leave after which I reported to Levin to do my basic training. This was the first course run at Levin and I was the only one on the course with military experience.

It was at Levin that I first met Joan, whose mother was a member of the Women's Division. It was the Women's Division who arranged dances for the boys in the camp. I went to this particular dance and noticed this young girl sitting with a distinguished looking lady who I later found out was her mother. I nervously approached and asked Joan for a dance. Later in the evening she invited me home for Sunday dinner and it was then that I met the family of my future wife.

In our training we were divided into squads and each squad member took a turn at commanding the squad for a week. The man appointed for squad leader the last week at Levin let it go to his head. He threw his weight around and yelled and shouted as if he was at least a sergeant major. When we were packing up to go to Ohakea he was chasing everyone around and yelling and giving orders so I said to him, "Just cool it off fellow. Just leave people alone. Don't yell and shout. You are acting like an idiot."

He threw a punch at me. Instinctively I threw one back at him that hit him on the nose. Unfortunately his nose wouldn't stop bleeding and he had to be taken to the medical officer. As a result I was arrested and taken to Ohakea in the Black Maria. At least I got a ride by myself and wasn't crowded in a truck with a load of others.

When we arrived at Ohakea I was put in the guardroom and had to wait three hours before I was taken before the adjutant. The Charge Sheet was written out and stated: 'he struck his squad commander in the face and broke his nose.'

Fortunately, the adjutant was human and asked, "What was the reason for this, Emeny?" I told him how this chap was bullying everyone around, how he had thrown a punch at me and how he had got his nose broken. "Well, if that is the case I don't think you should arrive at this place with a black mark against your name. We will just forget it."

We were at Ohakea for gunnery training, flying in those fabric and strut 'string bag' monsters called Vildebeests (the Vildebeest was a deer in Africa). This plane had been designed as a torpedo bomber and had a tremendously long wing. They were quite big aircraft and were meant to carry a torpedo underneath

The Vickers Vilderbeeste 111 was ordered by the New Zealand Government in 1933. When delivered in 1935 it was based initially at Hobsonville and Wigram but all were transferred to Wigram in 1937 to equip the flight training school. All 39 of the RNZAF Vilderbeestes had been scrapped by 1944.

(Royal New Zealand Airpower (Page 21) Matthew Wright Reed)

them. Its radial engine, when it was idling, just ticked over so it was possible, we were told, for a man to walk through the turning propeller without being touched. Its landing speed was only about 30 to 35 mph and its top speed about 90 mph. It cruised at 75 to 80 mph. It was real World War I stuff.

Ohakea could be quite windy and if the wind exceeded 35 mph the plane couldn't land. The pilot would fly it up to the hangar and the ground crew would rush up and grab the wings and when the pilot cut the motor it would settle to the ground.

The Vildebeest had a Lewis gun in the rear cockpit and we practised on this gun mainly against targets on the ground. The aircraft was fitted with a solenoid that automatically stopped the gun as it traversed so the bullets wouldn't hit the tail. On one occasion we were flying up the coast firing at targets and unfortunately for me the solenoid didn't work and I put a burst right through the tail. We were flying at about 100 feet and the old Vildebeest just rolled toward the water. The pilot yelled, "Throw everything out! Throw it out!" I had the gun off its mount in a moment and it, together with the ammunition, was over the side and gone. The pilot regained control, took it around, and landed safely.

I found myself on a charge of 'loss of His Majesty's equipment – one empty drum'. I was fined 10 shillings and confined to barracks for a week. I thought this grossly unfair as I only did what I was told.

Ohakea trained us well and the programme lasted for a month.

We were given six days' final leave. I went home and spent a couple of days with my parents. My older brother loaned me his Singer to drive to Karapiro to spend time with my sister Gladys and her husband on their sheep farm. At the end of my leave I set off at dawn to drive back to New Plymouth to attend a farewell social and dance for me that evening. The road

17

between Otorohanga and Te Kuiti was metalled and very bendy. Rounding a bend I met a car travelling on my side of the road. The driver was asleep at the wheel. Both cars crashed together and when the dust settled I found the driver of the other car was unconscious with a broken jaw and both wrists broken. I lifted him out of the car and waited for someone to come and phone the police to report the accident.

The police arranged for someone to drive me to New Plymouth to attend my farewell function. I enjoyed the evening and left next morning by train for Wellington.

My train stopped at Palmerston North and who should get on but Joan, the girl I had met at the dance. We chatted away until she got off at Levin. The train arrived in Wellington in the mid-afternoon. That night I caught the overnight ferry to Lyttelton and was soon at Wigram air station. In four days we were equipped to go overseas.

On 23 March 1940, 50 of us boarded the *Akaroa* to travel via the Panama Canal to England. Soon after boarding we had a sick parade. When the doctor reached me he asked, "What have you been doing? Have you been in an accident lately?"

"Yes Sir, I have. I was in a motor car accident."

"I can see you have had a knock. You have concussion. You are as pale as a ghost so I am going to admit you to hospital."

One of the first class staterooms had been converted

Off to War March 1940.

18

into a 'hospital' and I was kept there under observation for five days. I was the only patient and at the end of five days no one suggested I should move so I travelled to Canada first class.

We sailed across the Pacific and called in at Pitcairn Island and then on to the Panama Canal. When the ship stopped at Panama City all the boys were determined to get off and see the sights. This was the first time they had been out of New Zealand and the ship's crew had told them Panama City was a place that had to be experienced. Unfortunately, orders were given that no one was permitted to go on shore.

Just before dusk a small ship berthed alongside the *Akaroa*. It was Admiral Bryd's expedition going south. I had met the captain and mate of this ship in England when I was working on the cruise ship. I got out my torch and in Morse asked if I could visit them. They gave me a very warm welcome and later in the evening decided to take me into the city to see the sights. Meanwhile, the other boys still aboard the *Akaroa* were desperate to get into the city but all who had tried were arrested as they tried to leave the ship. Next morning they were fined and sentenced to extra exercises in the boiling sun.

We got through the Canal just as the Germans attacked Norway so were diverted to Cuasaga, a beautiful island. Several German ships, which had been seized by the British at the outbreak of war, were anchored there. Cuasaga had the most amazing clear water. You could see 40 feet down. After a few days' delay we set sail for Halifax to join a fast convoy to England.

At Halifax we were transferred to a Castle Line ship. As soon as we got on board I approached the officer in charge of the guns, told him of my gunnery experience, and that I would be willing to join the gun crew for the voyage. He gladly accepted my offer. He was even more pleased to accept my offer to do night duty. After seeing ships torpedoed in the Atlantic I felt I would rather be on deck at night than down below.

The convoy set out and on the third day we were hit by a ferocious storm that scattered the vessels. Our ship was the fastest in the convoy and our captain decided to go it alone. We sailed on, zigzagging across the Atlantic. We saw nothing and sailed up the English Channel a few days before the Germans attacked Holland and Belgium.

And so I was back in England again. I had left a few months previously as a gunner on a merchant ship. I returned as an air gunner in the New Zealand Air Force unaware of what was ahead of me.

Chapter 4

THE ROYAL AIR FORCE

When we landed we were sent to a place called Uxbridge, a receiving depot for RAF servicemen. Uxbridge was where I had been at the beginning of the war when I had tried to join the Air Force.

As soon as the Germans attacked in Europe the authorities decided that what military forces they had around London should be deployed at airfields and other strategic points. We were sent to a film studio in case parachutists dropped in. It was a beautiful place but had no strategic value that we could see. No films were being made but there was a lovely outdoor pool that the boys made good use of. We had been there a couple of weeks, quite enjoying the life, when I was recalled to Uxbridge and told, "We badly need air gunners as a lot have been lost over France. Your records show that you are a qualified air gunner and so we have decided you will have to defer your training as a pilot as you are badly needed as a gunner. You will be sent to 264 Squadron at Cambridge. The 264 Squadron had heavy losses over Dunkirk." Four other New Zealanders were sent there with me.

264 Squadron, Air Gunner Duxford.

When I arrived the senior gunnery officer said to me, "Well, you don't need much training. You are fully trained now. All we have to do is convert you from Vickers and Lewis guns to Browning machine guns."

I was given two days on Brownings. At the end of that time I could assemble it blind-folded. I was taken into a hangar where there were some wires on a wall and they gave me two sessions of two hours each operating a turret following the wires. The following day they sent me up with a pilot who had lost his gunner and was desperate to get back into operations. He was a very small man and the son of an insurance millionaire. He was popular because he tended to splash his money around a bit, particularly at the bar. He had a little MG that he drove like a maniac.

We went up and fired against a drogue (a target towed by another plane). He was supposed to come in at 200 yards and 100 yards but he came right in to 50 yards so the drogue was shredded with bullets from the four Browning machine guns that fired 2,800 rounds a minute.

We landed and taxied back to where we parked. The shooting was marked by the number of hits the drogue received. The marker said, "You have scored nil. There isn't a hit recorded, Emeny. There is nothing of the target left to count the hits. You have destroyed the target. Absolutely bloody perfect." I was given one more flight in a Defiant and became operational with only three hours flying training.

Immediately we were sent on convoy patrols on the east coast. It was that time of the year when there was a lot of low cloud and the Dornier bombers would come down out of the clouds right over the convoy, dive on the ships, let go their bombs and straight back up into the clouds again. We flew those patrols for five and a half weeks and never fired a shot because we couldn't get near them. Spitfires might have caught them but we had no chance of catching them. It was very frustrating.

The first day we spent so long on patrol that we couldn't get home to our base before refuelling so landed at another. This was about two o'clock in the afternoon. The officers went off to the officers' mess and the sergeants went off to the sergeants' mess but the five of us with no rank (three New Zealanders and two Englishmen) were left to look after ourselves. We found that between us we had enough money to buy a cup of tea and a pie each at the canteen. Every airport in Britain had a canteen open all day.

Refuelling Defiants, June 1940.

When we got back to our base the boys were complaining bitterly about this treatment so it was decided that I should go and see the gunnery officer and explain the problem. I asked him if we could go to the sergeants' mess to get a cup of tea. "Absolutely not. No of course not. It may not happen again." And that was that.

But it did happen again. It happened the next day. When we got back home the five us were upset by our treatment. I suggested we see the gunnery officer and tell him simply and plainly "no food, no fly" and because I had made the suggestion and was less in awe of the system I was again deputised to go.

The gunnery officer gave me no chance. As soon as I approached he said, "I'm not going to talk to you about that again Emeny. I spoke to you about it yesterday. It may never happen again."

I said, "But Sir, there is every possibility it will happen again and we are not prepared to put up with it."

"So what are you going to do about it? What can you do about it?"

"The boys and I have decided," I replied, "that the situation is simply 'no food, no fight'. If you can't bloody well sort this out you can stop the bloody war. We have not come over here to be treated like this."

He nearly fell out of his chair and commanded, "You stop here! Don't move!" and he rushed out and came back with the sergeant major and a couple of other fellows and I was marched up to the squadron leader's office facing a charge of mutiny. The King's Regulations and the Air Council Instructions said 'mutiny'. The CO was a very nice man. He had a few New Zealand friends in the Air Force and he had played rugby with them. He was thrilled to have New Zealanders serving in his squadron. He was always a polite and gentle-natured man.

This was not the first time I had met him. The day after we had arrived on the base the flight sergeant said: "You fellows had better read Routine Orders on the notice board in the guard room. There is something on it about you." When we read it we found that the sergeants had drawn up a list of aircraftsmen to look after and tidy their rooms for them.

I just ignored it but halfway through the morning the sergeant major approached me and asked, "Emeny, have you read the ROs this morning?"

"Yes, sergeant major!" I replied.

"Well why aren't you doing what you have been instructed to do?"

"Because I didn't come half way around the world to do that. If you want anyone to tidy and clean up after you go and pay someone or get one of your own flunkeys to do it. That isn't what I am here for."

"Is that so?" and straight up to the guardroom we marched. A short time later with the adjutant and then with the sergeant major I was marched into the CO's office and found myself on a charge. The charge was 'failing to carry out Routine Orders'.

The CO said, "Emeny, I believe you have just arrived from New Zealand and perhaps you are not aware of our system. Do you realise that our Daily Routine Orders are what the squadron actually does during the day and if there is anything on Daily Routine Orders for you, well that is what you have to do? It is a directive. An order."

"Well Sir," I said, "I wonder if you have today's Routine Orders?"

"No. I haven't."

"Well may I request that you get a copy and read them?" So he asked the adjutant for a copy. "I have asked you to read them Sir, because I hope you understand why I didn't take any notice of them?"

"Oh," he looked at me and said, "I don't think we need you any more, Emeny. You are dismissed." What he said to the adjutant and to the sergeant major I never found out but that was the end of free room service for the sergeants.

That was the first time I had met the CO. Now I had come up before him on a charge of 'mutiny'. The charge was read out and he said, "Have you anything to say? Have you any idea how serious this is?"

"No, Sir, I don't, because I don't think it is serious at all. I think it is just a load of rubbish." With that everyone tried to speak at once. When there was a moment's quiet I asked, "I wonder if I could speak to you privately on this matter. Would you mind Sir, if the others left the room?"

"It is a bit unusual. But all right," and he asked the others if they would leave. Then I told him what the situation was.

I said, "You know Sir, there is a perfectly simple solution. What you have to do is to give us a note to whatever station we land on so whatever sergeants' mess we go into can provide us with some tea. The other alternative is this. I understand that under wartime regulations all air crew are supposed to be sergeants so just give us our sergeant's stripes."

"No. I can't do that."

"Why can't you?"

"Well you are foreign troops and we have had no instructions what to do. Normally in the RAF an air gunner becomes a LAC and then after a period of time becomes a corporal and then after another period of time becomes a sergeant."

"Well I can understand that but doesn't wartime change all pre-war regulations and all air crew become sergeants."

"But that doesn't apply to you New Zealanders and I can't do anything about that."

"Well if you can't do anything about it Sir, I can. I suggest you phone our High Commissioner, Bill Jordan and explain our situation to him."

"Oh no. He is a foreign official. I couldn't ring him. I'm just a squadron leader and squadron leaders don't ring high commissioners."

"Well if you won't Sir, can I borrow your phone and do it myself?"

"No. No. I can see you are determined about this so I will do it."

He got on the phone and eventually got through to the High Commissioner and is stuttering, "I've … got hm … Clifford Emeny … ah … from N … hm … that we don't … hm … know what to do about New Zealand … we have a little problem …"

I called out, "Put me on Sir. Put me on the phone to him." I wanted Mr Jordan to hear my voice. I had met him in London before the war. Apparently the High Commissioner heard me and said, "Put him on."

I explained to him what was happening, "Bloody idiots! Put him back on."

All I heard was "Yes sir. Yes sir. Yes sir" six or eight times. When he put the phone down he said, " Emeny, go and get the other New Zealanders and the two English LAC gunners as well and go over to the stores and collect your sergeant's stripes."

The gunnery officer wasn't too pleased nor were many of the older sergeants who had had to wait years to reach their rank. The RAF at times could be so hidebound. From then on we had no problems when we landed on another airfield.

Tragically the CO, Squadron Leader Hunter, and the gunnery officer, Flight Lieutenant Ash, were both killed a few days later.

Promoted to Sergeant, 27 July, 1940.

Chapter 5

THE BATTLE OF BRITAIN

The Battle of Britain developed relatively slowly. We were doing convoy protection patrols on the east coast and we read in the newspapers about the developing battle far from us. Morale in the squadron was high and all were anxious to become involved in the developing scrap. There was no doubt whatever that we would give a good account of ourselves against the Germans.

Our squadron had done well over Dunkirk when it had shot down 65 enemy planes in one week. The 264 Squadron lost seven pilots and nine gunners killed, wounded or missing in this action. On one occasion the squadron got 37 enemy bombers without losing a plane.

It was at this time I heard that the *Wellington Star*, the ship I was a gunner on when she made her maiden voyage to New Zealand, had been sunk by a German U-boat off the coast of France.

Then early in August we were ordered to Hornchurch, right in the suburbs of London. The day after we arrived we were scrambled and did a patrol on the coast and had to land on a southern airfield to refuel. We landed with air raid sirens screaming and ran for some slit trenches for cover. Some low-flying German fighters swept across the airfield and destroyed 10 of our 12 Defiants.

Very shaken, we returned to Hornchurch by train. We were embarrassed as we were wearing flying suits and carrying our parachutes. Despite many looks of curiosity, not one person questioned us as to why we were dressed for flying, carrying parachutes and riding in a train. The next day, women pilots replaced our lost Defiants. They ferried the replacement planes direct from the factory to the airfield. We went up again. German fighters dived out of the sun and shot down three Defiants, including our CO, Squadron Leader Hunter. Other planes were damaged and some of the crews wounded. It happened so quickly that few of us even got away a shot. Discussing it on the ground we decided that the moment we started to look for fighters we would start firing so when we actually saw them we would have a bead on them.

The next couple of days we didn't see any Germans but we had to land on another airfield. When we eventually got back to our own we found that three of our boys had lost all their gear. We New Zealanders had a lot more personal belongings than the RAF chaps and I decided that no one was going to steal my gear. I had three uniforms, three shirts, in fact three of everything. I packed all my belongings in three big packs and the first thing I did each morning was to struggle across the airfield and pile them into the back of the plane behind the turret and tie them in with pieces of wire.

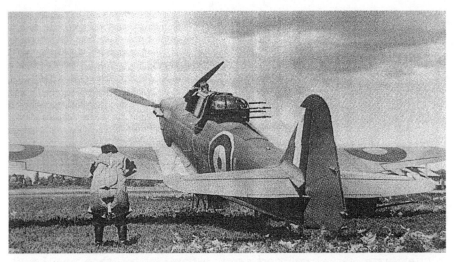

The power operated gun turret was the sole armament of the Defiant, with an arc of fire of 180 degrees. This made it defenceless from frontal attacks and from beneath. To enter the turret it had to be turned as seen here. Leaving it in flight was almost impossible.

The next day we went up and were again bounced by German fighters but this time we were alert. The moment we saw signs of their cannon shells coming at us we just flung our turrets around with everything blazing so they flew into a hail of machine-gun fire. We possibly damaged a couple of them but none of our squadron was damaged.

Two days later, high-flying German planes bombed Hornchurch airfield. The warning to take off came too late. There was a mad scramble as three squadrons took off from three directions at the same time just as a load of bombs crashed on to the airfield. As our grounded planes emerged from the smoke and clouds of dust and exploding bombs we saw only two had been damaged.

Three days of scrambles followed without any contact with enemy fighters. Then it happened again. Enemy fighters came diving out of the sun and two more Defiants were shot down with others damaged and more casualties.

Then came the final day. Incredibly our squadron managed to get beside a Heinkel bomber squadron and we began to inflict damage on them oblivious to the 50 or more enemy fighters high above us. I was in the mid-formation position and flying past the bombers only 100 feet away. We were gaining on a Heinkel but had to get past his wings to shoot him down. Barely 50 feet away I could see the German gunner furiously bashing his jammed machine gun. I kept my sight on him ready to blast him into eternity if he became dangerous. It didn't occur to me to shoot him. All I wanted to do was to bring the bomber down by shooting out its engines. A few more seconds was all we needed.

Then it all happened. The German fighters came down out of the sun and shot down the four Defiants behind us. They scored hits on us as they went past with cannon shells exploding in the turret. One exploded right in front of my face and I was momentarily blinded. Flying shrapnel cut my cheek, sliced through my nose and penetrated just behind my right eye. Smoke and flames filled the turret. Blood from the nose wound quickly filled the mike preventing me from talking to the pilot. He was yelling, "Bale out! Bale out!" and flinging the plane upside down to help throw me clear so I wouldn't hit the tailplane as I jumped.

I slammed the turret door release handle but shrapnel had jammed the doors and destroyed the turret rotating mechanism. My only chance was to escape down through the hatch below the turret but the guns had to be facing outward and were now pointing forward. The pilot was still yelling, "Bale out! Bale out! Are you out?" I just kept making gurgling noises through my blood-soaked mike to let him know I was still there, while he kept throwing the plane upside down to help me out.

The turret was filling with thick smoke and things were getting hot around my legs as I desperately tried to insert a small handle into a half-inch slot to try moving the turret by hand. All that throwing the plane upside down didn't help when I couldn't see a thing but I appreciated the pilot's concern to help me, and it probably caused the enemy fighters to leave us alone thinking we were goners.

Eventually I got the turret turned the right way and released the lower hatch. As soon as the hatch went so did all the smoke and flames. The fire was in the material just behind the turret. I ripped it out and we were safe again. My personal belongings in those three packs had saved my legs. They would have been blown off without the protection of the packs. Someone stealing our gear on the ground probably saved me from being mortally wounded in the air. I wasn't interested in baling out unless I had to. I established contact with the pilot by moving the guns up and down in answer to his queries about my wounds. The battle had moved miles away as it does in modern aerial warfare. So we returned alone to base. My wounds proved quite superficial although the piece of shrapnel that had penetrated behind the eye missed the optic nerve by a hair's breadth.

31

Slaughtered in Battle of Britain.
Cliff's plane is second from right.

That was the squadron's last sortie in the Battle of Britain. We had suffered 18 casualties of pilots and gunners in those eight days. This was the second-to-highest casualty rate of any RAF squadron. Our gunners claimed eight enemy fighters and bombers, either shot down, probably destroyed or damaged, but there was never time to be sure what really happened as the fighters dived on us so quickly.

We heard how the day before our last sortie the only other Defiant squadron in the battle had been wiped out on its first sortie. Bounced by German fighters coming out of the sun, they lost six out of nine planes. Only the lucky intervention of a Hurricane fighter squadron saved the other three from total destruction. So the Defiants were taken out of the battle and turned into night fighters. I later saw an RAF summary of the Battle of Britain that said 'only two Defiant squadrons participated in the battle. Both were annihilated'. How very true!

When 264 Squadron went into battle in the middle of August we had 20 aircraft and 16 crews. Eight days later we had lost 11 aircraft and 18 aircrew had been killed. There were in fact only five crews left. But how had this happened? In the Battle of France, 264 was one of the most successful fighter squadrons in the RAF. In one day this squadron knocked down 17 Bf 109s and 11 dive bombers without loss. This was a record number of enemy aircraft shot down by any squadron in one day.

Within three months the German fighters had changed their tactics. Instead of attacking in the traditional way of line astern and becoming easy prey to the Defiant's four Browning machine guns, they made frontal attacks or attacked dead astern and from beneath. In both positions the Defiant was defenceless. With this tactic they were completely safe from our machine guns with their 180 degrees arc of fire. It was a terrible mistake sending such a useless fighter into that kind of warfare. The Defiant should have been kept way up country, defending areas where only bombers without fighter escorts would have been attacking. There the Defiant would have performed more credibly having originally been designed and built as a defence against bombers.

There was one special incident that happened in this battle that had a profound influence on me. One of the Spitfire squadrons had a young Scottish pilot, whose fiancée had come down from Scotland to spend a few days with him and they decided to get married. A few of us attended his wedding service at nine in the morning. They had two hours together and then he took off with his squadron and was killed within half an hour of taking off. That evening we buried him. His young wife was grief-stricken.

After the funeral service we found his wife had an auntie living on the other side of London. The Kiwi boys put what money we had into a pool and I was asked to find a taxi and get her to her auntie. By this time it was dark and a bombing raid was in progress over London. The taxi driver wasn't too happy and I didn't blame him because bombs were coming down, shrapnel was pouring down and he kept saying, "Don't you think we had better get in a shelter?" I told him we had to drive on and the girl beside me was sobbing her heart out, devastated by her loss. Finally at 2 am we got to her aunt's house to find no one at home. I banged on the door of four houses before I found someone who knew where the aunt might be. I asked them if they could look after the girl as I had to get back to the airfield. They agreed and I left her there.

On the way back I made a vow that I would never mix marriage and war. I never wanted to be responsible for the grief I had just seen.

When our Squadron was pulled out of the Battle of Britain we were sent north to replace our losses and to train for two weeks as night fighters. We were sent back to London as night fighters, but had little success. The problem was that there were no inland radar stations. The system then operating was vintage World War I. The people on the ground listened with big ear megaphones to try and hear the bombers. By sound they tried to guess where the bombers were and at what height, then Fighter Command would try to direct us to where the bombers could be.

At night you had to be very close to a bomber to see it. If we were close to London we could sometimes see the enemy silhouetted against the fires on the ground but we weren't allowed anywhere

(Official post cards provided for men to write home on.)

near London because of the balloon barrages that went up 7 000 to 8 000 feet. Searchlights also surrounded the city. If occasionally we had the good fortune to see a bomber in the searchlights the anti-aircraft guns would open up and fill the sky with masses of bursting shells. It just wasn't safe to be in those areas.

We lost planes flying into 'ack-ack' and we lost two crews flying into balloons. Once my pilot and I got caught in a balloon barrage. Fortunately it was a moonlight night and I happened to look up and there was a balloon just above us. I yelled to the pilot who went into a steep turn and we were lucky enough to fly clear.

Then we were sent to Luton, a small city near London. The airfield was a small grass strip, on top of a hill next to the Vauxhall motor works, which made vehicles and tanks. Luton had a high population of Jews and they were very difficult people to get to know.

The ground crew lived in tents on the airfield while the air crews were billeted in houses close by. I was billeted in a house with another New Zealander, Les Wells from Marton. Just after we arrived the Germans pulled off a daylight raid on the Vauxhall works. Les and I were walking back to our billet in the mid-afternoon when the raid took place. We dived into a drain and heard someone running along the road. We looked out and there was a constable running down the road with a bomb bouncing along behind him. The bomb actually bounced right over him and off the road but the constable kept running.

Several bombs fell on the works but little damage was done because most of them didn't explode. The bomb disposal people found the bombs that hadn't exploded were duds.

One night the Germans bombed Luton with parachute mines. Just as they were arriving one of our pilots took off without putting his propeller in fine pitch. He got off the ground but couldn't get properly airborne, swerved and collided with two other planes and the three of them burst into flames. One was pushed in among the tents where people were sleeping. It was chaos with men whose clothes were on fire, running desperately trying to beat out the flames. The German bombers, seeing the fire, assumed this was the target and began to drop their parachute mines. They dropped silently; you didn't hear them but they were terribly destructive. A one-ton mine fell on a block of houses and when it exploded destroyed the lot.

My pilot and I were on flare-path duty and realised we had to get the lights out. Each one had an individual switch so we ran from light to light turning them off. I could see these mines floating silently down on the airfield and then I saw one coming toward us. It hit the ground, bounced three times, the parachute collapsed and the mine lay there. After a second or so we got over our shock and took off. The mine never went off. If it had it would have blown us to pieces.

Another mine landed on a hangar no one was allowed to enter. But it must have been left open because the mine floated through the door. The parachute got caught on the apex of the roof and the mine swung back and forth in the open doorway all night. The Navy came next morning, backed a truck under it, cut the parachute off, lowered the mine on to the truck and drove off with it.

Not a great deal of damage was done to the airfield but the town suffered terribly. The street we were billeted in was completely obliterated. The only thing left in the house we lived in was the dog, which was found under a heavy table. The couple that owned the house was killed. In the town 460 people were killed and over 1 600 injured.

Next day orders went out that no one was to go into the town. The people blamed the fire on the airfield for the German attack. By the end of the day the whole squadron had been sent to Southend on the coast at the mouth of the River Thames.

There we worked off another grass strip and lived in empty houses around the edge. We were given an army palliasse and two army blankets. There was no heating whatever and it was getting cold by November. I always slept in pyjamas with one blanket above and the other underneath me. You had to sleep between blankets otherwise any heat generated by the body evaporated. The English boys piled everything on top of themselves including their overcoats and then they took to going to bed in their clothes. When I got up I put on a pair of overalls and then my clothes and stayed warm all day. The other fellows, when they got up, were already cold and stayed cold all day.

We had some unhappy incidents at Southend. We went up every night but with no results. One night a pilot got disorientated, tried to land cross wind and cut a swathe through the trees. When the plane stopped it was a few feet from a tent where six ground crew were sleeping. It rolled on through one side of the tent and through the other side and remarkably never touched one of them.

Defiant Night Fighter Crash 1941.
Both crewmen survived the crash.

One evening I heard an aircraft coming in to land and thought "that fellow is not properly on the circuit". I rushed outside to see it crash into the trees and burst into flames. I ran as fast as I could and reached it to find four soldiers standing there watching it burn. In the turret the gunner was screaming and desperately trying to get out. Why the soldiers just stood there without jumping on the wing and trying to help the gunner out I can never understand. I grabbed a rifle from one of them, jumped up on the wing and smashed the Perspex windows and with the rifle levered the door open. The turret was on fire and everything seemed to be burning. The ambulance driver arrived and between the two of us we managed to lift him out and roll him on the ground to put out the flames. Unfortunately he died from his burns and injuries. His wife later gave me a silver goblet engraved with thanks for my effort in trying to rescue him.

One night I was taking a girl home after a dance. I delivered her to where she was billeted and then found I was three miles away from the airfield. There was no transport available at that time of night and I had to ask directions from a couple of locals who said, "You go down that street, across there and you will come to an alleyway. Go down there and you will reach the main road." My idea of an alleyway was an opening between two buildings. Their idea of an alleyway, however, was the bridge over the canal. With my coat pulled up over my ears, rain pouring and my head down, I found my alleyway before I found theirs. I went down past the buildings, missed the bridge and fell into the canal. With all my heavy clothing on it took me some time to crawl my way out and utterly exhausted I lay on the bank gasping for breath. I sloshed my way home. Back at the base the boys insisted the girl must have thrown me in. After that I was for a time introduced to any girl as, "This is Cliff Emeny. Be careful of him. The last girl he took home had to throw him into the canal."

When I got home I found I had lost my cap. It had on it the only New Zealand badge I owned so the next morning I went back to see if I could find it. I found the place where I had fallen in went up to the house beside the spot and knocked on the door. When a lady answered my knock I explained to her, "I had the misfortune to fall into your canal last night and I am wondering if you saw my cap lying around?"

"Oh," she said, "Were you the person who fell into the canal?"

"Yes," I replied.

"Well, we were in the air raid shelter near where you got out and we heard you swearing very clearly!"

From Southend we went to Biggin Hill in Kent. Biggin Hill was the famous fighter station of the Battle of Britain. By this time it was December and we were thinking of Christmas but the weather was terrible so we didn't do much flying.

The thing I remember most about Biggin Hill was the wonderful singing star Vera Lynn who visited the station to do a concert. To my amazement the CO came to me and said, "Sergeant Emeny, I want you to take a vehicle and driver, go up to London and pick up Miss Vera Lynn and deliver her here to the officers' mess. Will you do it?" Sometime later I asked the adjutant why I was chosen to go. He told me that Vera Lynn had an affinity for NCOs more than she had for officers and that the CO felt I could get her and bring her back to the base safely.

She was a lovely person. She chattered all the way to the base and when she was leaving after the concert she came to the sergeants' mess to find me to thank me for getting her there safely. I always remember Vera Lynn with real warmth.

Being near London I took the trouble to look up the name 'Emeny' in the telephone directory. I could find only one, so I got in touch with them and they turned out to be distant cousins of mine. In a way it was a strange family. The husband was a very small chap, quiet, almost timid. His wife was much bigger and quite domineering and she definitely ran the show.

They had two lovely daughters. One was married to a doctor and the younger daughter, still in her teens, lived at home on the edge of Black Hall Common. When I arrived I found that each night they slept in an underground railway station and hundreds of thousands of Londoners did the same. I decided to spend the night in the house and they decided, for the first time in weeks, to stay too. It was here I learnt how to fight incendiary bombs.

If an incendiary bomb fell on the roof you armed yourself with a wet towel and a bucket of sand. You picked up the bomb with the towel and threw it into the open street where you then threw the bucket of sand on it. Every street in that suburb had ladders and people prepared to deal with incendiaries before they burnt through the roof. I thought to myself I hadn't been much good in an aeroplane trying to help them so I might be of more use helping them on the ground.

I suggested to the Emenys that they make one room a little safer than the others so they bought a really solid table and put it in the dining room. We were there one night having a cup of tea when there was an almighty crash. I left my cup in midair as I dived under the table. Nothing happened, then a few minutes later another massive crash. I went outside to find there were eight-inch guns in action and they were firing practically over the house so we got the full blast. The big 'ack-ack' guns kept the bombers up higher. It was a massed barrage so the Germans had to fly at 15 000 to 20 000 feet. Above the smog they couldn't see what they were bombing so they bombed at random.

The 264 Squadron had been there virtually since the beginning of the Battle of Britain and had only managed to shoot down three bombers. The problem was that detection methods weren't developed to get us close enough to the bombers so that we could see them. We just weren't in the same part of the sky as they were.

As air crew we tried to think of a better method to get closer to the bombers. Over a couple of months we studied piles of combat and observer reports. It became obvious the Germans used a specific flight path to particular cities. They would make a landfall on the coast and then go straight to the target.

We came to the conclusion the answer was to have our night fighters on that flight path and so we sought co-operation with the searchlights and Army. The plan was that the searchlights would abandon attempts to illuminate the bombers but instead be stationed along these flight paths and put their lights straight up every few miles. Then the fighters would be sent up and would circle around the lights so the Germans would literally have to fly through us and maybe we could get close enough to see them and shoot them down. The anti-aircraft guns would be used as a barrage over the cities to try and keep the Germans high and hopefully shoot something down.

Regrettably we couldn't get the slightest co-operation from Fighter Command. In late October a conference on night fighting was held and our CO attended and took with him the plan we had worked up. All day he listened to cranky scientists come up with the most stupid ideas like having two aeroplanes flying along with a wire between them to catch either bombs or bombers. Another crazy idea that the conference spent time considering was to have a 'souped-up' two-engine plane with a light in front, with two Hurricanes formatting on it, but no thought was given to how they would see each other in the dark. They actually formed a squadron to do this but it was a complete and utter flop and did nothing and came to nothing. All these ideas had nothing to do with the task of night fighting. Only at 5.45 pm did they allow our CO to present our ideas. They allowed him 15 minutes to explain what was involved. Without discussion it was rejected. They had obviously had enough for the day and wanted to get to the mess for a pre-dinner gin. We called our idea 'Fighter Night Plan'.

In January 1941, just after my 21st birthday, my pilot Kay, decided to dump me as his air gunner and take on an officer air gunner who had arrived in the squadron and didn't have a pilot. It was terribly upsetting for me because I was left with nothing to do. There were no other available pilots at that time.

A week later I was posted from 264 Squadron to 255 Squadron. This was a new RAF squadron of Defiants still in the process of formation. Half the air gunners were Polish escapees who somehow or another had found their way to England. The other half was English and New Zealanders. I was to train them as air gunners.

I met a man a few years ago who was there when I arrived. He said, "I remember you Emeny. You came up to us and said, 'My name is Cliff Emeny. I've completed so many months in 264 Squadron. I have learnt how to handle the guns and have learnt a little about night fighting and I have been sent here to train you. I don't want any bloody trouble from any one of you and I want you to understand that from the word go'. And we didn't give any trouble either."

Only one of the Poles could speak any English but they had trained under strict discipline. I communicated through the one who could speak a bit of English and we had no problems or trouble. We got on well.

The presence of the Poles had a tremendous social impact on the community. A big station like Kirton-on-Lindsey had a lot of WAAFs serving on it and a big population of girls in the local town. Dances were held two or three times a week and the girls had been used to a fair bit of kiss and cuddle. When the Poles arrived the girls soon learnt they didn't kiss and cuddle with them without getting virtually raped. There was a surprising turnover amongst the WAAFs who obviously became pregnant and had to leave.

We did a few night patrols but still without success. The squadron became operational and the pilot allocated to me was

42

a Scottish sergeant. He had been in the Air Force a number of years. He upset me very much because when we were in the air and saw anti-aircraft shells bursting which indicated Germans, he would always turn away and fly in the opposite direction. This happened several times and it came to a head when we actually got alongside a bomber. It was dark and I had made a resolution that I would never fire at a bomber without definitely identifying it. There were 50 RAF bomber squadrons in that area and a number of our bombers had already been shot down by friendly fire.

We came alongside this bomber that I didn't recognise. A new British bomber had just become operational and because it had a twin tail looked very much like the German Dornier bomber. The pilot was yelling, "Shoot the bugger! Shoot him down!"

"I haven't identified him yet."

"No. No. Shoot the damn thing down!"

"Get closer then so I can identify it."

"I'm not getting any closer. It might shoot us down." No amount of talking would persuade him so I took the Very pistol and fired the signal for the day. Obviously the plane was a German because it banked away into the darkness and that was the last we saw of him.

When we landed the pilot said, "Well that is the last time you fly with me." He went to the gunnery officer to arrange for another gunner. It didn't actually help him because four days later he borrowed a Defiant to fly to Scotland to see his family and flew into a hill and killed himself.

I got a new pilot, Phyl Kendall, a Yorkshire man who had been in Malaya as a civil servant. He was a wonderful chap and he and I got on very well. He married a lovely girl from a wealthy family. It was quite a wedding. The bride had a younger sister who got bored at the reception. We went outside and had a swim in the pool in the park alongside the building where the reception was being held. Unfortunately some of my friends saw us swimming, whipped out and took our clothes and for a while things got a bit hectic.

Eventually in March 1941, in sheer desperation the RAF adopted our system of 'Fighter Night Plan' and the Battle of Britain was over in four raids. The German invasion of Russia might also have had something to do with the cessation of night raids on England. Be that as it may, there is no doubt that the number of German bombers shot down in the course of four raids was due entirely to the adoption of 'Fighter Night Plan'. In the course of these raids Phyl and I shot down two German bombers attacking Hull. The first night the plan was tried there were 11 bombers shot down. The next night 28 bombers were shot down, on the third raid 37 went down and on the fourth raid there were 44 destroyed. The Defiant had at last found an effective place in the defence of Britain. If the idea of 'Fighter

Victors of the night skies. 1941. Cliff Emeny with Phil Kendall, Pilot. Defiant Night Fighters RAF.

Night Plan' had been adopted in November 1941 the terrible losses of that winter could have been avoided.

After the war I was speaking to Ian Walker of Auckland who was one of the 50 young New Zealanders who left with me on the *Akaroa* in March 1940. In the Battle of Britain, Ian flew with No. 600 Squadron flying *Blenheims*. Later in the war he flew with Bomber Command in *Wellingtons* over Europe. He told me that over Europe the biggest danger was being caught in a cone of searchlights. There were two types of cone – an 'anti-aircraft cone' and a 'fighter cone'. The 'fighter cone' lit up the sky so that the fighters could see the bombers in the same way that searchlights spaced along the flight path in 1941 lit up the German bombers for our fighters to attack. Perhaps the Germans hit on this tactic themselves or perhaps they adopted the plan put forward by the air crews of 264 squadron in late October 1940 and adopted by Fighter Command in March 1941.

Chapter 6

CONTROVERSY DURING BATTLE OF BRITAIN

Three RAF Fighter Groups covered the area over which the Battle of Britain was fought. Sir Keith Park, the New Zealander, led No. 11 Group. It was in this area that the major battle was fought. He commanded seven squadrons of Hurricanes and one squadron of Spitfires.

No. 10 Group was in the southwest around Southhampton and Bristol. Ninety percent of the battle took place over No. 11 and No. 10 Groups. North of 11 Group was No. 12 Group based at Cambridge and led by Leigh-Mallory. He commanded five squadrons of Hurricanes and two squadrons of Spitfires.

Douglas Bader, the legless pilot, was in 12 Group. Squadron Leader Bader was to play a significant part in the controversy concerning tactics in the Battle of Britain.

The tactic of Sir Keith Park was sound and effective. His approach was to spend as much time as possible breaking up the bomber formations before they reached their target. His strategy was to meet them out over the Channel, ignore the fighters as much as humanly possible and go for the bombers. Often the British fighters buzzing around the bombers were enough to make them drop their bombs and go home. It was a successful tactic remembering that Park was greatly outnumbered by the Germans. Park had seven squadrons whereas the Germans had 40. Group 10 and Group 11 had 14 squadrons between them to cover the whole of southern England.

It was radar that made the difference and Park's tactic was dependent on radar. It was radar that allowed his squadrons to take off while the Germans were still halfway across the Channel. The squadrons weren't on patrol passively waiting. They went up purposefully looking for the enemy.

Park was an exceptional leader. He was a quiet, unassuming but a very capable man. He flew his own white-painted Hurricane. He would arrive at an airfield, where his squadrons were based at dawn, to talk to the pilots about the tactics he was employing and explaining how the battle was going. He was an amazing man. The air crews felt that he was one of them. He was tremendously admired and respected by everyone who had anything to do with him.

In mid-August the Germans made an all-out effort to destroy the Royal Air Force. They concentrated on the forward airfields, particularly 11 Group airfields. When Park's squadrons were meeting the enemy over the Channel, 12 Group was meant to come in behind and defend the airfields of 11 Group against anything that got through.

Squadron Leader Bader dominated the scene in 12 Group. He was a dogmatic, driving person who wouldn't take no for an answer. He was contemptuously critical of the tactics of Park and claimed it was useless attacking German squadrons unless you had parity in numbers. This meant six to eight squadrons fighting in one group.

To achieve this parity in the air meant that Bader had to circle over his own airfield to get them into formation, so the 'big wings' always arrived too late. Not only did he waste precious time but also assumed he was the only one who knew how to fight an air battle, so when he took off he did his own thing. On the first two occasions he spent his time chasing British fighter squadrons returning from battle over the Channel.

When the battle started over the airfields of 11 Group the bombers had already broken through and done massive damage

47

before Bader and his 'big wing' got on the scene. The effectiveness of the 'big wing' was severely diminished by its sheer size and by its slowness in getting off the ground. It was shown after the war that the number of German fighters it claimed to have shot down was four times higher than it actually was.

When Park complained his airfields were being left exposed by the tactics of 12 Group he was contemptuously ignored. Had 11 and 10 groups adopted the 'big wing' formations the Battle of Britain would have been lost. It was impossible to match the huge enemy formations with equal numbers. Big formations had little manoeuverability and were easy meat for high-flying German fighters.

We in air crew were very aware of the controversy raging at High Command over the tactics of Park to 'get the bombers' and the 'big wing' theory of 12 Group. We became very impatient with 12 Group because they were never there on time. The forward airfields were severely hammered for three to four days. We lost airfields and radar stations and were teetering on the edge of collapse. Had the Germans kept it up for another few days they would have forced the abandonment of these airfields.

Fortunately Hitler decided to intervene. One of the German bombers lost its way and dumped its bombs on a suburb of London. Churchill responded next night by sending a small force of bombers against Berlin. Hitler was so incensed that he ordered the Luftwaffe to destroy London. The focus of the attack switched from the airfields to London and that gave the RAF a period of grace to repair the radar stations and damaged airfields and get back into the fight.

The attack on London built up to its finality in the middle of September when the RAF had repaired its airfields and reorganised its radar.

Everyone involved in the battle knew that Park was achieving amazing results with the scarce forces he had available. We had not the slightest doubt that we would win because the bombers simply weren't getting through to their targets. His catch cry was "Get the bombers. Even if you only get at them once, get the bombers."

Immediately after the battle, late in October, the Air Council called a meeting with Sir Hugh Dowding, Commander in Chief of Fighter Command, and Sir Keith Park. They asked them to submit a report on what went right and what went wrong in the battle. Dowding and Park quickly prepared their report and arrived at the meeting. Sholto Douglas was chairman of the Air Council and said, "We have before us a resolution that Sir Hugh Downing be immediately retired from the Air Force and Sir Keith Park be immediately transferred to Fighter Training Command. All those in favour say 'aye'", and the majority voted for the resolution. The two men who had won the Battle of Britain were sidelined.

Sir Keith Park, now in command of fighter training, immediately straightened out Fighter Training Command and as a result better-trained pilots came forward. But what did they do with them? Leigh-Mallory, the former commander of 12 Group, took over Sir Keith Park's job and organised a series of sweeps in 1941 over the Low Countries, sending up Spitfires, either in pairs, or in large groups of 40 or more planes. In the course of it they lost over 900 planes and pilots whereas the Germans lost only 123. Far more pilots and Spitfires were lost in these sweeps than were lost in the whole of the Battle of Britain.

Soon after taking over Leigh-Mallory decided to have a practice run defending London. Within a short time he was hopelessly confused. The whole exercise was an utter shambles and had to be called off.

Later, when the Battle of Malta reached a crisis point, whom did they send out there to save the day? Sir Keith Park. Starting against great odds he finally won the Battle of Malta.

He was then transferred to the Middle East and for two years he was operational commander in that sphere and did much to achieve mutual co-operation between the Army and the Air Force.

Early in 1944 he was sent to Burma to command the air war in that theatre in preparation for the final attacks against the Japanese.

I served under him at the beginning of my Air Force career in England and at the end of my career in Burma against the Japanese. He was an outstanding RAF leader and a man I greatly admired.

Chapter 7

NIGHT FIGHTERS AND RADAR

In September 1941 I was posted to 409 Squadron, a new Canadian squadron training on Defiants. Before describing my experiences with this squadron, let me go back some months to when I was a member of 264 Squadron. After the heavy losses in the Battle of Britain more officers were needed. Five sergeants (myself included) were invited to apply for a commission. As part of the process we had to fill in a number of forms. The adjutant was an obnoxious type and he was supervising the process, walking up and down and watching what we wrote. He was looking over my shoulder and saw me filling in the question: 'What age did you leave school?' I filled in the space: 'age 12'.

"Well you haven't got any bloody chance, have you?" I saw red but didn't say anything. The next question was: 'What other education have you had?'

I would have answered, 'At 16 I enrolled in the International Correspondence School to study and complete a course on aero-engineering'. But before I could answer, again that sneering voice, "You haven't any chance have you?"

I leapt off my seat, tore up my papers and flung them at him saying, "I wouldn't join you bloody bunch of poofters for anything. You can stuff your bloody officers' mess" and walked out.

So I arrived at 409 Squadron as a sergeant. The squadron was just settling in. There was no armament section organised or training facilities arranged, and no equipment available.

The CO, Wing Commander Peterson, was a really fine man. He was naturally quiet and unassuming and I never heard him give a serious order to anyone. He told people what he wanted them to do in a most sociable way and he was such a decent fellow that his every request was carried out immediately. He was 32 and most of us were 10 years younger so as far as we were concerned he may as well have been 50. Among ourselves we took to calling him 'Pop'. He said to me one day, "Sergeant Emeny I hear that you sergeants have a nickname for me. I believe you call me 'Pop' when you are talking among yourselves."

"Yes Sir. We do," I replied.

"Well, I want you to know I consider it quite a compliment having 'Pop' as a nickname but please don't call me that in front of other people."

There was no gunnery officer in the squadron so over the next few weeks I set up a whole armaments section and training programme. We were just starting on the programme when the gunnery officer arrived. He turned out to be a drunken, useless lout and I was left to carry on the whole show myself.

The 409 Squadron was then converted to Beaufighters to be fitted with airborne radar. Four Americans came to the squadron to fit the radar sets into each plane. The Americans were civilians from Texas and were electronic engineers in civil industry. The Americans had been asked to install radar in our night fighters and in our submarine

Beaufighters, 409 Squadron (Cliff's writing).

planes. Britain didn't have the trained technicians to do this job. When they arrived Wing Commander Peterson called me in and said, "Sergeant Emeny we have these four Americans coming and there is a friendly rivalry between Americans and Canadians so I wonder if you would mind rooming with them. I'll put the five of you in the one hut. You will look after them, show them around and so on. If you like you can work with them. It will be better for you as a New Zealander doing this than a Canadian."

That was to be a great experience and I learnt a lot. They worked extremely hard and I learnt about radar from them. All we did was think radar, talk radar and play with radar.

The whole squadron turned out to see our first Beaufighter arrive. We had been waiting for its arrival for some weeks. It was a big, black twin-engine fighter and was being delivered straight from the factory. We all rushed up to get a closer look and then the pilot climbed out and we saw the smallest pilot any of us had ever seen. The boys started wisecracking, "Hi shorty! How can you see to fly little man?" and so on but the pilot walked steadily toward us, took off the helmet and we saw that it was a most petite girl delivering the plane. You never saw so many red-faced and quiet airmen as on that occasion.

The Beaufighter was really an adaptation of the Beaufort twin-engine bomber. It had been streamlined and fitted with more powerful engines and armed with four canons and six machine guns. They had been rushed into service quickly so that the RAF had something to put radar in. Because of its rushed production there were bound to be defects in the plane. The test pilots would test it under their favoured conditions but it was very different flying these machines at night especially when the weather was bad and putting them down on short strips. The Beaufighter proved to be unpredictable and unstable at slow speed.

We lost our first new plane on that first day when the CO, Wing Commander Peterson, took up the Beaufighter to try it out. He took with him his air gunner and the squadron engineer, who stood behind him. We saw him at 3 000 feet trying turns and banks and then trying to lower the undercarriage but the undercarriage wouldn't come down. He slowed and suddenly the plane flipped upside down and started to drop like a falling leaf and it came down and down and down. We could hear him over his radio telling us what he was trying to do to correct it and get the plane out of the spin but it was impossible. He couldn't get the nose down to get enough speed to regain control. It just came down and down until 'crash!'. It smashed into the ground on the other side of the airfield. There wasn't a mark on the three of them but they had all died with a broken neck.

Wing Commander Peterson was replaced by Wing Commander de Beaux, another Canadian who had done over 5000 hours bush flying. He owned a bush flying company. He was a very capable man and a tremendous pilot. He too didn't have the rigid military outlook of many of the senior officers in the RAF. He became annoyed when air crew saluted him. He told us quite plainly that the ground staff could salute occasionally for the sake of appearance but he didn't expect it from air crew.

We still had a few Defiants on the base and he and some others were going to do some air firing at Southenbridge and he took me as his air gunner. When we arrived over the range just after dawn a squadron from the Fleet Air Arm was practising, firing at towed targets. De Beaux asked, "Did you know anything about this, Emeny?"

"No Sir, I don't."

He put the Defiant down on a grass strip made for the much smaller Auster, got out and went to find out what was happening. He was told a signal had been sent to our squadron calling off the practice because the Fleet Air Arm squadron had suddenly been recalled to their aircraft carrier and had to get in some practice before they left.

De Beaux and I took off and arrived back at base. An hour and a half after we got back the adjutant rang to say, "Sergeant Emeny, the CO wants to see you and I don't think it is one of his best days. Come over as quickly as you can."

I walked across thinking, "It is not my fault. Why should I be in trouble over this?"

I knocked and entered his office. He asked, "Emeny, how come, after 18 months of operations, you haven't been commissioned?"

"Well Sir the last time the RAF talked to me about this they insulted me so much that I tore up their papers and told them to get stuffed!"

He said, "Oh, did you now? You are not saying that to me, Emeny. Get into the next room and fill out your papers." I found out later that the CO had found the gunnery officer in bed. As a boozer he never got up before 10 or 11 am and the signal was still in his pocket. The CO ordered him off the squadron. He took off that afternoon with a friend, fortified with drink. They got to about 400 feet, went into a spin, hit the ground and both of them were killed.

Now Pilot Officer Emeny – commissioned 29 November 1941.

I applied for my commission. The application began: 'What was your occupation before the Air Force?' So I listed all that I had done. 'What sport did you play?'

I wrote 'reading, tennis and swimming.'

"Great! Great!" said the adjutant, "but I see the CO says you are to be commissioned immediately without any fuss or bother."

So I said, "I don't suppose we need to go any further do we?" I was commissioned and took my place as gunnery leader of the squadron.

The new Beaufighters kept arriving and I had a young pilot not quite 20 years old. (A 21-year-old pilot was quite old.) All the young ones were coming straight from training. Six of these pilots (including mine) crashed on landing. The other five crews were killed but we luckily survived. It was a windy, stormy night and my pilot was trying to land on a very short strip. He must have got down just that little too slow and the plane flicked into a spin. Fortunately we were very low when we crashed. I suffered a broken foot but apart from that we were both uninjured.

My foot hurt dreadfully but I didn't report to the MO because I didn't want to give up flying. We held a dance each Friday night when the boys would stand around the bar and booze but I was a good dancer. Dancing on a broken foot was murder but I was seldom allowed to sit out a dance.

Soon after I joined 409 Squadron a group captain arrived from Group Headquarters to take over the area. He had been a night pilot in World War I and wanted to fly the Defiant at night. The CO asked me to go up with him because there were a few German intruders around and he didn't want the new group captain to get shot down.

We came in to land on a short strip with a very short glide path because the station didn't want to show up to any German intruders. The glide path indicator was a beam of light that showed white, green or red. If it showed white you were too high, green you were right and red you were too low. The first landing he attempted we lost touch with the runway and landed about 20 or 30 feet up. The plane crashed with an almighty bang on to the runway. The Defiant was a heavy plane and when we hit the ground the wheels were shoved up through the wings.

He did another couple of days' flying and on the third night we tried again. This time he was determined he wouldn't be too high because I saw him go through the white, green and into the red and down into the peat bog just before the runway began. When we stopped, the aircraft was buried in mud. We scrambled out of the plane and squelched through the mud to dry land and then squelched our way half a mile to the guardhouse at the edge of the airfield. We arrived there with the group captain very shaken. He tried to explain to the sergeant of the guard that he was group captain so and so and that I was his gunner and we had crashed. The guard was a Cornishman with a deep Cornish accent. He picked up the phone, called the CO and said, "Sir … there be … two funny men … here at the guardroom … all covered in mud. One claims to be a group captain … Sir … what will I do with them?"

The CO must have thought "Hell!" He jumped into his car, drove down and picked us up.

That was the end of that. He never flew a Defiant again and whether he took up his new appointment or not I never found out.

It was decided that air gunners could convert to Beaufighters as radar operators. The radar was very complicated. There were two cathode tubes, one went sideways and the other went upwards. One side of the set read 'up and down' and the other side read 'sideways'. There were five knobs on each transmitter and receiver. Your hands wriggled around these knobs and one eye looked at one side of the set and the other the other side. Only four gunners in the squadron had sufficient co-ordination to master it.

The four of us were sent to Scotland for a three weeks' course on radar. The second day I arrived there I had a terrible attack of tonsillitis and I was in hospital until three days before the course finished. I sat the examination, however, and passed. The time spent with the four Americans who had installed the sets in our aircraft got me through. So I became a radar operator and got my second set of wings.

We then commenced serious training with our Beaufighters, which had one serious design fault: it was very unpredictable at low speeds, and that caused some serious crashes. The fault was corrected by redesigning the tailplane and by replacing its engines with radial engines. Once these faults were corrected we had a new aeroplane, which proved sound and reliable.

By this time the Germans had attacked Russia and there weren't many German planes flying in English skies. The only planes that came over were fast reconnaissance planes.

All attention was given to building inland radar stations so that the whole of England was covered by radar. Our squadron did the calibrating work that took hour after hour. At the same time we were practising on our radar sets.

The only time an enemy aircraft came over our area the radar was operational. A call came to our CO, "We have a bandit for you." And he jumped in a Beaufighter, was vectored in and shot it down. The COs became aces and the rest of us didn't have a shot at anything.

Month after month of this went by and only once was I ever vectored on to a German bomber. Unluckily I was flying with a visiting wing commander who was going to take over 55 Squadron. At 16 000 feet I guided him perfectly behind the bomber with the assistance of the radar. At the close range of 150 yards he fired and missed. Immediately the German dived away but I got him back on my set and we got in behind it again. Again he fired and again he missed. The German was obviously experienced and very determined because he began his reconnaissance again. Again we got in behind him in the same position and again the pilot missed. This happened five times and he missed each bloody time. I got in as close as a 100 yards and he missed. He just couldn't shoot. He had no ability whatever – luckily for the German. The only time I had a chance to shoot a bomber down we missed out. The other memorable experience with 409 squadron

Radar Operator Night Fighters 1941/42.

happened at night at 23 000 feet when my pilot went to sleep. I noticed the plane go into a diving turn. I yelled at him to wake up, which he did with a start, heaved the stick back and we flipped upside down, and started coming down in a flat upside down spin. He yelled at me to bale out.

That day some goon from Group Headquarters, in charge of parachutes, noticed that the observers in 409 Squadron had the same parachutes as pilots. He must have thought, "Can't let this damn thing happen." With nothing better to do he rushed over in a truck, took our parachutes away and left in their place bomber navigator parachutes. In a bomber, navigators wore a jacket and the parachute was clipped on to the wall of the plane and when needed they put it on. We had the same seats as the pilots so we sat on the same type of parachute.

When it came to go on duty that night our parachutes had gone so we took the one left in its place. We found that it needed a couple of folded blankets to fill up the seat and the parachute had to be placed on the floor beside us. When the plane flipped over the parachute shot up to the tail. I unfastened my straps to reach it but the plane was whirling around in a spin and I whirled with it. My feet were caught in the ammunition rack at the top and I was being swung from one side of the aircraft to the other.

My pilot was still yelling, "Bail out! Bail out!" and I was shouting back, "Do something! Do something! I'm trapped!" I must have been knocked out because I remember hearing vaguely in the distance the voice of my pilot calling my name and I thought, "Hell, I'm in the next world and Robbie is here with me." Then I became aware of the pain in the back of my neck. Robbie had stuck with the aircraft and he doesn't know how but he got it out of the spin 400 feet above the water. Then he circled around and around trying to wake me up so I could tell him where we were. My feet were still trapped in the ammunition rack in the roof and my head was crammed down between the drums of the two cannons with all my weight on the back of my neck.

I dragged myself up the wall of the aircraft but found I couldn't pull my foot out with one hand so I let go and used both hands. I got one foot out and crashed down again on to the ammunition drums with one foot still trapped, I crawled up again and got the other foot out and crashed down again with the middle of my back hitting those same ammunition drums. Meanwhile Robbie was climbing for height. He got a fix on our station and we headed for home.

When we landed and walked inside everyone stared at us because our faces were absolutely chalk-white with shock. We were admitted to hospital and after a couple of days we were given a week's leave.

Glasgow 1941 with Gene Skninner on leave.

Cliff with Billy Watson, Glasgow, 1941.

By this time I had done nearly 100 patrols and there was talk of sending me as an instructor to one of the training commands. This was the last thing I wanted to do so I decided to try again for pilot training.

The station had a Magister, a light communications plane, and I persuaded Sergeant Robbie to teach me to fly it. It had an open cockpit with the two seats one behind the other and it wasn't equipped with inter-communication.

Robbie instructed me on my first take off, "You just go to the end of the runway, open the throttle and go!" But the Magister didn't want to go. It didn't want to travel along the runway. It wanted to go to the right. By the time I left the ground it was at right angles to the runway. With a sense of accomplishment I finally got it into the air but by the time I came back in to land I really had problems, I had been used to flying in a big Beaufighter where the maxim was 'Keep them well up and well out', so I did a Beaufighter's circuit. Robbie waved his arms about and then, from behind me, grabbed the controls and took me close in so I could try to land the thing. I was used to sitting up high in a Beaufighter so I attempted to land the Magister about five to six feet above the ground. We landed with a few big bounces and then took off on another circuit. After a few times I got the hang of flying it.

Cliff with Robbie, 409 Squadron 1941/42.

I had about 10 hours up when one night in the mess I was sitting near the CO. He turned to me and asked, "Cliff how are you getting on with the Magister?"

I thought, "Hell. He knows!"

"All right, Sir."

"I'm pleased about that, but don't you break the bloody thing or there will be hell to pay." What he was really saying was, "You can go on doing it, but don't damage it."

A short time after that the Magister was replaced with a Blenheim, a light bomber used at the beginning of the war but now outmoded and used as a communications plane. It wasn't long before I was flying the twin-engine Blenheim and having no trouble. I had 30 hours' flying up and asked the CO if I could be trained as a pilot. He said, "You leave it to me, I might be able to do something about that." Shortly afterwards I found myself posted to an Initial Training Wing – a Tiger Moth Flying School. This place was used to see if you had an aptitude for flying before being sent to the training school in Canada.

The CO of this school was a fellow I knew in the Battle of Britain. I flew the Tiger Moth without any trouble and in the five weeks I was there did the whole elementary course including some night flying.

The Tiger Moth had no night-flying instruments but I was used to flying at night.

The CO arranged for a short strip to be made available a few miles away. Lights were set up and I had two or three landings and then, when I was still in the air, a German intruder arrived. Just as I was coming in for my final approach all the lights along the runway were switched off. Everything was blacked out except the beacon, which I could see in the distance about seven to eight miles away. I flew toward the beacon and circled it for 20 minutes. I had read the course and the time to the beacon. When I got back over the airfield they tuned back on the lights and I landed safely.

Cliff flying Tiger Moth. Cliff was officially accepted for pilot training on 1 January and posted to No. 22 EFTS, Cambridge for a grading course.

I tried to persuade the RAF through the CO, and also sent a message to the AOC to the effect that I had so many hours on the Magister and Blenheim and could be sent to an OTU where I could get experience on twin-engines and quickly become operational.

But no! You had to get in and become part of the system. Anyone who was going to train as a pilot had to go to Canada. Possibly there was another reason why they wanted me to go there. On the ship were 150 airmen going to Canada for training and they wanted two officers in charge so I would be one of those officers and they wouldn't have the expense and trouble of getting me home again.

Before I embarked for Canada in mid June 1942 I visited 409 Squadron to say my goodbyes. My experience with 409 Squadron was the happiest I ever had in the Royal Air Force. It was a fantastic squadron. The Canadian squadrons were so superior, in every respect, to any other squadron I served with. They looked after their people very well and looked after their physical health. They ran a well-organised physical and sports programme. They were the only pilots in the RAF who had physical exercises. In other squadrons the only exercise was bending the elbow at the bar, but not in Canadian squadrons. Once a week everyone did a mile run and I found I could still run the mile in four minutes forty seconds, the same time I used to run it around the Trentham racecourse in 1938.

The adjutant of 409 asked me if I could do the squadron a favour and personally deliver the personal effects of the six Canadian air crew in the squadron who had been killed on active service. Of course I agreed and the adjutant arranged for me to have 10 days' leave when I arrived in Canada and expenses paid and he would write to the families telling them of my visit. I thought this was a great idea; 10 days' leave and all expenses paid and to tour eastern Canada sounded almost too good to be true. Little did I realise what was involved!

Chapter 8

CANADA

My first call in Canada was to a widowed mother and her daughter. They were still grieving deeply the loss of an only son and brother and wanted to know the details of his death and information about his life in Britain. It was then that I realised I was on no happy holiday assignment.

All they knew about him was what was contained in the awful telegram informing them of his death. Somehow I managed to answer their questions and they were very grateful for my visit. Until I was shot down over Burma late in 1944, this lovely couple sent me a gift parcel each month, which was very welcome and most appreciated.

The next visit was to the father of another pilot, again an only son. This man was the Chief of Police on the Canadian side of Niagara Falls. He showed less outward grief but it was obvious how deeply he felt the loss of his son.

I spent a great couple of days with him. We talked a great deal about his son's life in Britain and he took me out on patrol with him and showed me the sights of Niagara.

The next person I visited was Wing Commander Peterson's widow. He was a man who was respected by the whole squadron and a man whom I admired deeply. I knocked on the door of their Hamilton house and a most gorgeous blond woman answered the knock. I asked her if I could see Mrs Peterson and she answered, "I am Mrs Peterson. You must be Cliff Emeny. Please come in."

The thought flashed through my mind, "How could a man old enough to have the affectionate nickname 'Pop' have such a glamorous young wife?"

This was to be my hardest interview. Mrs Peterson was deeply grieved and shocked at the loss of her husband, especially as no one could tell her exactly what had happened. She had written to the top brass in Canada and the RCAF in England and all she got back was that his death 'was a training accident'. But how could he be killed in a training accident when he had done over 1 500 hours of flying? It seemed to her to be a terrible waste of a good man and a good officer. Everyone had told her that night fighters were the safest way to fight a war and his chances of being killed were slight. She was obviously an intelligent woman and wanted to know exactly what had happened.

I told her the details of how her husband had been the victim of the unpredictable instability of the Beaufighter 2 and how he had died checking out the first Beaufighter 2 that 409 Squadron had received. I told her how it had suddenly flipped upside down and came down in a flat spin he couldn't correct and how all the time he was transmitting on his radio the steps he was taking to pull out of it. The tragedy happened when the whole squadron was watching his fight to regain control.

She asked me how many other Beaufighters had crashed. I told her that, including my own survival, there had been six other crashes caused by the inherent instability of the planes at low speed and under difficult conditions. Then she wanted to know why the RAF used such defective, dangerous aeroplanes. I explained to her that German bombers were blasting British cities night after night. Hundreds of innocent people were being killed and every raid was injuring thousands. The RAF had rushed into production the Beaufighter 2 to carry radar.

Then she asked, "Well, why wasn't it fully tested before it left the factory?" I explained that the factory test pilots were far better trained and more experienced than wartime-trained pilots. Test pilots did their testing on good runways and did not fly at night in rough weather nor did they try to land on narrow, short landing strips as operational pilots so often had to do.

I told her how we knew the RAF was working hard to improve the stability of the Beaufighter but until the better model arrived we just had to do the best with what we had. We owed that to the thousands of victims of German air raids. All accidents, except her husband's, had been landing crashes at night in stormy or difficult conditions.

I told her again how her husband had told us so calmly over his radio what he was trying to do to control the spin until he finally crashed into the airfield. His bravery had helped reveal an undetected design fault in the plane and so he had saved the lives of many other Beaufighter crews.

Over lunch she asked me about my own wartime flying and then drove me around to see the city. She became much more relaxed and asked me to be her guest at dinner. My train didn't leave till 10.30 so we dined and danced and talked about the war and the Air Force in Britain. She was charming company.

In the taxi to the station she took my hand and thanked me for coming to see her, telling me that I had answered her questions and had filled in all the gaps. She now understood much better what the war was all about and she was no longer going to wallow in self-pity and anger. "If nice young men like you are going to keep on risking their lives I am going to get involved to help win the war." At the station she gave me a hug and a kiss and with tears in her eyes said, "Please be careful. God bless you and bring you safely home."

After that experience the next three visits were easier to get through. All of them were visits to family members who just wanted to know so much more than the brutal telegram they had received that had told them of a husband, son or brother's death.

The last interview had an interesting extra. After I had been in this home an hour or so, a very good-looking girl arrived. I recognised her immediately from her photograph as the fiancée of a 409 pilot. Her name was Paula and she was plainly uptight about something. When I found myself alone with her, she blurted out, "Is my fiancée being faithful to me in England?" What could I say? I knew he wasn't. I reassured her that all the officers in 409 Squadron loved her. Every time we had a party it always ended with us all dancing around her photograph and singing the popular love song 'Anna Palau', but using her name 'Paula' instead. She said, "How wonderful!" And seemed quite happy and relaxed.

Two weeks later I began my flying training. I arrived at the training establishment to find an instructor calling the roll for the new entrants. I took a seat at the back of the room and when the instructor called, "Emeny" I replied "Yes".

He obviously didn't see me or hear me and called again, "Emeny! Where are you? Stand up man." So I stood on a chair and when he saw I was an officer he looked nonplussed, paused and then went on calling the roll. Shortly afterwards I was called to the CO's office. He asked me, "How come you are here? Who sent you?"

I replied, "The RAF sent me to do pilot training."

"But we don't have officer cadets here. We only have LACs."

"Well," I replied, "I can live in the officers' mess as well as in the airmen's mess."

"No," he answered, "It is not as simple as that. It is a real problem. I don't know what I am going to do about it."

A couple of days later he called me back in and said, "Well, I have found the solution. Just north of here, halfway to Edmonton, there is a civilian flying school. We will send you up there. Actually they are going to expand the school and we are going to send some instructors up. An English squadron leader will arrive shortly to run it. We will send you up there and your rank won't matter so much."

So I travelled up to Bone and arrived the day after the new CO arrived. He was in the process of settling in and turned out to be another of those obnoxious, officious officers that turned up all too frequently in the RAF.

"Well then," he said without any hint of greeting, "Let me see your log book." He looked at the entry where I had done my flying training in England. "Oh, so you think you are above average do you?"

"Well Sir, that is not my opinion. That is the opinion of the officer commanding who checked me out and judged my abilities."

"We will damned soon see if you are that here."

That was my welcome and I knew from the outset I was in trouble. He decided to be my instructor. Three weeks later, when everyone else had completed 15 to 20 hours I had completed only four. We were flying Stearmans, an American trainer with a 300 horsepower motor, much bigger than a Tiger Moth. It was a real aeroplane. After three weeks I had done very few familiarisation flights. I knew the time had come for me to confront him.

Cliff with a Stearman at the finish of his elementary pilot training.

I threatened that unless in the next week I was brought up to the same level of instruction as the rest of the course, I would leave and go straight to the AOC and report to him personally what was going on in this training school. After this I began to get my training.

Canada was a fantastic experience: wide open spaces, towns and cities all lit up at night, but the west had problems with dust storms. Four planes were up when a storm developed. I was on a cross-country flight and could see I had no hope of getting back to the airfield before the dust storm hit. I decided I had to get on the ground as quickly as possible. I landed in a wheat field and taxied up to the big grain silo elevators and buildings and parked the aircraft on the lee side sheltered from the wind. The workers there helped me to tie it down with ropes. Of the four planes up that day I was the only one that survived. The others were caught in the storm and crashed.

I finished the course and the CO marked me down at 72.5 percent which was 2.5 percent below above average so he had the last laugh.

I went from there to Calgary, and instead of Harvards, chose to fly twin-engine planes because in the back of my mind the aeroplane I wanted to fly when I got back to Britain was the twin-engine Mosquito.

Flying Officer Emeny (promoted 1 October 1942) in front of Airspeed Oxford, advanced training plane.

At Calgary I started my training on Oxfords. I was there a month when the whole unit was moved to Saskatchewan in the middle of the prairie. The airfields there were all along the railway line so it was quite easy to navigate. Suddenly autumn was behind us and winter came with all its chilling cold and snow. Once a snowstorm was over, there was brilliant sunshine but the temperatures could be as far below as 30 degrees Farenheit. The Oxford engine would not fly at that temperature so we got very little flying in. The time we could fly was when another snowstorm was approaching and the temperature would rise to about zero. The big panic was to get everyone to do some cross-country flying before the storm hit and made flying impossible. I finished up acting as navigator/pilot to help pilots get back home before it snowed again.

We graduated the day before Christmas Eve. The day before Christmas, however, I flew four times as navigator to four pilots who still had their cross-country flight to do.

My roommate and I decided we would have some fun before we left. We cooked up a scheme where we would fly

up the railway line after dark with boxes of toilet rolls and fly up and down the main street of Medicine Hat and line the street with toilet paper. Medicine Hat was about 50 to 60 miles from our base. I was flying in the late afternoon and got back just as it fell dark. Everybody was tearing off to their Christmas Eve parties and my roommate asked me, "Are you still on for this game?"

The third 'Wing' at last.

"Yes." Because even if it was snowing the railways were lit up and we knew the course and so away we went to Medicine Hat. We flew up the main street at about 50 feet high and dropped the toilet rolls behind us. By the time we got back to Swift Current it was snowing like hell and you could hardly see anything, but I knew the exact course from the clock tower to the end of the runway. Landing was going to be the problem because we couldn't see a thing. I flew over the runway four times, getting a little lower each time. Unbeknown to me the CO was up in the tower and said on my fourth run, "If that son-of-a-gun doesn't come down next time shoot him down with some rockets." The fifth time I got it right and came out of the murk just a few feet above the ground and right at the end of the runway. We taxied to the hangar, jumped out, grabbed a vehicle and raced into town. No one ever did discover who flew low over Medicine Hat dropping toilet rolls all over the place.

A couple of days later who should turn up to Swift Current but Group Captain Tiny White, a little New Zealander in charge of all New Zealanders taking part in the Air Training Scheme in Canada. I was called up to the CO's office and Group Captain White said, "Emeny, I am pleased to meet you. I have been reading your record and the CO and I have been discussing what we are going to do with you. I have decided that you are to return to New Zealand as an instructor. You have a lot of qualifications and experience we don't have in New Zealand."

I objected, "I have only just got my wings, sir."

Yes, but you have air gunnery, you have radar, you have night fighter experience – all the things we may shortly need in the Pacific. You have been away now for nearly three years so we think that the best thing we can do is send you back to New Zealand."

He was quite adamant about it and nothing I could say would change his mind. "I've arranged with the CO for you to stay here. It might take us a few months to arrange a passage for you. In the meantime you will be an instructor here and get in as many flying hours as possible."

Unhappy and frustrated, I took a week's leave and decided to travel to Texas to visit Gene Skinner. Gene was one of the civilian electronic engineers who installed the radar in our Beaufighter 2 in 1941. When he returned to the States with the other three Americans he told his sister how I had roomed with them and learnt from them about radar and his sister wrote me several letters. So I made my way to Dallas, Texas, and had a truly wonderful time there. Gene and his family made me very welcome and the Texas War Veterans Association welcomed me as one of their own. I was asked to speak to 5 000 workers in the factory making Mitchell bombers and Mustang fighters and tell them how we had won the Battle of Britain. I never mentioned to this large group the slaughter of the Defiant squadrons. I spoke about the achievement of the Spitfires and the Hurricanes and the value of radar and the development of the night fighter.

After two weeks' leave, I decided to ignore Group Captain White's orders and to make my own way back to Britain via Halifax, Canada. It was from Halifax that the convoys sailed to begin their journey across the Atlantic. On my way to Halifax, bad weather put me down in Boston forcing me to take the 11.30 pm train to Canada.

I enquired at the Services Information Centre about what I could do and see in Boston. The kindly middle-aged lady behind the counter asked me my age. When I told her it was my 23rd birthday that day she almost begged me to return to the information centre at 5.30, which I did. She invited me to dinner at her home, which turned out to be a birthday party for me. There were a dozen young people of about my age there and we had a great time. They all came to see me off on the train at 11.30 pm.

That thoughtful lady then wrote a lovely letter to my mother and included some snaps taken at the party.

As I got closer to Halifax I began to worry how I would

explain away having no embarkation papers. When I arrived I was surprised to find very few airmen walking around and then I was told a severe blizzard had stopped all traffic from western Canada for over two weeks. I explained that I had made my way to Halifax from Texas and the embarkation officer kindly gave me 250 dollars to cover my expenses while I waited for the first ship to England. No one asked to see my embarkation papers.

After the war I met Tiny White socially in New Zealand. He was surprised to see me, "Oh yes, I remember you. You disappeared from Swift Current but I never bothered looking for you. I was sure you had simply decided to go and fight your own war. Later in 1944 I saw that you had been killed in Burma. You must have been lucky to survive all that." He was quite right. I was lucky.

Apart from that first week visiting those grieving families, my visit to Canada was a wonderful, restful experience. What a contrast to the difficulties of life in wartime Britain with its food shortages and blackouts. In Canada all the towns and cities were lit up at night and there was no shortage of good food. The people were friendly and sociable. It was a huge interesting country. I arrived in summer and stayed through to winter experiencing the heat of summer, the gold of autumn and the searing cold of winter.

Being both commissioned and operationally experienced I had both time and money to see a lot.

While in Alberta for instance, I went to Banff Springs, an imposing resort in the middle of the Rocky Mountains. There, both good and bad luck befell me. I met a group of American diplomats on holiday who had been in Europe when war broke out. In the group was a beautiful girl named Elaine. We decided to go horse riding together. On the second floor of the hotel I bought a film for my camera but when we reached the first floor and I went to pay for the horses I found my wallet had gone from my hip pocket. Someone had picked my pocket as we came down the stairs.

Elaine insisted on paying for the horses and was delighted

75

to find I could really ride. We rode through forest paths high in the Rockies and thoroughly enjoyed ourselves. Back at the hotel she introduced me to her father and told him how I had lost my wallet. He immediately invited me to join their party as his guest. This was so typical of the hospitality I experienced while I was in Canada. With them I went to a lovely lake resort higher in the Rockies. I spent four and a half days with them instead of just the weekend I had originally planned.

I also attended the great Calgary Stampede Rodeo with all its Wild West features, very different to anything in New Zealand. At Calgary I was invited to join a group who were rifle shooting. I got a score of 9.5 bull's-eyes. I thought I was doing great until I discovered that this shooting contest was the Canadian National Rifle Shooting Championship and only the hits in the small circle in the centre of the bull's-eye counted. I was eliminated in the first round.

The final thing I would like to mention about my stay in Canada happened at the air station at Swift Current. There I hired a girl typist to type up my diary I had kept since I had left New Zealand. I had written it in pencil and it was beginning to fade. I swore her to secrecy about its contents but I suspect that some of the other girls in that town got a little information from the nature of the questions I was asked and by the attention given to me at the local dances. When I finished the course at Swift Current the girl who had typed my diary gave me lovely brevet wings she had stitched in silver thread. It must have taken her hours of work and it looked quite splendid. Regretfully I later had to give it away.

Trained as a Pilot 1942-43. Canada.

Awarded his pilot's 'wings' on 24 December. Embarked at Halifax 3 February 1943.

Chapter 9

BACK TO THE WAR AND COURT MARTIAL

Late in January 1943, I was on my way back to Britain on a modern, fast Castle Line ship. I immediately introduced myself to the second mate and told him about my service on the *Wellington Star* as a seaman/gunner and offered to assist in the defence of the ship. He was delighted and incorporated me in to the 6-inch gun crew. I was equally delighted because it meant that I was on deck at night when the danger of submarine attack was greatest. No way did I want to be below deck at night.

Early on we ran into a nasty storm, which scattered the convoy at night. At dawn we found ourselves alone in the Atlantic. Rather than search for the convoy the captain increased speed and headed for Britain zigzagging all the way. We sailed practically at full speed all the way, faster than any submarine could go and so we safely reached Liverpool.

From Liverpool I travelled by train to Bournemouth on the south coast of England. What a changed lifestyle! Complete blackouts at nights, a sense of drabness, especially women's clothing, limited and rationed choice of food, uniforms everywhere and no heating in our quarters even although once it was a smart tourist hotel. It was certainly back to the war all over again.

The usual wait at Bournemouth before being posted was six to eight weeks. Not being prepared to take potluck as to where I would be posted I took leave and went to London. There I looked up some former Battle of Britain acquaintances in the Air Ministry and asked about the possibility of being posted to a Mosquito squadron. I was steered to the right Air Ministry office and finally got to see someone who knew about Mosquito night operations over Germany. He was an ex-Battle of Britain pilot and eager to help. He told me about a new Mosquito night intruder course being organised and arranged for me to be sent to Grantham in Lincolnshire for more twin-engine flying on Blenheims and Beauforts.

I returned to Bournemouth. A bunch of Aussie pilots and navigators arrived from Canada and they immediately challenged the few New Zealanders there to a game of rugby. I played on the wing. Unfortunately, the referee knew little about rugby and nothing about its rules. It was a wild, free-for-all game. Anything went. No one was safe. We played like crazed lunatics and wide-spread injuries were the result. I ended up with a dislocated shoulder, damaged ribs and numerous bruises. It took three weeks of painful massage to get me mobile again. After that match, rugby was banned at Bournemouth.

On 30 April I arrived at Grantham to begin flying twin-engine aircraft. I put my foot right in it the first night I was there. Sitting at a long table at dinner I heard someone further along the table emphatically shooting his mouth off about how good these pilots would have to be if they wanted to fly Beaufighters. I heard him say that the Beau was a real tough fighting plane but quickly killed off any dud pilots. And so he went on and on. I got more and more annoyed until finally I interrupted for all to hear, " Bloody bollocks. What a lot of rubbish you are talking."

To which the sharp reply came, "What do you know about Beaufighters?"

"I did a tour on Beau night-fighters not 30 miles from here. What you are talking about happened to the Beau 2. But the

Beau 6, which is now flying, is a very different plane. It is free from all the dangerous faults of the Beau 2. It is a very stable plane. You should be bloody well ashamed of yourself talking such rubbish to these young trainee pilots."

The fat was really in the fire. He turned out to be a squadron leader and deputy chief flying instructor and I knew I was in trouble right from the start of the course. I found out later that this man who caused me so much trouble, had been in Training Command most of the war. He had only had one flight in the Beaufighter 6 and that was standing behind the pilot, not actually flying it himself.

I was the only one in the course who had been on wartime operations and this didn't endear me to him. I think jealousy played a big part in our relationship. The students had many questions they asked me, particularly about combat. I tried to answer their questions as truthfully as I could without affecting their morale. The squadron leader hounded me all the way. The planes in the training school were old and many were worn out and I seemed to get the worst of them to fly. Three times I had

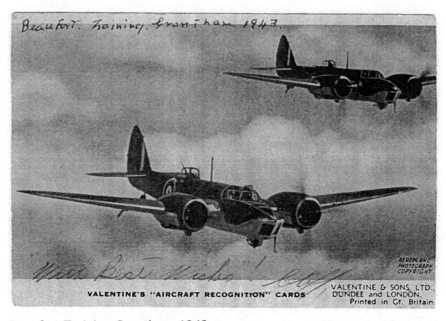

Beaufort Training Grantham 1943.

to refuse to accept one until it was airworthy. After each flight he was loudly critical of me. He not only unjustifiably found fault with my flying, but also was very sarcastic about me personally. I soon learnt to just keep quiet and let him rave but that seemed to make him worse.

Then without warning, halfway through the course, I was posted to a torpedo Beaufighter operational training unit. I think he found out that I was to go on the Mosquito Night Intruder Course but he was determined that I wouldn't.

I was given a few days' leave and went straight to London and looked up my friend at the ministry. He made some uncomplimentary remarks about the squadron leader and gave me a note requiring me to finish the course. He told me to return to Grantham as the intruder course was not quite ready to begin and I need all the flying experience I could get on twin-engine planes.

So I returned to Grantham, handed the squadron leader the memo and continued on in this very unhappy atmosphere. Two weeks later I was posted again to the same torpedo operational

The Course at Grantham. Emeny fourth from right in back row.

training unit. Again I went to London and got the same memo to take back.

I tried delivering the memo to the chief instructor but was curtly told by his staff that all communications had to come through my flight commander, the squadron leader. As far as Training Command was concerned there was no such thing as a war. They insisted I follow the same system and the same procedure as existed prior to the war.

The squadron leader never gave up. I never received the flying I should have and there was certainly no pleasure in it for me. Two weeks later I was again transferred to the same Beaufighter unit. Back to London I went. This time my friend in the ministry decided on a new strategy. He told me that the Mosquito conversion course would commence in three weeks' time so he gave me three weeks' leave and told me to report back to Grantham when my posting to the Mosquito unit would be through.

It was then I had the idea of visiting Southern Ireland. I borrowed some civilian clothes from a London friend and travelled to Belfast on the steamer and then got on the train to Dublin. In my compartment was a well dressed, middle-aged man. We introduced ourselves and I found I was travelling with a supreme court judge. He invited me to his home in Dublin as his house guest. He had three teenage children and I had a great time with them. This family had a 30-acre farm south of the city and so they didn't go short of bacon and eggs, butter, cream, cheese and meat, which were so scarce in the rest of Ireland.

The two oldest children were twins, a boy and a girl. Both were graduating from university at that time and they invited me to go with them to their graduation ball. The men wore tails and the girls ball gowns so I borrowed a suit of tails and off we went to a wonderful night of celebration. The Irish certainly do things in a big way when they celebrate. We rode home on the train next morning, still in our tails and ball gowns and sharing the train with people going to work. No one seemed to take the slightest notice of our dress. Such is life in Ireland.

With these connections I saw a lot of Dublin and learnt much about Ireland. The Irish were interested in New Zealand and very hospitable to a young New Zealander who had come so far from home to be involved in England's war. The English they definitely didn't like. I found their music great and the lovely Irish colleens great fun. I sadly left my new friends feeling that Ireland was a lovely country and the Irish were lovely charming people.

When I returned to RAF Grantham I found myself in serious trouble. The squadron leader had put me up for Court Martial on a charge of 'lack of moral fibre' (cowardice) for refusing posting to a torpedo Beaufighter training unit. I was immediately confined to my room under military guard. In vain I asked to speak to the commanding officer or the chief instructor but neither would see me. A junior officer was assigned to defend me and told me I didn't have much of a defence. He was helpful, however, in that he agreed to call three of my former squadron leaders from 264, 255 and 409 squadrons as defence witnesses. The CO of 409 was now a group captain commanding a Typhoon wing.

Within a week the hearing took place. The squadron leader accused me of 'continuous disobedience, poor application to my training and poor performance as a pilot'. The junior instructors who gave evidence were all complimentary of my efforts. Reports from my official records from the three squadrons I had flown operationally with were all highly complimentary. By this time the station commander was beginning to look decidedly uncomfortable.

Then the group captain spoke. He really got stuck in to the stupidity of the whole business. He spoke highly of my work with 409 Squadron. He concluded with, "If the RAF is so stupid as to waste Emeny's two years' operational experience in night fighters by sending him to a Beaufighter torpedo squadron I am

Blenheim, Grantham Training 1943.

immediately going to demand that he be posted to a Typhoon training unit. Without doubt he will shortly be one of my flight commanders."

When he sat down there was absolute silence. The CO seemed not to know where to look. He adjourned the hearing and I was escorted back to my room. Within 20 minutes I was told that the case had been dismissed. Next day I was posted to RAF High Ercall to begin training in night intruder interception, flying Mosquitos. It was a happy ending to a very stressful experience.

Chapter 10

THE MOSQUITO

The Mosquito was the most streamlined twin-engine plane produced in the war. The motors were only geared for low-level work with a maximum speed 350 mph or 280 mph fully loaded. It was armed with 4 x 20 millimeter cannons under the nose and 4 x 700 machine guns also in the nose.

It carried 2 x 500-pound bombs in the body and for short trips 2 x 500-pound bombs under the wings. For long trips the bombs under the wings were exchanged for long-range fuel tanks. The cannons reduced the size of the exit door by half. The crew had to push their parachutes in first and then crawl in afterwards. Escape by parachute was only possible with height – rarely possible from low level.

It was quite a compact cockpit. The crew consisted of a pilot and navigator. The pilot's seat was on the left side and the navigator sat slightly further back, on the right just behind the exit door.

The de Havilland Mosquito was the best performance bomber and fighter bomber of World War II for load capacity, versatility and speed. Everyone wanted to fly it. I was thrilled to be posted to a Mosquito Training Unit where we were trained to attack German airfields from where their night fighters operated. This reduced their effectiveness in shooting down RAF night bombers. Flying low level over enemy country at night called for special knowledge of the variations of terrain, and of many unknown obstacles about. It also required a high navigational ability to find these airfields deep in enemy territory.

Training Course. Emeny, front row right

The course comprised 15 pilots and 15 navigators. It was a mixture of British, Australians and Canadians. I was the only New Zealander and the only one with previous night fighter experience.

The course began with a series of lectures for the pilots about flying the Mosquito. The CO insisted no one would begin flying training until he was word perfect going through the flying manual. He gave us four days to master it and told us emphatically that if any pilot damaged a Mosquito in any way he would be sent to Aldershot (the RAF Detention Centre). He was a typical Colonel Blimp!

I was first to master the manual so began dual flying training on the afternoon of day three. My first take-off in a Mosquito was most disappointing. I had seen it streaking across the sky and imagined it to be a twin-engine Spitfire. It seemed to take a lot of runway before getting airborne but once in the air it was lovely to fly. There was no comparison between the Mosquito and the old Blenheims and Beauforts at Grantham.

We did all the conversion checks – steep climbs and stalling and then take-offs and landings. With all its power the Mossie had a tendency on take-off to pull to the right so full power was applied to the right motor and half power to the left motor. When speed was sufficient to hold the tail straight the plane quickly became airborne.

I did the first solo flight of the course two days later at 10 am. Everybody from the CO down was watching. The take-off and circuit couldn't have been better and so I approached the runway for landing. I put the Mossie down nicely on the main wheels and left her standing with the rudder high. Suddenly the left wing began to go down and nothing I tried could stop the wing hitting the ground. The plane swung off the runway and the right undercarriage collapsed. It came to a stop on its belly in a cloud of dust. Quickly I flicked off the switches.

I was shocked and terribly disappointed. My first solo a crash! I made no attempt to leave the plane. I just sat there wondering what I had done wrong and all my dreams of flying a Mosquito seemed gone forever.

In a few moments the first tender arrived. The crew leapt on to the aircraft and began smashing the cockpit window around me, obviously thinking I was injured and needed rescuing. I released my straps, climbed out through the broken roof and dropped to the ground.

By this time there was quite a crowd around the wrecked plane, including the CO. Slowly I walked toward him remembering what he had said about Aldershot. The chief engineer was talking earnestly to him. As I approached I heard him say, "I was watching through my binoculars Sir. I saw the left undercarriage fold up. His landing was perfect. The undercarriage locks must have failed."

First solo Mossie flight. U/C lock failed after a good landing. Not my fault!!

I began to breathe again. So it wasn't my fault after all! The CO looked at me and merely asked, "Are you all right, Emeny?" I replied, "Yes, Sir." Then the doctor arrived and suggested I travel in the ambulance to the sickbay and be checked over.

Later that afternoon my instructor checked me out on a circuit and landing. Then I went solo again. This time all went well. I was greatly relieved. At last I began to feel that my longing to fly the Mosquito looked like becoming reality and I wasn't going to Aldershot prison!

The next week gave me more flying with the Mosquito, most of it solo. Then I was to commence the induction course. This meant I needed a navigator.

During this time the navigators had been doing their specialised training. Usually pilots and navigators teamed up haphazardly when drinking together but not being interested in alcohol I chose a different approach. I called at the navigator leader's office and told him I was looking for a good navigator.

His answer was, "Well the best we've got is a quiet, tall Canadian. He has the highest marks. He comes from another Operational Training Unit. Apparently he had two pilots reject him there after a short time but no one seems able to tell me why. Because of his good exam results they sent him here."

I thanked him and called at the sergeant's mess to find him. (This was something not done by officers in the RAF.) I knocked on the door and asked for the duty sergeant. I asked him to find Johnny Yanoto for me. He did and ushered him into his office.

John arrived looking rather serious. I told him I was looking for a navigator and had heard that he had good marks and would like to suggest that we team up for a while to see if we suited each other. Johnny seemed speechless. His mouth opened but no sound came out. Then I suddenly realised the enormity of the situation. Here he was, probably feeling rather down after being rejected by two pilots being summoned to the office wondering what the officer wanted him for, then being offered the opportunity to fly with the most senior and experienced pilot on the course. It was all a bit too much at once. He stammered out, "Yes, Sir! Yes, Sir!"

I replied, "That's great Johnny. I'll contact you when we can do some flying together. In the meantime good luck with your studies." I then left. I was quite prepared to take the navigator leader's word that John was a good navigator.

Once we pilots could safely fly the Mossies we proceeded to learn about the armament, guns and bombs. We were to start doing practice attacks on each other, using a camera instead of firing the guns.

The system used to teach aiming and judging the distance to the target aircraft was based on a system I had used extensively when training gunners on 255 and 409 Squadrons.

Regretfully, I found our flight commander was the CO's son-in-law, who had flown Hurricanes in the Battle of Britain and had been transferred to Training Command after a bad smash. He was confused about the whole business of camera attack exercises. After the first rather confusing lecture I went to his office, told him about my experience and offered to help. He told me, "Mind your own business, I am running the flight." I quickly left.

When we arrived for the second lecture after lunch he arrived half an hour late, looking rather dishevelled and smelling of alcohol. He walked to the front and announced, "I'm not well. Flying Officer Emeny will take this lecture" and stumbled out.

So I became the armament lecturer. I soon found part of the important camera/gun equipment was missing, which probably caused some of the squadron leader's confusion. I continued explaining tactics, sighting, etc. over the two days it took to get the missing items.

When everything was fitted to the Mossie the squadron leader decided he would fly the camera-equipped Mossie and I would fly the target aircraft.

We climbed to 3 000 feet, with the squadron leader 500 feet higher and behind, flying at 260 mph. He was supposed to make a 290 mph approach and fire the camera at 400 yards, 300 yards and 200 yards. Then break off. I asked Johnny to keep a close look out on his approach. He reported the squadron leader coming in very fast indeed, much too fast and closing very quickly. I flung our Mossie into a full bank diving turn as he flashed past. I shoved the throttles through emergency for four seconds. Our speed shot up to 350 mph as I dived for our airfield. I flashed across it at 200 feet with the squadron leader close behind. Then I hurtled up in a steep climbing turn on to the base, letting down the undercarriage and flaps and landed well ahead of him. I parked in my right bay and walked to the flight. The squadron leader said nothing to me, nor I to him.

I rather fear he imagined himself back in the Battle of Britain and I was a German bomber he was attacking.

I managed to see that he never flew the camera plane again. Regretfully, he was holding a position he was not really suited for.

I continued the training and provided him with continuous reports as it proceeded. I procured my supplies from the stores officer. Nothing was said but we both understood the position.

I really enjoyed the extra training because in my lecturing I was really training and learning myself. I had to keep one step ahead of the class to get us through the schedule.

Bombing was completely new to me but I found the armament officer helpful as well as the navigation officer. In fact all the staff officers seemed to understand our squadron leader's problem. We soon began to work well together despite 'Colonel Blimp', our CO. (Colonel Blimp was a term coined by cartoonist George Lowe and used during World War II, to describe senior officers who acted in a domineering manner as though they were serving in the 19th-century Army.)

Having mastered armament use, the next step was to practice cross-country flights at night to simulate low-level raids on German airfields. This was where the navigator's skills were vital. I had always been interested in navigation. From the beginning of my flying in Defiants, as an air gunner I always carried maps and a compass to keep track of where we were. By listening to radio instructions given to the pilot, timing the flight in that direction and plotting the course, I usually knew where we were. Even at night I followed our flight mentally.

One night flying with the CO of 409 Squadron, the radio receiver failed and the pilot was concerned about our position. I was able to give him an accurate course back to base. He was very appreciative of my unexpected skills.

So Johnny Yanoto and I took off for our first cross-country and I was soon to learn why two other pilots had dropped him. It was a nice night with half a moon. Our first leg took us from High

Ercall to Oxford. Knowing the country well I was able to follow the track. Johnny's course was wrong and he missed Oxford. He became noticeably busy and then began praying softly to the saints in the Catholic religion. I assumed that being nervous, and trying too hard, he had made an error in calculations. I said, "You seem a bit confused. I know exactly where we are. Your course is out by a few degrees. Just go right back to the beginning, find the error and give me a course to Oxford. I'll just circle until you get it right, and no more praying. Those saints know nothing about navigation."

He got to work with his gear and soon gave me a course to Oxford, which was exactly right. From then on we did the rest of the trip perfectly. When we landed I said to Johnny, "I know you were dropped by two other pilots. Now I know why. Don't ever do that to me again. If you have a problem just tell me and we'll sort it out together. I happen to know something of navigation myself."

Johnny never made another mistake. His navigation was always spot on. I could not have had a better navigator. When we ran into severe problems he never lost his cool and brought us through. I always made a point on these occasions of thanking him for his efforts. But whenever we got into battle situations, Johnny would pray softly to his saints. I didn't mind that and told him so.

Although I didn't place much reliance on praying myself, as long as he applied himself to his duties he could do as much praying as he liked. Life must have been pretty scary at times for him, especially when attacking defended targets at low level. Then he would be looking right down the barrels of guns firing at us from only a few yards away and feeling bullets and shrapnel striking the aircraft as we flashed across the target. I was too busy lining up on the target to have time to think but poor Johnny had to just sit there and watch what was coming up at us and there was absolutely nothing he could do about it. At times it must have seemed sheer hell and I can understand him lapsing into prayer.

Near the end of the course we were scheduled to do the longest run from East Anglia, Scotland, Northern Ireland, Wales and back to High Ercall. Take-off time was 11 pm.

At 10.30 pm rain and heavy wind arrived and by 10.45 Control was recalling the planes already out. I suggested to Johnny that we put our parachutes and gear away. The squadron leader was standing close by and ordered us to go out to our Mossie and take-off at the scheduled time of 11 pm. I was both angry and annoyed. I just grabbed the form 700 that pilots must check and sign before take-off. I signed it without checking it fully expecting to be recalled as soon as I called Control to takeoff. But we were cleared for take-off into the teeth of a howling gale and heavy rain.

It was terrible flying and the storm increased in violence. It was a three-and-a-half-hour flight. Very soon we were the only aircraft in the sky over Britain. With the help of bomber beacons over Lincolnshire and Yorkshire, Johnny did a great job of navigation under appalling conditions.

On the last leg, half way across the Irish Sea to Wales at 600 feet in pouring rain and howling winds I changed fuel tanks. The motors stopped dead. No fuel in the reserve tank! Quickly I dived to the sea and changed back to the main tank. Luckily the motors picked up again 100 feet above the sea. We climbed again to 600 feet. I did a quick check and decided that we might not have enough fuel to reach Wales so I made a mayday distress call.

Western England Flying Control replied. I explained the situation and called for illumination by searchlights over the nearest airfield in Wales. I reduced speed to the most fuel efficiency possible. So the drama continued. A safe ditching on that stormy sea was out of the question. It was a case of reaching Wales or die.

Tossed about by the storm I tried desperately to keep the plane level. Control got on to the top engineer in Rolls Royce and from his bedside phone he advised how to get the best out of our dwindling fuel supply. I was already doing everything he suggested so I just repeated his advice back and thanked him.

Control told me to broadcast at one-minute intervals. All I did was to give my call sign and leave the message to Johnny. (He was praying flat out to all the saints in Catholicism.)

Soon we saw searchlights come on and were told that the airfield was under the lights. The gauges were back at zero and any moment the motors would stop. As we got closer and closer to the light, Johnny left off his praying. The airfield was right on the coast. We had to get right there, or go down in the stormy sea. Finally I was at the point where I could glide in. I closed the throttles, put down the undercarriage and flaps when almost on the runway and landed. We rolled to a stop and the engines stopped. We had made it! What a relief when we stopped. I turned to Johnny and said, "Thanks for the prayers. She has been flying on them for the last six minutes." He just grinned. We sat there in the rain and wind until a truck came out to collect us and took us to the tower.

Everyone was saying, "Whew, that was close!" We agreed. The controller handed me the phone. It was our squadron leader, full of booze at the other end. He started abusing me for signing the 700 for a plane that had not been refuelled. I just put the phone down and cut him off. I heard later that he had sat in his office drinking whisky, listening to all our radio conversations.

Apparently, because they heard the others being stood down and because of the weather, the mechanics hadn't refuelled the plane. They never expected it to be flown that night.

When I got back to base the next day the squadron leader didn't say anything. Neither did I. We had survived so what was the point. No trouble either from Colonel Blimp!

During his early lectures about not damaging a Mossie the CO also forbade any booze parties in the officers' mess, adding that parties may be all right for operational squadrons who were having casualties, but not for trainees. He ended with, "There will not be any footprints on the ceiling". It was common practice for parties in the officers mess to end with putting soot on the feet of a WAAF officer, upending her and walking her across the ceiling, leaving black footprints across it.

One morning, three weeks into the course, the black footprints appeared on the ceiling. We all waited for the CO to arrive. He took one look at the footprints and glared furiously around the room. Then a girl's laughter broke out. He opened his mouth to speak then abruptly left the room. The laughter came from his 20-year-old daughter. They were her footprints. She was a very pleasant and sociable person. The ceiling was clean by lunchtime.

The same girl featured in two other incidents. One evening we had a discussion about 'What is a gentleman?' One of the WAAF officers, a schoolteacher and a very bright lass, came up with the idea that we should write down what we thought proved a man a gentleman. The girls would judge the best answer and the prize would be a night out with one of them. The boys thought it a great idea.

Next evening all the entries were in and the girls were reading them. They were doing a deal of laughing. Much to my surprise I was announced the winner. The schoolteacher lass thanked all the boys for their entries, commenting that some of them must have had very strange girlfriends. My entry, she said, was the only one that all the girls supported as it was of great importance for girls all their lives.

My entry read, 'I have no idea what girls feel makes a gentleman. I feel everyone will have different ideas as to what makes a gentleman. To me a gentleman is the man who always cleans the bath after him!'

The girl chosen to be my companion was the CO's daughter. She came over and gave me a little kiss. We attended the pictures and several dances together and enjoyed each other's company.

On one of those evenings we came back to the bus, which was to take us back to camp. It was full and although the motor was running, the driver seemed in no hurry to get going. He was enthusiastically fondling and cuddling a WAAF in a doorway a few yards away. Thirty minutes later he got into the driver's seat to take us back to base.

My companion was really annoyed and the next day she had the driver on 'the mat'. The charge read, 'Fondling his WAAF companion for 30 minutes with his motor going, and while a bus-full had to wait'. The word got out and she was ragged for some time about a WAAF fondled by a bus driver while his motor was going.

My course lost three Mossies plus my crash. The other three crashed with each of the crews killed. They had been trying to out-fly American Lightnings, (twin-engine fighters) training at a nearby airfield. The Lightning was the only twin-engine fighter in World War II that could match the performance of single-engine fighters. Two Mosquitos failed to pull out after trying to out-turn the Lightnings. The third turned in a tight turn and crashed. Bravado in the air can be a dangerous thing.

Only one pilot got sent to Aldershot. An Aussie was taxiing into a holding bay on a wild stormy night. A mechanic with a torch was directing him. Because of the pouring rain the pilot hadn't noticed that there was already a parked Mossie in that bay. Walking backwards the mechanic walked into the stationary plane and panicked. Instead of giving the pilot the stop signal he just rushed around waving his torch. The pilot, seeing nothing because of the rain, continued on until his props chewed into the parked aircraft.

Next day the CO had the pilot transferred to Aldershot RAF prison in a 'Black Maria'. But the day, after he was back. He had contacted the Australian High Commissioner in London who clearly told 'Colonel Blimp' what the score was.

When the course ended on 24 September I had flown 72 hours on Mosquitos. Both Johnny and I were rated 'above average', but with no thanks from the CO or the squadron leader for all my extra work. The other officers I had worked with were very forthcoming with their thanks.

Next day there was much news. We were posted to 418 Canadian Squadron that had been especially set up for night and day intruder low-level operations over Germany. Everything seemed wonderful. We flew to an aerodrome near Bristol to pick up our new aircraft and then join 418 Squadron. Just before take-off I was ordered to land at High Ercall.

Here my dreams were suddenly shattered. We were met when we landed by the adjutant who took me straight to the CO's Office. There I found a wing commander and a group captain from the Air Ministry. They told me my posting had been changed.

Instead of joining 418 Squadron, I was to lead a flight of Mosquitos to India, to try them out on operations over Burma against the Japanese and to see how they stood up to tropical conditions.

I was shattered. I was so close to achieving my heart's desire to see it suddenly vanish. I asked about the kind of operations we would be doing. The answer was attacking Japanese communications. Mostly daylight raids on river and rail communications.

I protested emphatically that I was especially trained for night intruder work over Germany and definitely didn't want to go to Burma. Both the wing commander and group captain insisted that I had special qualifications for the job. My records showed that I was adaptable, very persevering and exceptionally good at assuming responsibility for newly formed units with good leadership qualities.

They quoted Group Captain Paul de Beaux, my former CO in 409 Squadron as saying 'He only needs to be told the job to be done and he quickly works out how to do it'. They persisted that I had proved to be a very good pilot and I had a wide range of experience that would be invaluable over Burma.

I still protested and pleaded that they must have more experienced people than me. They then focused on the promises. It would only be a three-month operation and then back to Britain and when operations commenced I would be promoted to squadron leader. They would personally send orders to that effect to India. Finally the CO most emphatically demanded, "Let's not have any more of this arguing, Emeny. You've got your orders. Just bloody well get out there and do them."

With a heavy heart I had to give in. My immediate orders were for Johnny and I to return to Fulton to test fly the Mosquito being prepared for the trip. Johnny was just as disappointed as I was. So we moved to Fulton.

Two days later I was ordered to take a group of ten airmen to Manchester for inoculations prior to sailing to India.

On getting there at 11.30 am I was told quite rudely by the flight sergeant in charge that we could not be done that day and would have to come back in two days' time. He insisted that no signal had arrived booking us in. I went into the office and found the signal lying on his desk. The WAAF clerk commented that he had come in late and had not looked at his desk.

I returned to the flight sergeant, showed him the signal and suggested that the party be done over lunchtime as two nurses had offered to help. It would only take 30 minutes to inoculate the whole group. He again rudely refused to co-operate. So I made him stand to attention and emphatically told him, "You are a flight sergeant. I am an officer. I order you to dose these men over lunchtime or do you want me to march you immediately to your commanding officer on a charge of refusing to obey orders?" He grudgingly capitulated. I was the last in the line. He just drove the needle into the bone. It was most painful and bled

U.K. Night Intruder Training.
High Ercall. U.K. 1943.
Before Flying To Burma.

Cliff was posted to Burma on the 18 November 1943 and promoted to Flight Lieutenant on the 29 November 1943.

considerably. A nurse bandaged it for me. (Over recent years the wound has opened up on occasions and bled profusely.) The other men were going on final leave before embarkation and needed time to get over the jabs before their long sea trip.

Johnny and I tested seven Mosquitos for endurance and performance and made them ready for the flight to Gibraltar, Morocco, Cairo, Baghdad, the Persian Gulf and finally India. Before departure we were given a few days' leave.

When I returned from leave I found a strange letter waiting for me. It was written on a piece of folded brown paper from my older brother Bert. He had written from Leros, an island between Crete and Turkey. He was serving with the Long Range Desert Group who usually operated behind German lines in the desert.

But Bert's group had recently been spying on German-held islands between Crete and Syria, where the Allies feared the Germans were preparing an offensive from Crete to Syria. The Long Range Desert Group was trapped on Leros too far away for Allied air support.

The guns of the Mosquitos had been unloaded to carry more fuel so that we could fly around Portugal to Gibraltar. Both Spain and Portugal were neutral and we were only to fly over Spain in an extreme emergency. Bert's letter had been given to the last pilot to leave Leros. On reaching Cairo he gave it to a pilot leaving for the United Kingdom where he posted it to me. By passing military censorship the letter had taken only six days to reach me. To me this was an extreme emergency. If Leros was under attack when we reached Cairo maybe we could give them some air support

I arranged for the guns to be re-loaded and planned to fly over Spain. I reckoned they wouldn't have anything to catch our Mossies. So we flew to Portreath in Cornwall. Portreath was the last RAF airfield leaving the United Kingdom for Gibraltar. There we refuelled for the trip. With full tanks we had just enough fuel to reach Gibraltar by flying over Spain. No one supervised my arrangements. They were used to groups of planes flying out to Gibraltar and everything was left to whoever was leading the flight.

So we set off, out over the Bay of Biscay, and then past France. Our only fear was German fighters based in France. I flew at the most economical speed and took a wider curve than usual to avoid the fighters. It took longer but was safer. We were not intercepted and arriving opposite the Spanish coast I turned and flew across Spain. Gradually we lost height but kept at high speed. As we reached the Spanish/Gibraltar border I had each plane stop and feather one engine. We all landed with one engine stopped.

As soon as I got out of my plane a big black Rolls Royce drove up. Out stepped two senior RAF officers complete with much gold braid.

They explained that I was in big trouble; "You flew over Spain and we have their senior officers yelling at us in my office! Why did you do it?"

I shrugged my shoulders and explained that we had a massive emergency. Didn't they notice that all the flight landed with one engine stopped? We were very short on fuel. They began to relax. Running out of fuel in the air was certainly an emergency.

Then another car arrived. The Navy officer who stepped out confirmed that the flight landed with one engine stopped. The Navy officer was also covered in gold braid. "Come on," he said, "We'll soon sort out these Spaniards!" He seemed to be enjoying it. They took me with them.

They asked me why all the engines stopped and I blamed fuel contamination in our reserve tanks. I explained that as we switched over to them to fly around Portugal, all the planes had one engine stop. Our only hope to reach Gibraltar was to fly over Spain. Besides we were unarmed and could do no harm. After a lot of talk, the Spaniards accepted the explanation and apology. When the Spaniards and the RAF officers had gone the Navy officer invited me over to dinner suggesting that I could now tell him what really happened, which I did. He commented, "Shades of Admiral Nelson lives on in the RAF I see." Then with a laugh he said, "If you try that, it will shake the buggers up in Cairo! Good luck to you."

Next day all the flight had both engines running and we took off for Rabat in Morocco, where the Americans had invaded and built an airfield in the desert by laying metal sheets on the sand. We were to refuel here and fly on to Castille Benito in newly conquered Syria. Rabat was our first introduction to the East but we saw only our quarters – stucco buildings, no windows, open doors and none too clean.

Next morning as I took off, the control on the left engine failed and produced uncontrollable fuel power.

Unable to control the successive swing to the right I shot off the metal strip into the desert. I couldn't afford to cut the switches to shut off the fuel and I concentrated on saving the plane. The sand quickly reduced the speed and the motors stopped in a cloud of dust. When it settled we found ourselves 500 yards off the metal strip and the plane settling in the desert.

It took all day getting the Mossie back on the runway and back to the workshop. I made a sledge to pull it on and towed it safely back to base. The mechanics found the faulty engine part and radioed for a spare from England. It arrived two days later and we took off for Castille Benito. The weather was cool inland so we flew low all the way around North Africa. We passed Roan, Algeria, Anabar, Byerte and Tunis. Flying low over Tunisia we saw the wrecked guns, tanks and vehicles of the defeated German army. The wreckage stretched over 100 miles.

At Gibraltar en route to Burma November, 1943.

Johnny's navigation was excellent and we landed at Castille Benito where we refuelled for the trip across Libya to Cairo. In the air again we passed over the battlefield of El Alamein. The wreckage of machine warfare stretched for 50 miles. The area of the initial battle was covered in shell holes from the terrific British bombardment. I tried to imagine what it must have been like to be a soldier in that battle. The New Zealand Division had fought with the 8th Army in this decisive battle under Montgomery and had played a significant part in the defeat of Rommel – the first major British victory on land since the beginning of the war.

As soon as we landed I asked about Leros Island and was told that it fell to a German airborne attack six days earlier. I began to feel bad about Bert's fate. When I asked if any Allied troops had escaped it was suggested I check with New Zealand Army Headquarters in Cairo.

Seeing Leros had fallen I had the guns unloaded so that we could carry more fuel for our long flight over the desert to Karachi. I also requested the electrical fault in our machine be fixed.

Everyone was helpful. Now the Germans had been driven out of North Africa life was much easier on airfield bases.

Early that evening we all travelled into Cairo. I went straight to New Zealand Army Headquarters seeking information about Bert. The orderly officer directed me to the Intelligence sector. I found everyone very evasive about anyone escaping from Leros. I was left with the impression that they knew something they wouldn't tell me.

I met a pretty WAAC Corporal just going off duty and asked her to show me around Cairo. She readily agreed. As we moved around from place to place I generously supplied her with wine, taking little myself. It was quite a night! By 3 am she had told me what I wanted to know. Some New Zealanders had escaped from Leros and were being held in a secret camp on the Lebanese/Syrian border. I took her back to her quarters and gave the guard some money to take her safely to bed. I then went to look for Johnny.

I found him at 4.30 am. He hadn't long been asleep when I woke him up and told him I wanted to fly out at dawn and look for this secret camp for the Leros survivors. He agreed so we took a taxi to the airport and were airborne 30 minutes after dawn, flying up the coast to Palestine.

Suddenly I saw gun flashes on the shore and looking around saw splashes way out to sea. We were flying through an artillery firing range. Immediately we dived to low level and got through safely.

Finally we reached the Lebanese/Syrian border and flew along it. We came to a camp of tents, laid out in military order. Being very early in the morning there was little sign of life so I 'beat-up' the place, flying only a few feet above the tents. On the fourth run some men came out and shook their fists at us. I saw their berets and knew I had found the right camp. Johnny marked it on his map.

The nearest airport was Lydda in Palestine. We landed there and Johnny went to the sergeants' mess after I had told him to be very secretive about our movements. I took the map and set off to hitchhike to Bert's camp. Luckily I soon got a ride in a truck driven by two young Israeli women. They were carting munitions to Russia. They passed me on to other travellers and I eventually reached the camp at 11.30 pm. The guard took me to the commanding officer, woke him up and introduced me to him. I asked him if Bert was present in the camp. "Yes," he replied. "He's here. Come in and sleep in my tent and we will look him up in the morning." The guard procured for me an army straw-bag bed and two blankets and being exhausted I went to sleep and slept soundly on the ground in the CO's tent.

After breakfast we set off through the scrub to find Bert. Suddenly there was someone running and Bert burst through the scrub. He grabbed me and lifted me off my feet. Bert was over six feet tall. He had heard I was in the officers' mess and took off running to find me. What a great reunion we had! I was so happy to find him alive and well. In the three and a half years since I had seen him he had grown a big moustache and had become a sergeant.

Back in the CO's tent I asked if Bert could have a few days' leave and come back to Lydda with me. His CO agreed and gave him a pair of officers' epaulets to wear, and said, "When someone salutes you, don't drop dead. Just wave back." We had a good laugh together. A vehicle took us to the main road and we soon hitched a truck ride to Lydda. I took him to the officers' mess telling him, "Let me do all the talking. Just relax."

Lydda was a big peacetime RAF base. It was full of Colonel Blimps and humbug rules and officers who seemed to have little or nothing to do. That night at dinner the adjutant came over to our table and sternly asked who we were. I eyeballed him and replied, "That's not for you to know." Rather taken aback he then told us that officers didn't wear battledress to dinner.

I replied, "Haven't you heard yet that there is a bloody war going on? We only have battle dress." Then he rather tartly informed us that when we entered the mess we must come to attention and bow towards the CO's table. To which I replied, "Sorry, we didn't know the Germans had occupied Lydda. I suggest you tell that humbug to the troops in the desert, or in the jungle. We are not interested." He left and we noticed him talking to the CO. Next evening we just stalked into the dining room and made a little move towards the CO. He never came near us.

Bert admitted he felt worried about his young brother's belligerence. He naturally never felt at ease suddenly becoming an officer and we had landed amongst the stuffiest people imaginable. Breakfast and dinner were the only times we mixed with the other officers. One asked Bert what outfit he belonged to. Bert truthfully replied, "The Long Range Desert Group". That reply would most certainly have got back to the CO and confirmed we were something special.

For three days we went into Haifa and sat alone in a café on the waterfront. We sipped an occasional drink and talked about home and our experiences since we had last seen each other.

Bert told me what had happened at Leros. "It was a balls-up," he said, "from beginning to end. We had no air cover and no air support." I found out subsequently that it was at the Casablanca Conference in January 1943, that the decision had been made to recapture Rhodes and the Dodecanese Islands.

Bert explained to me that the Islands had been occupied by Italian troops and it was thought that if they were re-taken it would take the heat off the invasion of Sicily. A full-scale operation was mounted in September and all the islands were captured by the Allies within a few days. Then the Germans counter-attacked. The Allies had no effective air cover and the Island of Cos was quickly over-run. Out of a force of 1500 Allied troops only 100 escaped from the island. One by one all the other islands seized by the Allies were re-taken. The Germans invaded Leros in November and a few days later our forces were forced to surrender but not before the Germans had suffered heavy losses. Eleven hundred were killed out of the 3 000 invasion troops. Even so, Bert and his mates were very lucky to get away.

I realised that Bert had been engaged in no small skirmish. Later I read a description of this little-known episode as a 'flawed and forgotten campaign'. It was flawed because it was attempted without adequate air cover. The Luftwaffe had air superiority. Most of the Allied air forces were heavily engaged in the Italian campaign. They could give little help in the Aegean, which was seen very early in the planning as little more than a sideshow. The question is why did the Allies attempt it at all and why hadn't they learnt the lesson of air superiority?

At the end of our third day together I phoned Cairo and arranged for them to send the other Mosquitos to Lydda. They asked me if I would also take some Spitfires out to India to which I agreed.

Next morning the Mosquitos and Spitfires arrived and we topped up their tanks for the trip to Baghdad. When all was ready I took a jeep to control to get final clearance only to be told that all flying was cancelled. They wouldn't tell me why but when I saw them rolling out the red carpet I knew someone important was coming.

Three DC 4s (large American transports) landed and taxied up to the carpet. The place was loaded with gold braid, including the CO. Out of the plane stepped the Chinese leader Chiang Kai-shek, accompanied by several senior American officers.

I was standing near the carpet with some army photographers. I had with me my own camera and was about to take a photograph when a hand banged down on my shoulder. It was the adjutant. "Put that bloody thing away," he said.

Immediately I got into the jeep and tore off to the planes. I called all the pilots to me and told them that we would take off immediately, and 'beat up' the airfield before we left for Halbanya.

Mosquitos and Spitfires roared low over the visiting party making four runs each. One of the Mosquitos had to return to the airfield soon afterwards with a fuel pump problem. He was told that Chiang Kai-shek and the American officers thought the 'beat up' was put on especially for them. Even the station CO was pleased about it.

The Chinese and American leaders were on their way to meet Churchill in Cairo to attend a war-planning meeting.

As soon as we took off Bert got on the road to return to camp. He took off his officer epaulets, happy to become an ordinary soldier again. It was just as well. The United States General Stilwell landed at Lydda a day or so later and heard that a Long Range Desert officer was on the base. He had everyone out looking for him, but Bert had just disappeared.

The flight to RAF Halbanya was uneventful, flying low over desert-looking country all the way. Even the mountain ranges had little forest on them. It was hard to imagine that across this land developed the cradle of humanity and civilisation. Either the ravages of thousands of years of human habitation, or maybe just natural climatic changes and erosion had left a desolate-looking landscape as far as we could see from 10 000 feet.

The Spitfires were getting low on fuel so we were pleased to land at Halbanya. None of the Spitfires had endurance tests on them before the flight so I sent them up for one-hour endurance tests at different cruising speeds from this airfield. That gave us a lot more information to work on.

Because it was a long flight to Bahrein Island, in the Persian Gulf I told everyone to use the toilet just before we left. There was a large group of us and as we wanted to leave together we used both men's and women's toilets. Then there was a great yell from some officer, "Can't you bloody fools read or are some of you women?" I replied, "Don't you bloody fools know there is a war on!" We heard no more from him. Halbanya was a very old RAF base with plenty of Colonel Blimps there also. So many staff officers around in cushy jobs with little more to do than to see that no one of the wrong sex went into the wrong toilet.

There were two unmanned emergency airfields on route to Bahrein. Just before reaching the first base a Spitfire called reporting lost fuel pressure. We guided him to the base. Just as he touched down his plane burst into flames. He threw himself out, enveloped in flames. He hit the ground while the plane was still moving and the speed rolled him over and over and put out the flames – but he didn't move. We had to leave him there. I called Halbanya who sent a rescue plane to pick him up and thankfully the pilot lived.

In 1943 Bahrein was just an Arab Sheikdom and not the great oil city it is today. When we landed it was a new refuelling stop for RAF planes flying to India. There were only two RAF people there: one officer to supervise refueling, the other to keep the Arabs happy. He informed us that we were all invited to a feast with the Sheik that night.

This officer gave us a thorough briefing on the dos and don'ts.

The dos were: eat like you were starving, make a lot of noise while eating, make much noise of appreciation of the belly dancers and sit quietly on the cushions provided.

The don'ts were: don't allow anyone to get you talking about the planes. (There were certainly to be German or Japanese spies there.)

There won't be any alcohol. Don't be persuaded to have any in secret; it will be the spies supplying it. Don't take any interest in the harem. They will be watching behind a screen. The Sheik won't like you showing interest in them. Stay in a group and leave together.

When we arrived at the Sheik's huge tent we were ushered into a large area and seated on lush cushions that held you six inches off the wooden floor. The Sheik and his family (a dozen boys, aged from 10 to 16) sat on bigger cushions. Bowls of warm water were handed around to wash our hands in and then towels to dry them.

After the hand washing and drying they began bringing in the food in large bowls, about 20 inches across and nine inches deep. Fortunately they fed the Sheik and his family first so we were able to follow their example. They just took a bone covered with meat from the bowl and holding it in both hands proceeded to tear the meat off with their teeth. I thought to myself, "Just like people did a thousand years ago."

I just used one hand to eat with, keeping the other clean. I watched the Sheik and his family licking their hands clean but

I couldn't follow their example and resisted the temptation to wipe my hand on the cushion.

The meat tasted like wild game, possibly young goat. It was quite tender. The servants kept coming around with bowls until no one took any more. I was surprised at how much the Arabs ate. Then the servants brought in bowls of warm water and small towels to wash and dry our hands.

The music increased in volume and tempo and several lightly dressed belly dancers began their routine to the beat of the music, which gradually increased in tempo. The girls were all young, slim and good-looking. As the tempo of the music increased the Arab men showed more pleasure and made more noise. Although we didn't know what the dances meant we followed our instructions and made plenty of noise too. The servants circulated among us offering dates, dried fruit and nuts.

I sneaked a look at the harem (behind the screens) and they were smiling at the dancing.

When the dance finished the Arabs seemed busy talking to each other. After a short while the political officer came over to us and told me that the Sheik's favourite son wanted my pilot's wings. When leaving the UK I had changed my standard RAF wings on my battledress tunic, replacing them with the silver badge, made for me by the girl in Canada. They had the letters NZ instead of RAF. I figured the Indian RAF might just assume they were standard NZ wings.

I cherished those wings because of the effort the girl had put into stitching them so I declined his request. The officer insisted, "Let him have them. Keeping these people happy is important to us. He will give you something valuable in exchange." I looked across to the Arab youth who was watching me. Maybe he knew I was leader of the flight and that these silver wings represented a higher rank. I raised my hand in a small wave, and he waved back. I agreed to let them go.

The RAF officer carefully snipped the stitching off and carried the wings on a cushion to the youth. He took them and placed something back on the cushion, which was brought back to me. It was a miniature Arab scimitar wide-bladed sword with a jewelled grip. It was obviously quite valuable. I looked across at the youth, smiled and gave him another light wave. He waved back. I was reluctant to send it back to New Zealand by ship in case it was lost so secreted it in my case. But it was missing when the case was returned to me after getting away from Rangoon.

About one and a half hours after entering the Sheik's tent we left. We all agreed it was an interesting occasion, if a bit primitive. The RAF officer was pleased at how we had conducted ourselves.

Next day we left for Karachi, the last leg of our trip from Britain. The flight was planned to take four hours and 55 minutes, leaving 20 minutes of fuel reserve. On take-off the weather was good but we had no idea what to expect further out. The weather was critical for the two remaining Spitfires.

Finally we reached the border of India (now Pakistan) where there was an emergency landing strip but with no facilities, so we made the decision to carry on with the Spitfires to Karachi. The trip took four hours and 50 minutes. We flew at only 250 mph to extend the range of the two Spitfires. Fortunately we had a light following wind. They had only 10 minutes of fuel left when we landed. The RAF had taken a big risk in sending them out, especially as they hadn't bothered to do any endurance trials. Johnny's navigation was again right on.

Arriving in India was a cultural shock to all the crews. We were the first occupants of a new transit camp. The camp consisted of long rows of buildings. Each building was divided into small rooms just big enough for two narrow beds. There were no windows or doors. The base of the bed was plaited material, which was all right for light people, but they sagged somewhat

110

under heavier bodies. We were issued with a typical army mattress: a sack filled with straw, two blankets and a mosquito net. Without that net it would have been impossible to sleep and we would have been eaten alive and probably become malaria cases.

Amazingly there were no feeding arrangements in the camp. We were expected to hire local servants who would buy our supplies, do our cooking and look after us generally. No one bothered to brief us about this. The RAF truck just dumped us off with our gear and left us to fend and find out for ourselves.

What a shambles! The locals were soon around us, jabbering away in a confused sort of pidgin English. We had no idea of the name for water or for food nor had we any idea how to employ them or how much to pay them. Everyone talked so loudly and fast and all of them obviously wanted work.

I decided to do nothing until I could find an English-speaking person, preferably a European, who could explain how we should handle the situation. We had no local money, only English and Egyptian from Cairo. All I could feel was, "If this is a sample of the organisation of the RAF, God help us! No wonder no-one in the UK wants to come to India."

So we decided to go into the city to find some help. Then there was another bout of shouting and yelling and jabbering. Finally we got into some rickshaws, not realising how far it was into the city. We were also surprised that one man was in between the shafts and another walked beside him. There were two of us sitting in each rickshaw and it must have been quite heavy to pull. Periodically the one walking spelled the one between the shafts. We left a couple of guards behind to mind our gear.

Arriving in Karachi was an even greater cultural shock. There were crowds of people everywhere with the bustle and the noise and the dirt and filth, and the bargaining. You bargained for everything, whether it was riding in a rickshaw or buying food. We were quickly conscious of being strangers in a strange and different world. Whereas the war dominated our lives in Britain, Europe and the Middle East, here the war just didn't seem to matter.

I realised we needed some good advice quickly. I had some UK money to change and walked into a big building that looked like a bank and asked to speak to the manager. Again I was lucky. He was a very approachable, helpful and knowledgeable person. He was delighted to know that some modern fighter-bombers had arrived in India to fight the Japanese. He told me how most military people in Karachi called themselves the 'forgotten army'. They were desperately short of modern weapons and supplies.

He told me that the 'forgotten army' could only hold the Japs on the Bengal/Assam borders but had no scope for offensive action to drive them out of Burma. "You'll find plenty of unemployed officers hanging around waiting for something to happen," he said. How right he was!

He warned me of the many dangers for Europeans living in India. Food, drinking water, hygiene, disease and the danger of 'tummy bug' (a form of dysentery), all presented danger. "Eat only in well-established places," he advised, "and keep out of the brothels. Venereal disease is rife in Karachi." He warned us to make sure our possessions were always well guarded. "The most reliable guards are retired Gurkha soldiers," he said.

"Above all, never carry any quantity of money on you. Certainly never show a wad of notes. There are pickpockets everywhere, often just small children.

"Don't give to beggars. Never accept the first price quoted for anything. You can usually get 25 to 50 percent off. When you want to get into a rickshaw tell him where you want to go and bargain a price. Do not rely too much on the police. They have a price for everything too."

As if this wasn't enough, he added, "Never go around alone. Always go in a group. It is very easy for a lone Englishman to be waylaid in an alley and mugged and robbed."

So the list went on. I began to realise even more why no one in the RAF wanted to serve in India and why an unsuspecting New Zealander was picked to bring the flight of Mosquitos out to the 'forgotten army'.

I had the empty, sad feeling that there would be many problems to be faced before we could fire our guns against the Japanese. Nine weeks had already passed since the High Ercall course had ended. If I had stayed with 48 Squadron I would probably have 20 raids under my belt by now. Still we had flown from England to India, something that just a few years previously would have been hailed by the newspapers of the world.

I signalled RAF Headquarters in Delhi that the Mosquitos had arrived at Karachi and I urgently requested further orders.

Two days after we landed a flight of Soviet biplanes, the antiquated Po-2, arrived. They had been spraying locust swarms further north. I took their flight commander for a short ride in a Mosquito. He was most impressed but refused to allow any of us to even look inside their old planes.

We could fraternise away from the planes but a solid wall went up as soon as anything about the military was mentioned.

After four days of inaction I became impatient. Next morning Johnny and I took off for Delhi. We reached RAF Headquarters at 9 am. I spent all day sitting outside one office after another trying to see someone who knew anything about the plans to use our flight of Mosquitos. Each person I saw just handed me on to another. The Karachi bank manager was right when he said we would meet many unemployed officers in this part of the world.

That evening at dinner in the officers' mess I sought out the senior officer wearing wings. I told him of our arrival and asked him how it was planned to use our flight in operations against the Japanese. He was affable and pleasant. He thanked me for the signal I had sent when we arrived at Karachi and for then

113

coming on to Delhi. He suggested I get myself settled in because I would be staying some time. He explained that a list was being prepared of officers who wanted to have a flight in the Mosquito. After a pause, he said that I would probably start the operation next day.

Looking him in the eye I remonstrated, "That is not what we have come to India to do."

He just smiled and said, "Don't be in a hurry. You will have your share to have a crack at the Japanese with all in good time." He excused himself and walked away.

I was dumbfounded. I thought of Jean Watson and her mother in Scotland working 12 hours a day, seven days a week making Rolls Royce engines for our Mosquitos. I thought of the seamen manning tankers bringing fuel to India at great risk. So many of them had died terrible, fiery deaths when their ships had been torpedoed en route. Now that precious fuel was to be wasted giving joyrides to this group of RAF officers with nothing to do except boast they had flown in a Mosquito.

Feeling annoyed, I bought my usual shandy, half beer and half lemonade, and looked for somewhere to sit. The only table available was already occupied by a squadron leader without wings. As I sat down he said, "Hello," in a broad Scots accent, "What brings you to Delhi?" I told him as briefly as I could and then asked him what his job was. He was an engineering officer co-ordinating equipment needed for planes operating from India. He had received no notice of the arrival of the Mosquitos but now that he knew about them he would look out for them.

I asked him what would happen to them? "Simple," he replied. "They will be sent to the central main base unit at Allahabad in central India and stay there until they are allocated to a squadron." When I asked him how long it took to get to a squadron, he replied, "Rarely less than four weeks. Sometimes much longer. It all depends what plans the planners have for them." We chatted on for a couple of hours. He came from Glasgow and we talked a lot about Scotland. Before leaving him I checked on how to contact him if I ever had need to.

That night I made a decision to immediately take the Mosquitos to Allahabad. By seven next morning I had contacted Johnny and at 8 am we took off for Karachi leaving the Delhi officers to whistle for their joyride in a Mosquito.

In the air I began to realise that a sore throat was beginning to develop. That night it was really nasty and I knew I was in for a real attack of inflamed tonsillitis similar to the one that had laid me low in Scotland in 1941. Maybe the infected dust of Karachi had caused it.

Next morning I reported to the RAF medical officer. He informed me that I was the second one to become infected. The other was a Russian officer flying a crop-spraying plane. He had been operated on at the local hospital for the removal of his tonsils but had died. Immediately I decided that hospital was not for me. I would go to bed in my own quarters and rest there. The MO gave me some sulpha tablets. My throat was too sore to swallow any food so I stocked up with suitable fluids and tins of preserved peaches, which I found I could swallow.

By the evening I was semi-delirious. Everyone had gone into Karachi. After dark the dogs, both local and wild, arrived on the scene. They made a tremendous noise snarling and growling. I got my revolver, loaded it and waited in the darkness of my room that had no doors or windows. Finally a big dog stood in the doorway, beady eyes staring at me, only about four feet from where I lay. I let him have the whole six rounds, as fast as I could pull the trigger. The wounded dog rushed out yelping loudly. Immediately there was absolute pandemonium as the other dogs attacked it. Next morning all the boys found was a few bits of hair, bone and bloodstains.

I rested for seven days before the fever subsided and I was able to eat normal meals.

Once I felt well enough I contacted the engineer squadron leader in Delhi and suggested the flight fly to Allahabad. He agreed and told me that no one had mentioned the Mosquitos to him but added, "Don't tell anyone that I agreed they should go to Allahabad."

Next day we took off for Allahabad. Here I requested the CO to signal Delhi that the Mosquitos had all arrived safely. He hadn't heard anything about the arrival of a flight of Mosquitos but signaled Delhi. He was most interested in them, especially after I gave him a flight in one that afternoon. I noticed eight Beaufighters parked there too. He told me that they were waiting for 10 more to arrive before they went out on operations.

So we settled down to wait. Christmas 1943 arrived and I went with Johnny to a big Catholic Church for the Christmas Day service. It was a long, formal service, mainly in Latin, but a little in English. Johnny was happy and seemed very much at home and now I could say that I too had been to a Catholic service.

Cliff and Johnny Yanoto, Canadian Navigator. Christmas Day 1943.

Early in January the Beaufighters left for Agartala in Bengal but there was still no word about the Mosquitos. Then we were asked whether they had been air tested and the necessary modifications carried out on them. Some armourers arrived and studied the guns and bomb fittings and we knew that someone was taking an interest in us. In December and January I had only completed eight hours of flying.

Shortly after the Beaufighters left things began happening in earnest. Groups of mechanics arrived and they were obviously familiarising themselves with the Mossies. They seemed to have files of paper to work through and seemed to be very thorough in what they were doing. They were fresh from the United Kingdom and the officer in charge was sociable but very busy. Then on the 9 January 1944 we got the news we had been waiting for. We too were going to Agartala to join up with the Beaufighters as a composite squadron. Apparently the idea was to try them both out together against the Japanese.

Chapter 11

No. 27 SQUADRON

On my 24th birthday (11 January) we took off for Agartala, which was to be our operational base for the next four and half months. We were to operate against the southern front where the Japanese were trying to advance into India with Calcutta as their ultimate goal. This border area consists of several mountain ranges, covered by thick jungle and stretching to the Bay of Bengal. It was terrible country to fight a war in.

Our airfield was a long, single strip. The reddish gravel produced a great cloud of dust on both take-off and landing. There were no bomb-proof shelters for the aircraft and all buildings were of light bamboo construction. No doors or windows had been installed but we were assured that they would be by monsoon time. Never having experienced the terrific daily deluge of monsoon rains we were blissfully ignorant of the importance of that promise.

We lived in a long bamboo structure, divided into rooms just big enough for two single beds. One building was for officers, another for sergeants and another for ground staff. The third building was simply a dormitory.

Officers were issued with two sheets and a blanket. The nights were unbearably hot and sticky. Our beds were covered by a white mosquito net that rolled down at night to protect us from the swarms of malaria-carrying mosquitoes. We all took quinine tablets to ward off malaria. Many American servicemen refused to take the quinine tablets as they didn't like looking yellow and as a result they suffered much more from malaria than we did.

The ground crews and sergeants were fed by the RAF but officers came under the old British Indian Army system where they employed their own servants to organise their meals, water supplies, bath water, washing of clothes and so on. Each officer was expected to have at least four or more servants. Four of us really upset the system. We insisted we would pay one man twice as much to look after the four of us but there was so much trouble that we finally went along with the old system.

As an officer you purchased your own folding canvas bath that was about three feet square. The bearer (servant) poured three buckets of water into it. You then stripped off and sat in it trying to splash some of the three inches of water over yourself.

Everything you owned had to be guarded night and day or it would be stolen, so we had to hire guards.

The commanding officer of this composite Squadron No. 27 was Wing Commander Nicholson, VC. He was the only fighter pilot to be awarded the Victoria Cross by Fighter Command during World War II. He had won his Victoria Cross in the Battle of Britain when he encountered the Luftwaffe for the first time. (Pilot Officer James Nicholson was leading a section of Hurricanes over the Southampton area at 18 000 feet when it was bounced by Bf 109s. Nicholson was wounded above the eye and in the foot and his plane was on fire. He was struggling to bale out when he saw a Bf 110 ahead of him. Though badly burnt on the face and hands he sat back in his seat, attacked it and shot it down. He struggled free and parachuted to earth.)

I had heard stories about him that had made him unpopular in England but I found him to be an excellent commanding officer. I imagine that a great deal of his problem was jealousy over his VC.

In August 1943, with the rank of wing commander, he was appointed CO of No. 27 Squadron. He solved the many problems of operating a rare mixed squadron under very difficult conditions and showed good leadership on the operational side. As well as Hurricanes he had flown Beaufighters on operations in the United Kingdom.

Now that we had at last reached our operation's squadron I began to wonder about the operational experience of the Mossie pilots. That evening I asked around and was startled to find that none had ever bombed, nor had they ever fired the guns of a Mosquito. Our flight commander had been a Blenheim bomber pilot over Burma but had not flown for 12 months since the Blenheims had been withdrawn from service. He had only 20 hours experience on Mosquitos and had no operational training on them. His appointment must have been by 'the old boys' network'. We were all untrained amateurs at daylight low-level operations with Mosquitos. I alone had been trained on its guns.

Next morning I called in on Wing Commander Nicholson and asked him what our schedule was. He told me our first trip over Japanese territory was scheduled for 24 January and he was leading a Beaufighter operation the next day. I asked him what the schedule was for the Mosquito flight. He replied that it would be local flying, familiarisation and some formation flying practice. Then he asked me about my RAF service. I briefly told him about being a gunner with 264 Squadron on Defiants.

"Hell!" he exclaimed, "not the Defiants that were slaughtered in the Battle of Britain?"

To which I replied, "Yes. I was one of the lucky survivors." I told him how we had changed to night fighting with very poor results and how I was sent to 225 Squadron in January 1941 to train the gunners. I told him I became operational there and got two victories. Then I was sent to 409 Squadron (Canadian) to train its gunners, where I received my commission. The 409 Squadron was converted to radar-equipped Beaufighter 2s and

I spent several months with them as a radar operator before training as a pilot in Canada. Then returning to England I had trained on Mosquitos for night intruder operations over German night fighter airfields but that the RAF sent me to India instead. I covered my RAF history in about 10 minutes and even managed to tell him how I ran the gunnery and bombing training course in 409 Squadron.

The wing commander seemed quite impressed saying, "You've certainly had quite a range of experience."

I replied, "But none at low-level daylight strafing and bombing." Then I added, "But I'm not alone. I'm the only one in the Mossie flight who has fired its guns at a ground target. The rest are all bomber-trained pilots; even our flight commander has only 20 hours experience in Mosquitos and has no operational experience on them." He was visibly shocked. He told me he had so much trouble getting the flight of Beaufighters operational that when he was informed a flight of Mosquitos was coming to join his squadron only the week before, he assumed they would be all operationally trained crews. My comment was that they had all proved to be good crews on the way out and our flight commander was already experienced on light bombers over Burma.

"We have 12 days to give the whole flight some valuable practice. After that they will have to learn on the job, which I am sure they will," he said.

I asked if he minded if I made a suggestion?

"Of course not."

I suggested that he give orders to the Mossie flight commander to immediately set up a suitable ground-firing target for all pilots to practise air-to-ground firing. I offered to help him because of my experience doing this in Britain adding, "We haven't got the time for the squadron leader to learn by trial and error."

He agreed with my suggestions and thanked me for bringing the problem to his notice. He explained he would be tied up for the next two days getting the Beaufighters into action and asked me to report to him in three days' time on our training.

Within 30 minutes the squadron leader had sent for me and asked for my help in setting up an air-to-ground training programme. We got off to a good start and by nightfall had everything ready to begin with a lecture by me the next day. After each lecture I would take a pilot to show him how to execute a low-level strafing attack on the target. We would only use our four machine guns to save our short supply of cannon shells for the Japanese.

The training programme was a great success. It fired everyone up wonderfully and they threw themselves into it with enthusiasm. Even the ground crews worked like troopers keeping the planes flying and the guns re-armed.

We had no camera guns so after taking them all through the practice run, I stationed myself near the target and made notes of each pilot as he attacked. On the ground I could share with him what he was doing right and what he was doing wrong. As a group we met and discussed the results and then each pilot was provided with a list of corrections he needed to make to his firing. It was encouraging to see how quickly they learnt the basis of air-to-ground attack.

On the third day Wing Commander Nicholson was delighted with my report. He thanked me for taking this off his shoulders when he was fully stretched with the Beaufighter situation. Each crew reported to the intelligence officer after each operation and I asked if I could read these reports myself to learn from their experiences and save us learning the hard way. It could possibly save casualties. He agreed that the two groups should share their experiences.

Then we returned to discussing the training on the Mosquitos. I suggested that after five days we should give the pilots a change by some formation practice using the full flight on a larger target.

I expressed concern, however, that our squadron leader might want to teach the old bomber formation of two 'vics' of three planes when really the fighter system of four was much better for our operations. He confirmed that the Beaufighters used the 'fours' system and he would be instructing our squadron leader to do the same.

Then he asked, "What comes after that?"

"Low-level speed bombing before they do it in action," I suggested.

"But we haven't any practice bombs," he queried.

"Remember the Mosquito doesn't have any bomb-sights. They have to make a split-second judgment when to let the bomb go as they approach the target. The bombs have an 11-second delay before they explode to allow the aircraft to fly clear of the explosion. If they are flying in line astern, as we will be doing, they must be able to judge the 20-second gaps between each aircraft. This requires training. We don't want to lose any Mossies blown up by our own bombs."

Nicholson commented, "Thank God our Beaufighters don't carry any bombs. I'll happily leave that to you."

Good weather allowed the whole training programme to go through without a hitch. We had two spare days before our first operation. Regretfully the Beaufighters lost one crew to ground fire. It had a sobering effect on all crews. We suddenly realised we were fighting a war again and could be killed over enemy territory. During these two days we studied the Beaufighters' combat reports to learn as much as we could about flying over Japanese territory and attacking our targets. We were very grateful for this valuable source of information.

Finally came the fateful day for our first Mosquito operation over enemy territory: 24 January 1944, exactly four months from when I finished the night intruder course at High Ercall. My total flying time in Mosquitos was 117 hours; 75 of these had been on

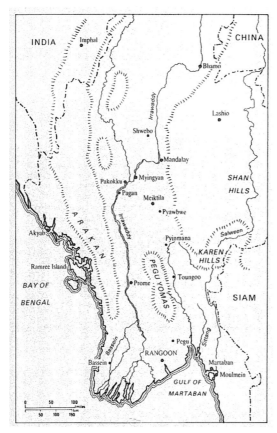

training and 42 on the flight to India. However I did have more than 500 hours flying in Defiants and Beaufighters.

To keep the Mosquitos separated from the Beaufighters we were given the area south of Akyab. North of Akyab was where the Japanese invasion had stalled. Both the Japanese and the Allies occupied steep, jungle-covered ridges and neither was strong enough to dislodge the other in such terrible country.

Our orders were to attack river, road and rail transport behind the Japanese front.

First we flew to Ramu to refuel for the sortie over Japanese territory. Then with wing tanks full and with two 500-pound bombs in the bomb bay we set off with the squadron leader leading and myself as his number two. Our route took us over the Irrawaddy River at Minbu then down the river to Kensada, following the main Rangoon road and railway.

When we reached the river the squadron leader fired at a group of sampans and hit some. I suspected they were local Burmese so I left them alone. One day we might want some Burmese friends. He was flying quite low, between 100 to 50 feet. I reformed at 200 to 300 feet so I could see the target earlier and get in a good burst before having to pull up.

Nothing else showed up on the river. Next we came to a road and saw a truck coming our way. The leader was too low but I got in a good burst causing it to crash and burst into flames. Then we reached the railway. Again the squadron leader was too low to hit the first train we saw. I got a good burst of cannon in starting two wagons back from the engine and finishing with several hits on the engine itself. A cloud of steam and smoke erupted as we flashed over. Looking back, Johnny reported it was stopping.

As we sped on the leader turned towards a small group of bamboo buildings. I saw the smoke from his cannons as he opened fire. At the same time I saw a light anti-aircraft gun emplacement firing on his plane. I went straight for it firing from about 500 yards. My shells enveloped the position in dust and we flashed over. Johnny, looking back, yelled excitedly, "You got him! They look to be all dead!" We sped on. There was another locomotive ahead. The squadron leader only touched it before he had to pull up. I was able to put a good burst into some wagons and the locomotive. Again the locomotive burst into a cloud of steam and smoke.

A few minutes later the squadron leader radioed, "My oil pressure is gone and the temperature is rising on my port motor." He had been hit by fire from the gun emplacement.

I asked Johnny, "What is the course to Ramu and how far away?"

He replied, "285 degrees and over an hour away."

I called the leader, "Fly 285 degrees. What is the situation?"

He replied, "No oil pressure. Temperature getting high."

I suggested to him, "Let go your bombs and feather the motor. You may want it later in an emergency." He dropped the bombs, stopped the motor and feathered the propeller. The Mosquito flies well on one engine but the speed reduced to 180 mph. We were over an hour from Ramu on two motors. On one it was going to be a long trip home.

Johnny gave us a definite course to fly. There was only one thing I could do. I pulled up to 2 000 feet up sun so that I was above and behind the damaged plane and maintained a gentle weaving flight to keep a good lookout behind. If an enemy fighter arrived and attacked the damaged Mossie I would be able to dive upon it and hopefully bring it down. Flying at a constant speed I kept position and conserved fuel so that we would reach Ramu. So we continued steadily home. We climbed over the ranges and got closer and closer to safety. Every now and again the leader called us up claiming he couldn't see us and I would reply, "Granny has you in sight." Luckily no Japanese fighters appeared and we reached our front line without further incident.

By this time Johnny and I were becoming worried about our fuel supply. Ramu appeared as our gauges were getting very low. I called the squadron leader telling him my fuel was low and that I would like to land first.

"No. Follow me in."

I was concerned that if he pranged on landing and obstructed the runway we would quickly run out of fuel and maybe lose both planes as I still had the bombs on board. With this thought in mind I just put our nose down, dashed past him and landed. The trip took five hours – 90 minutes longer than we had planned.

Wing Commander Nicholson was delighted with our sortie. "This will give the Japs something to think about having their roads and rail system attacked only 60 miles from Rangoon. The Mossie really has legs. It means that now we can attack the main Japanese air base in Burma, Mingaladon, anytime we want to. They will be worrying about that and will keep their fighters down there now."

He congratulated us on the results we had achieved and how well we had handled the emergency. "We will all learn something from your experience." The crews were all excited about our sortie and were just itching to have a go themselves.

The squadron leader and I had a long discussion with the wing commander on how low to fly and where number two should be. I advocated flying at 300 feet so we could easier recognise targets in time to get lined up to attack effectively. Flying lower and closer in formation would be suitable for a formation attack on a known target. I felt that the risk of ground fire was balanced by the ability to recognise targets in time to make a successful attack.

Wing Commander Nicholson agreed that this would be worth trying. He admitted the Beaufighters were flying low and having problems getting successful attacks on small targets like trucks and locomotives. It was decided that we would all try a period of flying at 300 feet with a more open formation.

That night as I lay enclosed in my mosquito netting I began to think of the Japanese reaction to our penetration to within a few miles of Rangoon and our successful attack on their transport system. What would our reaction be if they suddenly appeared with a new, fast, effective and unknown plane and attacked the road and rail traffic out of Calcutta? We would immediately take steps to meet this threat. We would concentrate fighters in the area and quickly set up an early warning system on the route flown by these new attackers. If the Japs reacted in the same way the next sortie into the area could fly into great danger.

I began to think of ways to minimise these risks and still get the same results. I eventually came up with a plan to reduce the amount of time we spent flying over Japanese territory by changing the route out to Kasada and back. This would make any Japanese early warning system useless because if they did report the Mossies overhead they would be going home and not going towards Rangoon. It would also make interception by fighters from Mingaladon impossible. Even if they took off as soon as our Mossies were reported at Kasada they would be at least 40 miles behind and below the Mossies and would never catch them.

I got out my typewriter and in the light of my kerosene lamp I typed out the details. The Mossies leaving the Ramu refuelling strip, would proceed to the coast behind our own army's front, then fly out over the sea at about 200 feet in a straight line to Kasada, turn inward and commence their patrol along the road and railway line away from Rangoon eventually reaching the Irrawaddy River and then head home. Unless the Japs had fighter patrols up over the area we wouldn't be intercepted.

Next morning I was at the CO's office when he arrived. He read the report and with a great grin said, "Who needs wing commanders on this job?" Then added, "You know I hadn't given a thought to all the things you've got in this plan but I see what you are getting at. What do you want me to do with it?"

I answered, "If you feel the plan is worth using I wonder if you could find time to brief our Mosquito crews on it?"

His reply completely floored me, "What do you think about your flight commander? Why don't you take it to him?"

I replied, "There are two reasons why I brought it to you. First, the squadron leader is a career RAF man and is used to getting instructions from above. I have the feeling he prefers not only to be told what to do, but how to do it. Secondly, he is in a completely unfamiliar role flying Mosquitos. He may be too afraid of making mistakes to take any serious initiatives. We need to try and help him in any way we can but in a way that doesn't embarrass him."

He replied, "All right. I'll accept your comments as your frank opinion. We'll see how things develop as we step up operations. In the meantime I will give some serious thought to your plan and your request."

Later that morning I received a request from the squadron leader to be at the briefing room at 11 am and to bring Johnny and his navigation log of our last sortie. The CO was talking to him when we arrived. He greeted me without referring to our earlier meeting. Hanging on the wall was a big map of Burma.

The CO began by congratulating Johnny on his work in the first Mosquito sortie and asking if he would mind showing his track in and out of Burma. He explained this would be a great help in planning the next sortie. Johnny made a great job of it. He had noted a good log of why the change of course, the time of the course itself and he had marked every incident accurately. The CO then explained that he and the squadron leader were expecting an aggressive Japanese reaction to this attack so close to their main base at Rangoon. They were considering some changes for the next sortie. He described everything that was in my submission as though the two of them had worked out the plan. Then they turned to the map and worked out the distance of flying down the coast and back to Ramu allowing for patrolling the road and rail from Kasada and up the river. It turned out to be 10 miles shorter than actually going overland all the way in and out. He explained why they felt it much safer to fly down the coast and patrol coming back, just as I had written in my plan.

In quite a short time the whole trip was planned in detail on the map. Arrangements were made to brief the crews that afternoon for the next day's sortie. The wing commander would do the briefing.

As we walked back to our quarters I thanked Johnny for his great help. He admitted he had been rather nervous.

That afternoon the CO gave a great pep talk to our Mossie crews. He told them how impressed he had been by our training results and by our first sortie. Then he went on to explain how we were planning to outwit the expected Japanese reaction to our successful raids in southern Burma and to give the crews the best chance of getting home safely. He used the map to explain in detail the flight down the coast and areas of patrol along the road and railway and showed how these ran close to each other along the river. He also covered heights, formation and distances. He stressed the importance of the navigator keeping a good look out astern in the patrol area and observing results of attacks.

In all he gave a thorough briefing and the crews really responded to his leadership. When he finished I noticed the squadron leader showed no sign of speaking so I got out of my seat and thanked the CO for his help, especially in view of his big job with the Beaufighters.

As he passed me going out he gave me a big wink with a broad smile on his face. Then Johnny and I got beside the two crews who were to do the sortie next day and we went over their plans with them.

They had quite a successful sortie and not the slightest sign of fighters or ground fire. They claimed successful attacks on five trucks, two locomotives and several rail wagons. They also sank several small power-driven boats on the river going north. They left two hours earlier than our sortie the previous day and this may have caught the Japs napping. I felt that varying the time as well as the route and the day was wise. This would confuse the Japanese defence plans and the rescheduling of train and truck timetables.

I rather suspect that the CO may have had a quiet word to our squadron leader after the briefing. He was a changed man from then on. He called me into his office and said, "It is clear we are breaking new ground out here with our Mosquito operations. I would appreciate it if we could work together to make a success of it. What do you think?"

I replied, "I fully agree with you. It is going to take a lot of learning and thinking to get the most out of our Mossies. Burma is not like the war in Britain where there is a great deal of back up from specialist services. Out here we are really on our own and know practically nothing about the Japanese forces or tactics. However, I would like to emphasise that I am only in this war to win it. I have no ambitions for a career in the RAF. I prefer to leave the administration work to you. You know the systems. I would like to concentrate on how we can best beat the Japs and bring our fellows home alive."

He was very happy with that and from then on he always called me by my Christian name but I always called him 'Sir'. He showed me instructions from Group Headquarters and together we would work out how to implement them. It was a most amicable relationship. We realised we were in a battle of wits with the Japanese in their efforts to maintain the supply lines to their forces in the coastal front and in northern Burma where they were trying to close the Burma Road to China.

We had started something we didn't have the resources to finish. With only six Mosquitos and six Beaufighters it was quite impossible to close up the Japanese supply lines. All we could do was to try and inflict constant damage and use every tactic possible to confuse the Japs and save our crews.

We should have been out every day attacking road, rail and river transport but our supplies of fuel, spares and ammunition made that impossible. We had to avoid any form of regularity that could enable the Japanese to organise their transport when it was safe from attack. It was for this reason we adopted persistent but irregular attacks. We constantly altered patrol times to just before dawn and darkness at night. We changed target areas so that the Japanese could never be sure where their trucks, trains and boats would be safe from attack. Results from patrols varied considerably. Some sorties found good targets and others little or nothing to attack but a steady attrition of Japanese transport took place.

After a month the Mosquitos were ahead of the Beaufighters' tally of trucks, trains and boats attacked. We had lost no Mossies and only suffered a little damage from ground fire. The Beaufighters, however, had lost two crews and began to complain of declining targets in their sector. The Mosquitos patrolled nearer to Rangoon and got to the target first because Rangoon was the point where all forms of transport started the journey to central or northern Burma.

By the end of that first month no Mosquitos could find anything to bomb. I suggested we didn't carry bombs unless we had a specific target to bomb. That would save 1 000 pound in weight and thus increase our speed and range and improve our ability to manoeuvre. The bombs were in short supply and dangerous to have on board when landing. Wing Commander Nicholson agreed to the policy of carrying no bombs unless to a specific target.

In case the Japanese were moving trains and trucks at night Johnny and I did three patrols covering the area just north of Rangoon to Meiktila but we found no trucks or trains. We shot up some signal boxes just to let them know that we had been there.

It was easy to fly over Burma at night. With the moon we could see road, rail and rivers quite clearly and ground attacks would have been possible. Regretfully we didn't find any targets and gave up after three nights.

Chapter 12

TACTICS AND STRATEGY

The Allied Army had sent information that at night small, heavily camouflaged coastal ships were delivering supplies to the enemy. Johnny and I went to investigate as soon as we had another moonlight night. We carried a full bomb load of two 500-pound bombs. We flew down the coast up-moon so that the moon shone on a large area of the sea. We both saw a small dark spot on the surface that looked like the fluorescent wake behind a powerful vessel but we could see no sign of the ship's profile.

I made a low approach from stern to bow. There appeared to be a fluorescent bow wave about 100 feet long. We came in low for a beam-attack and dropped the two bombs, which both exploded and within minutes there was nothing left on the surface. In all probability it was a small vessel but two further night patrols failed to find any more. We gave up night patrolling, as we couldn't afford the fuel, or Mosquito flying time, on wasted patrols.

It was decided to make a combined Beaufighter and Mosquito attack on Meiktila airfield. This was the largest Japanese airfield in central Burma in support of the Japanese Central Army Headquarters.

The Beaufighters went in first and we followed hoping to find something to bomb. We had a recent photograph taken by a Beaufighter navigator with his hand-held camera. It showed the layout of the buildings we planned to bomb.

The Beaufighter was a quiet plane and they went in low, doing strafing runs. We were concerned about anti-aircraft fire but the Beaufighters were through before a shot was fired. We came in at 300 mph at 300 feet to see our target better and made a diving attack reaching 340 mph at pullout. This time the Japanese were ready and the air seemed full of anti-aircraft shell and machine gun fire. The tracers were obvious but you also felt you could see the bullets coming right at you. We could hear them thudding into our Mosquito. All the planes in the flight were hit but none were brought down.

It was quite a terrifying experience for the crews who had never been fired on from such close range before. There was a lot of patching to be done on the planes and we were interested to find that no hits had been scored on the Beaufighters. They didn't carry bombs and were quite happy to go in first. Several of the bombed buildings were completely blown away but only one small fire had resulted. We had no way of telling how much real damage had been done. The Beaufighter crews were disappointed to find no parked aircraft to fire at. Either the Japanese planes were well hidden or had been removed to Rangoon to counter Mosquito attacks there.

It was a quiet and subdued debriefing. We realised we needed more up-to-date information on Japanese activity at Meiktila so we could strike at a time when aircraft were on the ground. Without this information it would be too costly for our small force to risk losses going through that hail of anti-aircraft fire when so little might be achieved. We were extremely fortunate not to have lost half our Mosquitos.

So we returned to our patrols against road, rail and river transport. Only twice were we intercepted. I was the first to experience this. We had just come in from the sea and begun our patrol, just north of Kasada when Johnny yelled that fighters were diving on us from behind and above. I had begun to transmit the moment he yelled to inform our number two who was 400 yards behind me to our right. I then slammed the throttle right

134

through the 'gate' for four seconds of emergency power and dived down to 50 feet above the ground. Our speed shot up to 350 mph. The Jap got to about 500 yards astern before he lost the momentum of his dive. He fired a long burst at us but failed to get any hits. As we pulled away I reduced power to stay safely ahead of him with number two flying abreast of me about 400 yards away. The Jap kept up the chase for another 30 minutes and then turned back either from fuel shortage or an over-heating engine. He was obviously flying at full power at 300 mph.

We resumed our patrol and scored hits on six trucks and then a train that we raked the whole length of with cannon fire. A small fire developed in one wagon and the locomotive was a mass of flame. We could see no boats but boats were becoming very scarce and difficult to find.

A week later another sortie pair were intercepted, indicating that the Japanese were doing standing patrols. The Mosquitos saw the interceptor in time, followed the same tactics that I had and got safely away. The number two of this sortie was tempted to pull across and make a beam attack on the Japanese fighter. Discussing this later I strongly advised against it. The Jap could just as easily turn into the Mosquito and get in a head-on attack. Our policy must be not to risk our few Mosquitos in combat with Japanese fighters unless we were forced into a fight.

No more interceptions took place but we continued to vary both the time and route of the sortie to further confuse the Japanese. We felt our strategy of flying south out to sea must be making it hard for the Japanese to intercept us. Our tactics meant that we suddenly arrived on the scene without warning. If we had flown all the way over Japanese territory they would have had more than an hour's warning. Wing Commander Nicholson was very impressed by our tactics and the Japanese must at last have begun to realise how fast the Mosquito really was.

Then we had the first loss of a Mosquito. That really shook me because I was sure it could have been avoided. By this time the Beaufighters had lost three planes. Delhi sent orders that they wanted a Mosquito to do the longest possible reconnaissance flight, from Rangoon to the Port of Moulmein, southeast of Rangoon, and to fly at 15 000 feet to the target and back. This height was chosen because the Merlin motors were not supercharged above 15 000 feet and performance fell off above that height.

I wasn't happy about this proposal as it exposed the crew to a long time over enemy territory as well as flying twice over the same route making interception by Japanese fighters from Rangoon much easier. I couldn't see the point of it. What did they expect us to find out that we didn't already know? We had already done constant recess to within 50 miles of Rangoon. Beyond Rangoon was the tidal delta of the Irrawaddy and Sitong rivers with only a single road and railway skirting its edge. It would have been a different matter if we had had a specially equipped camera Mosquito that could photograph Rangoon Harbour and Moulmein Airport. Then the trip would have been worth the risk. A camera plane was faster and had a longer range than an operational Mosquito because it carried no guns. Our crew would see very little detail at 15 000 feet.

I made these concerns known to the squadron leader but the trip had to go ahead. I offered to fly it but he insisted that the next rostered crew should go. Maybe he thought I would fly south over the sea and return overland. Perhaps he didn't want to risk losing me. Whatever the reason, the crew duly took off and was never seen or heard of again. They were simply listed as 'missing'. I was very saddened by their loss. It was a needless loss brought about by lack of operational understanding at Fighter Headquarters. It was to be the only Mosquito loss our flight suffered during the four months we operated in Burma.

I duly found out what happened in 1966 when I visited Johnny in Canada. It was there that I met the commanding officer of the Japanese fighter force in Burma. He told me how an Oscar fighter was flying at 5 000 feet near Rangoon as the Mosquito was returning home. It took the Japanese fighter, on full power, 50 minutes to catch up with it. The Mosquito flew a straight line without variation. The Oscar came in behind and below and when very close opened fire. When the Mosquito slowed down the Japanese pilot pulled close alongside and signalled it to follow him down but the Mosquito continued on the same course steadily losing height. They attempted a crash-landing but the aircraft burst into flames and the crew died in the crash. This crew died because they had ignored the most basic safeguard of weaving every few minutes to check for fighters below.

I am sure that if I had flown the operation I would have seen the pursuing fighter and easily avoided it. That the missing Mosquito took no evasive action when attacked might have meant that the pilot had been wounded and couldn't dive to get away.

To save flying hours on the planes and to save fuel we started doing single aircraft patrols. Both Mosquito and Beaufighters patrols found road and rail targets becoming more and more difficult to find. Johnny and I went out twice at night to check whether the Japanese were travelling by night. On both occasions we flew quite close to Rangoon and towards Meiktila but we saw nothing, not even a single light.

I decided on a campaign to destroy small rail bridges to hinder any transport movement by rail. This was easier said than done. Our first attempt at a low-level approach was almost fatal. We released the two bombs at 250 mph. A few seconds later Johnny let out a yell; there was a bomb flying alongside us. It must have hit something very hard and bounced back to our height. I instantly hauled back on the stick and the plane shot skywards. The bomb exploded below us and heaved us skywards. Fortunately we suffered no damage but we learnt a valuable lesson. Low-level bombing flying straight and level was too dangerous and ineffective.

I suggested to the flight that only one bomb at a time be dropped from 500 feet but even at 500 feet we failed to avoid being flung around by the explosion of the bombs. We finally found 1 000 feet to be the ideal height. Fortunately there were plenty of small bridges that were in use. It was the monsoon season and the heavy rain filled every stream. By picking the bridges without concrete abutments it was possible to leave a big hole that had to be filled in before it could be used again.

It took two to four days to repair the damage. I made a habit of attacking two big bridges 40 to 60 miles apart on each trip. The effect must have severely disrupted Japanese rail traffic.

About this time we received information that High Command suspected the Japanese would be moving troops from central Burma to the Arakan front. We took our four Mosquitos and went out looking for them. We found the convoy of trucks moving through a cutting behind the front. We were at 300 feet. I called on the radio, "I'll take the front two. Number two take the rear and the rest of you make sure you get the rest."

We achieved complete surprise. Probably the convoy had been on the road for hours, with heavy noise and tired troops. They hardly knew what hit them. I took the first two, a continuous long burst on each of the trucks, which were enveloped by cannon and machine gun fire. Both slewed across the road and burst into flames. Such concentrated fire must have killed all the troops in the trucks instantly.

I swung around and returned to the scene followed by the other three planes. Every vehicle was on fire and there wasn't the slightest sign of life. No one appeared to have gotten out of the trucks. It was total slaughter. The crews were rather shocked when we got home but I reminded them that it took one killed and one wounded of our troops to kill every Japanese soldier. In that one sortie we had saved hundreds of Allied lives.

Although more patrols were carried out no more trucks were seen in that area. If they did use the road it must have been at night. Later the Army reported that the expected Japanese offensive did not eventuate.

Our next big, combined offensive with Mosquitos and Beaufighters was a bombing and strafing attack on the Burma Shell Oilfields and refinery.

I had done a lone 400 mph sortie at 1 000 feet three weeks before. Johnny used my own high-quality German 35 mm 500.2 shutter-speed camera and he got two good pictures. When these photographs were enlarged they clearly showed all the buildings, installations and some of the gun emplacements. It was obvious the Japanese were getting fuel from the field. Burma Shell had only just begun operations in the area when war broke out. It had been assumed the staff had wrecked the place before they were driven out of Burma in 1942. Obviously the Japanese had repaired it enough to start pumping oil again.

As soon as we got the message from Group Headquarters to attack the airfield I began to think how we could successfully carry it out and still bring all the aircraft home safely. I did not accept the RAF light bomber force philosophy that the bombers roared in, diving straight for the target, fatalistically ignoring everything that the anti-aircraft gunners could throw at them. I accepted that some would not make it but by careful planning many would bomb the target successfully and get home safely.

Because it was a combined operation with the Beaufighters and because my squadron leader had shown no interest in the raid, I took my plan directly to Wing Commander Nicholson who was leading the Beaufighters.

He read the plan without a word and then said, "Let's take a look at the photographs and the map." He agreed that the first Beaufighters should concentrate on destroying the heavier anti-aircraft guns. The Beaufighters were so quiet at low level they might just catch the Japanese unprepared. Though the gun positions were well camouflaged we felt fairly sure we had located them all on the photographs. After 45 minutes we had everything planned and the wing commander briefed the crews that afternoon. He was very good at the job and we couldn't have had a better leader.

This time everything was better organised and all the crews were much more experienced. The Beaufighters were to go in at 300 feet, concentrating on the defences and going for the bigger guns. The three bombing Mosquitos would go in at 500 feet targeting the refinery. Three more Beaufighters would go for the guns again, or other installations if the guns had been silenced. Then the three Mosquitos would come around again to finish off the refinery and oil well. Then both Mosquitos and Beaufighters would all come back and do a high-speed strafing-run on any storage tanks left standing.

It was a highly successful raid. We left the place engulfed in smoke and flames including the three storage tanks. So extensive was the smoke and flames, probably a lot of it from ruptured pipes, that it was difficult to be sure how badly the main installations were damaged. The Beaufighters had made a good job of wiping out the heavier anti-aircraft defences so the only damage was from machine-guns. There was very little machine gun fire on the last run.

It was an excited and happy group of crews that landed back on base. The wing commander had led the Beaufighters and I had led the Mosquitos. The squadron leader was away organising supplies. The Beaufighters were the hardest hit with several bullet holes in each, possibly because they were slower than the Mosquitos and their targets had been defended with machine guns.

Two days later I flashed across the target at 400 mph to photograph the results. The developed photographs showed total demolition of the target. The Japanese would get no more oil out of that field for some considerable time. I heard later that Mosquitos bombed it subsequently in 1945 and thoroughly wrecked it again.

On the evening of the raid the crews were drinking, noisily celebrating the fact that they were still alive. I was sitting alone in a quiet corner. I just wanted to relax now that the raid was over. The wing commander came over to where I was sitting and sat down with me. He asked, "Did you volunteer to come out here to Burma or were you pushed like me?"

I replied, "I was very definitely pushed. Despite my protests I was commanded to lead the flight out and I was made all sorts of promises that never eventuated.

"Now thinking about it later I can see a little of their reasoning. They obviously tried to get experienced Mosquito pilots to come but experienced pilots were all tied up with the new Pathfinder Bomber Force. The CO of Bomber Command wouldn't release any of his experienced pilots so they came up with the idea of sending pilots from Australia, Canada and New Zealand, who could be interested in having a go at the Japanese. Having got two Australians and three Canadians they probably enquired of the CO at High Ercall for someone to lead the flight and were told that I, a New Zealander, and Johnny, a Canadian, were top of the course. They would then check out my credentials with Group Captain de Beaux, formerly CO of 409 Squadron and now leading a full-blown wing. They had quoted de Beaux at my interview with them. He had praised my leadership abilities. 'Emeny is the sort of officer who only needs to be told what the job is and he can be left to successfully work out by himself how to do it.' After that they told me to go to Burma."

To which Wing Commander Nicholson commented, "Just as bloody well for us." Then he told me a little of the problems he

141

had got into in the United Kingdom. He felt he had definitely been exiled to India.

"I've been lucky here because no one in Delhi seemed to want to lead a mixed Mosquito/Beaufighter squadron. It probably seemed an impossible job to them." And then he paid me a compliment. "It would have been a hell of a lot tougher if you hadn't come along. Just imagine how much tougher my job would have been if it had been left to your squadron leader to try and lead the Mossie flight into action. It could easily have been a shambles."

As both Mossie and Beaufighter flights were coming to the stage of a complete maintenance overhaul, it was decided to carry out three days of maximum effort on single-plane patrols to both confuse and inconvenience the enemy. Afterwards four crews from each flight would have seven days' leave in Calcutta while the servicing was being carried out. The Japanese were still rather quiet at this time so we inflicted little damage on them.

Johnny and I got fed up with the lack of targets so we bombed the largest building in the main street of Pegu, 40 miles beyond Rangoon. The building collapsed in a cloud of dust. Unbeknown to us at the time we had bombed the HQ of the Japanese Army in the area.

While our Mosquitos were being re-serviced the whole flight took the train to Calcutta. There were 16 of us; eight navigators and eight pilots. All the pilots were officers and the navigators were sergeants but we decided to stay together.

It was a slow trip from Agartala to Calcutta. The train was ancient with wooden seats and carriages. Our carriage wasn't crowded like the others with people even clamouring for space on the roof. There were obviously no tunnels on this line. We heard that those who travelled on the roof paid the train crews and the officials. I doubt if on the whole journey this long train exceeded 30 mph.

We travelled through the generally flat delta country most of the way. Small towns and small houses seemed to be everywhere. Much of the open ground was planted in rice or some other grain. The density of the population exceeded anything I had imagined. The only animal I saw was a number of water buffalo. The wild animals that once must have lived in this place had long since been replaced by hordes of densely packed human beings, barely surviving on their tiny plots of land.

The train took all day to reach Calcutta. Taking the advice of the 'old hands' we had taken with us all the food and water we would need on the train. Europeans are very prone to 'tummy bug' from food or water bought from native vendors. Everywhere the train stopped, which was frequently, it was besieged by a crowd of yelling, demanding people all trying desperately hard to sell food and drinks. What a noise and what confusion, with people wanting to get off and people wanting to get on the train, and others yelling their heads off wanting to sell us food, clothes and trinkets. Never have I heard such noise and witnessed such complete chaos. We stayed put in our carriage, very grateful for the safe food and drink we had brought with us. Fortunately the crowd was not allowed to enter our carriage.

The Indians travelling in our carriage were well dressed and also had their own food and drink and were well looked after by their servants. We had been told not to fraternise with the Indians when travelling so we were left to ourselves. They all seemed friendly enough and whenever our eyes met they smiled and we smiled back.

When we arrived in Calcutta we travelled by rickshaw to a place for European officers and sergeants. It was built like a barrack. The officers lived in one dormitory with beds along each wall and a small cabinet between each bed. The sergeants lived in a similar dormitory. It was clean and air-conditioned with good eating facilities. After a long trip, and arriving late at night, we settled down for a good night's sleep.

Next morning we travelled in rickshaws down the central boulevards of Calcutta. The boulevards were wide with one-way traffic each side. Wide lawns, gardens and shrubs were planted down the centre of the boulevards with large, well-kept buildings on each side. It was a beautiful area. It was hard to imagine that Calcutta was only a few grass huts 200 years before when the British first arrived. It is even harder to imagine that Calcutta was the scene of the infamous 'Black Hole' at the time of the Indian Mutiny.

As we passed down the boulevard I thought I saw a bank I recognised. Then I remembered the bank manager I had found so helpful in Karachi. The bank in Calcutta had the same name so I went in and made an appointment to see the manager, leaving him a note telling him that I had been told by the Karachi manager to call. I signed myself from 'New Zealand, RAF Operation Leader of the new, modern fighter/bombers so heavily engaged attacking Japanese forces close to Rangoon'. While I waited the rest of the boys went off to see the bazaar.

Within minutes I was ushered into the manager's impressive office and given a warm welcome. He explained that a little news of these super planes had spread around business circles but no one knew much about them. He was amazed that the leader of this mystery force should suddenly call on him. He offered me alcohol but I declined and asked instead for a cup of tea. He was full of questions and I told him that we could only speak about things that security allowed. I told him about raiding Japanese lines of communications close to Rangoon and north and central Burma and emphasised that nothing about our operations must appear in the news media.

Then I told him how a group of us were spending our first leave in Calcutta and asked for some advice on how we should spend it. He immediately invited us, as guests of the bank, to lunch at one of the most expensive hotels in Calcutta.

I set out to round up the rest of the boys. A well-dressed Eurasian in Indian robes who spoke perfect English came with me to guide us to the hotel. Eventually I collected everyone together and we set out in the rickshaws, organised by our guide. Little did we know that we were headed for one of the most fabulous occasions imaginable and one that none of us were ever likely to forget.

We finally arrived at a large impressive hotel. Regretfully I can't remember its name but I am sure that none of us had ever experienced anything like it before. The staff were obviously expecting us. Most of the boys carried purchases made from the bazaar and these were quietly taken and put into secure storage. Then we were escorted to the dining room.

It was a large room with the most impressive furnishings. The huge chandeliers, the richly coloured drapes that hung from ceiling to floor, the ornate pillars and the thick carpet underfoot spoke of money and luxury. The tables were covered with well polished silver set on fine, white starched tablecloths, with flowers arranged tastefully on each table. It was all quite overpowering. The room was full and everyone was formally dressed.

As we entered, and were being shown to the far side of the room, diners and staff stopped talking and we became the centre of attention. The boys were seated at two tables but I was led on to a raised stage where about a dozen people were seated, including the bank manager. He rose from his chair, welcomed me and introduced me to his wife and his teenage daughter and then to the other guests at the table who all seemed to be civil dignitaries. He must have made all the arrangements for this marvellous occasion within the couple of hours since I had left his office.

The bank manager (I can't remember his name or that of the bank) rose and welcomed all the people who were present. He then announced that they were all there to have the opportunity to greet and show their appreciation to this special group of gallant airmen who had for two months been fighting hard to protect Calcutta.

"We have all heard a vague impression of something happening in the Burma war. Now we find these mysterious Allied servicemen in our midst and we welcome them to Calcutta."

He then read out the name and country of each of the airmen. When he finished I asked them all to stand and they were given a rousing round of applause. When he introduced me he told them that I had fought in the Battle of Britain then in night fighters and now I was out here as one of the operational leaders of this mysterious force. He concluded, "His job is to plan and lead them over Burma. What he does I am not allowed for security reasons to talk about, so I will ask him to speak to you himself."

I felt trapped. Never for a moment had I expected this. When I got up to speak there was great applause. The whole thing seemed so unreal. As I remember it I said something like this:

"I have to tell you that we are all overwhelmed by this wonderful welcome you have given us here today.

"The RAF has taught us many strange things such as flying super aeroplanes and using terribly destructive weapons, but the RAF never told us what wonderful people live in Calcutta who have given a few combat airmen such a welcome to your city. Please don't tell the Japanese in Burma that we are here. We are hoping that they will wake up each morning terrified that we are going to shoot hell out of them each day.

"Such is your welcome that I am sure any of us lucky to survive this war will remember this occasion for the rest of our lives. Our host is right not to speak of our activities. We trust that you too will be the same. We cannot tell you how many there are of us or where we are based, or what planes we fly, their performance or the armaments they carry because the Japs are desperate for such information. But what I can tell you is what we are doing to the Japanese. They know what we are doing to them and it must make them very afraid.

"Victory over the Nazis in Europe and over the Japanese in the Pacific and here in Asia is only a matter of time but there is still a lot of fighting to be done and a lot of casualties to be suffered before the final victory.

"It has been decided by High Command to begin sending out to Burma the vanguard of the latest weapons. Our task is to become familiar with them in tropical conditions. Though the Burma war has been a stalemate for some time the exceptional bravery and perseverance of Allied troops on the borders of Bengal and Assam has kept the Japs at bay. Our arrival, two months ago now, must be a great worry to the Japanese. Suddenly they have found us sinking their river boats, constantly attacking their trains, destroying their rail bridges and blasting their trucks off the road.

"For example, we recently caught a convoy of eight trucks, loaded with troops, heading for the southern front. In one minute four of us destroyed all the trucks and killed every Japanese soldier on them. Not one of the 400 to 500 troops survived the attack. Talking to our Army friends they told us that to kill that many Japs in the jungle would cost our troops over 1 000 casualties killed, wounded or suffering from illness in the terrible conditions they must fight in. There has been a scarcity of Japanese trucks ever since in that area in daylight hours.

"I am able to tell you that we have completely destroyed the Burma Shell installations from which the Japanese get their oil and petrol supplies. We have also struck at some other vital resources of the Japanese in Burma and some quite close to Rangoon itself.

"Over all, we are very pleased with our capacity to strike widely at the Japanese, and just as importantly for us to come back alive. All efforts so far on the Japanese side have failed to counter our attacks. After two months of this activity we are grateful for a few days' leave and to enjoy our leave in your great city. We have to admit, however, that travelling here on your train took a lot longer than we could fly here.

"We thank you again for this wonderful welcome to your city."

As I sat down there was another great round of applause. Then we were served a sumptuous lunch. Afterwards everyone mingled together for an hour or so. Several came up and introduced themselves and told me they would be contacting the bank manager to make some arrangements to help us enjoy our stay in Calcutta. So it was that each day someone arranged a bus trip for us to see something of importance in Calcutta. Someone else organised lunch for us at a lovely restaurant or hotel. In the afternoon we enjoyed another free tour. In the evening someone else paid for our entertainment at a good nightclub. Food, music, good shows, dancing partners and 'special partners' for keen amorous young men – what more could we want?

On our second night in Calcutta we were enjoying ourselves at a nightclub when the boys decided they must get me involved in everything that was going. I normally drank little or no alcohol but I enjoyed dancing. So I was persuaded to dance with the 'extra favour girls'. They all ganged up on me to make me change my puritan ways. To do this they kept plying me with drinks, most of which I poured into the flowerpots when they weren't looking. Halfway through the evening someone started a competition to find a nickname for me. 'Mary' was suggested but I declined and then one of them climbed on a table and loudly exclaimed, "We should call him 'Homer' because he always brings us home safely."

There was a round of applause and I found great difficulty in dodging a bottle of wine. One of them was determined to christen me with it by pouring it over my head. I ended up tying this persistent chap to a chair with my belt.

They picked out a girl who I should enjoy the 'extra favours' with. She was about 26 and very attractive and sophisticated. She paid me a lot of attention and became rather sexually suggestive. I thanked her for her offer and declined. She was obviously put out but later I saw her going upstairs with one of the boys. She must have been very expensive because next morning he was borrowing money from us all.

On the final night a special dance was held for us at a very pleasant venue. It was obvious that several important families were there. It was a dinner-dance put on especially for our benefit. A very good meal, ample wine and a good band playing all the hits of the time made for a great evening. It was rather formal but the boys were kept busy being introduced by parents to their daughters. It was a most enjoyable farewell. I had to make another speech and more or less repeated the first one.

Regretfully, 56 years later, I can't remember now the details of the places we saw on our trips. Far too many events have clouded them out of my mind. At the time I took lots of notes of places we visited and people we met and later wrote many pages about them in my voluminous diary. When I was shot down over Burma, however, my CO of the time took my diary and it was never seen again. Such diaries were part of the deceased belongings to be returned to his next of kin after the war but mine simply disappeared.

Finally, a dozen people including the bank manager, his wife and daughter, saw us off at the station. The journey back was similar to the first, except for one exciting event in which we experienced personally the campaign to force the British to leave India.

Our train suddenly stopped in the open country far from any station. There was a lot of yelling and shouting coming from a large group of people who aggressively approached the train. An Indian man in our carriage yelled, "We are being attacked by an anti-British mob. They will burn the train."

I told everyone to remain in the carriage. I jumped on to the ground and ran towards the engine. The crew was out of the engine looking frightened and bewildered. I introduced myself and found that one could speak English. I asked, "Which carriage has English troops on board? Show me!"

We pushed through the yelling mob and I found 30 armed Indian troops with a sergeant in charge. I suggested I take command and that we show ourselves to the mob and demand to speak to the leader. No one took the slightest notice so I ordered the soldiers to fire a volley in the air. The crowd became silent and the sergeant yelled in Indian for their leader to come forward. Six people stepped out. The sergeant then demanded to know why they had stopped the train. They gabbled away excitedly, throwing their arms around and then became quiet. He translated that they demanded that the British leave India immediately.

I instructed the sergeant to tell them that I had 100 armed soldiers on the train. If they attempted to damage the train we would fire into the crowd and kill many of them. I climbed on to the step of the carriage and told the sergeant to translate exactly what I said and so he translated, "Your quarrel with the British will have to wait. What your leaders haven't told you is that there is a huge Japanese Army on the Burma/Bengal and Assam border. This Japanese Army is being kept out of Bengal by the British and Indian Armies fighting the Japanese in the jungle. If the Japanese win they will come here, burning all your homes, destroying all your crops, killing most of your men, raping and killing your women and children as they have done by the million in China.

"Only by keeping these trains carrying the supplies that the British and Indian Armies need can the Japanese be kept out of Bengal and keep you safe. If you insist on attacking these trains why should we keep on risking our lives to protect you? Take your choice! Either you let the trains carry the supplies to our

Army or we let the Japanese come here – burning, killing, raping and enslaving.

"If you have never heard of this Japanese Army then ask your leaders in Calcutta. We advise you to leave your quarrel with the British until the British and Indian army has defeated the Japanese and you are safe from them here."

I doubt if any of that mob and their so-called leaders had ever heard of the Japanese. They argued with the sergeant for a while then quietly walked away, calling the others to go with them. The train crew came rushing up to us and we told them to get the train moving.

The sergeant saluted me and said, "You are a very brave officer, sahib. Good liar too! Thirty does not make 100!"

I answered, "Better a lie than bullets." He agreed. We met at the next station and he asked me what unit I was with. When I told him fighter bombers he saluted again and said, "Great sahib! Great!" And that was the last I saw of him.

Finally we reached Agartala and returned to our airfield. All was quiet when we arrived at dusk. I was handed a note from Wing Commander Nicholson telling me that he and the squadron leader had to go to Delhi and would be back as soon as possible. He ended the note with "I hope you enjoyed your leave. Just take over and do whatever you feel is necessary". It was a mark of our growing friendship that he addressed me by my Christian name and signed with his own.

Checking with Operations while we had been away I found there had been single Beaufighter and Mosquito sorties every second day covering our regular frontal areas. It was enough to keep the Japs on their toes so we continued the same operational pattern until the two senior officers returned. I was not overly familiar with the capabilities of the Beaufighters so I found it a little strange talking tactics with the pilots. We had no losses or problems and I knew much more about Beaufighter operations by the time Wing Commander Nicholson returned.

The two senior officers arrived back on a transport plane and the wing commander asked me to his office. My reports on the operations since my return were already on his desk. So also was a detailed report of our leave in Calcutta, including the incident of the train. He read the patrol reports and laughingly commented, "I told you once before this unit doesn't need wingcos. Now you have proved it. Many thanks for looking after the show. Well done! I will read about your leave later."

That night in the mess I told him about the amazing reception we had been given on leave in Calcutta. He was just as surprised as we had been. I told him that the bank manager had invited the remaining four crews to contact him and he would see that they enjoyed their leave in Calcutta too. He commented that he wouldn't mind going himself to which I replied, "Can't you think of an excuse to go to Calcutta?"

He replied, "No, not at the moment. But if I ever do go I won't tell them in Delhi."

He did eventually go and although they did not have the big welcome reception we received they got the same tours, lunches and night entertainment. Nicholson had to make a speech on one occasion and said that it was easy because he had a copy of my notes in his pocket and he just added few extras of his own. He told me our group had made a big impression.

"Everyone seemed to be asking about you, especially that pretty young daughter of the bank manager. She asked if I thought you would survive the war? Maybe she has dreams about you! What a gold mine you dug for all of us when you called on that bank manager. He must be one of the most important men in Calcutta. I doubt that the City of London gave Sir Keith Park anything like the reception that Calcutta gave your crews on your visit there. The bank manager told me that you chaps gave a lot of people a real boost to their morale. I bet all the gold braid in Delhi would be green with envy if they knew what a wonderful reception we all got in Calcutta but I certainly won't be telling them."

Then he told me about his trip to Delhi. He and our squadron leader had been told to report to Delhi but not told why, and to bring a summary of the squadron's combat activities, those that went well and those that didn't.

He told me he had missed me because the squadron leader had made very hard work in giving the report on the Mosquito operations. In fact Nicholson felt that he had had to do most of the talking for him. "He obviously left most things to do with operations to you and you weren't there so he sounded at times as though he was doing a great job. They'll probably give him a DFC on the strength of it. But even if you had written the report yourself it would have gone in under his name. That is how the RAF system works."

There was silence for a few minutes and then he continued, "Anyway, when we got there the air commodore's man took the report and that was the last we heard of it. No one came to talk to us about it so we spent our time looking into supplies for the Beaufighters and the Mosquitos and that is where your squadron leader shone. He knew the system inside out. You and I would have been utterly frustrated and wouldn't have got anywhere. He seemed to have a secret code and doors seemed to open for him. These people seem to live in a different world to us.

"We finished up with a Scottish engineering officer who knew you and asked after you. I told him you were doing a great job on operations.

"He said, 'Pity! The 'old boy network' doesn't like him. He's got a very big black mark against him here. They have not forgotten nor forgiven him for disobeying them. Little things can become very important to them.'"

The engineering officer was obviously referring to how I refused to give them a ride in a Mossie when I first flew into Delhi and left against orders the next day.

Nicholson told me that as a result of their visit to Delhi they received a limited promise of supplies. This meant that some changes to 27 Squadron were pending but they weren't telling us anything yet. All we could do was carry on the best we could until, in their own good time, it suited them to tell us what these changes were going to be.

I was surprised no one in Delhi HQ was interested in talking to Nicholson about our operations. We could only assume they were satisfied with our combat reports. Maybe it would be different if we were having big problems or suffering heavy losses but being the first modern, high performance unit on the Burma front you would expect the staff to be interested in our activities.

Then Wing Commander Nicholson made a strange comment, "Maybe they plan to do a Hugh Dowding/Keith Park on us." Air Vice Marshall Keith Park was the New Zealand Commander of 11 Group, the fighters who fought off the German attacks during the Battle of Britain. Air Marshall Hugh Dowding commanded Fighter Command before and during the Battle of Britain and was responsible for conserving fighter strength before the Battle of Britain began, when it was in danger of being frittered away in the vain fight for France.

I expressed my ignorance as to what Nicholson meant.

"I can see you don't know what happened after the Battle of Britain was won. Dowding and Park were asked by the RAF Air Council to submit to a special meeting, in November 1940, a detailed report on where the RAF did things right in the battle and where things went wrong. They came to this special meeting expecting a deep discussion on their reports. Instead the reports were accepted without comment. The next item on the agenda was to strip Keith Park of his command of 11 Group and relegate him to Fighter Command training. They then immediately retired Hugh Dowding from the Air Force.

"The Air Council's 'old boys' network' just brutally dumped the two leaders who had successfully saved England from invasion and filled their places with their own cronies. Air Vice Marshal Leigh Mallory of 12 Group took over Park's 11 Group. Leigh Mallory was the man who had failed so miserably to carry out his responsibilities in the Battle of Britain. Another far less competent crony replaced Hugh Dowding. Between these two men they lost nearly 1 000 Spitfires and men during 1941 with very little to show for it.

"If the 'old boys' network' can do that to such great men we haven't much hope of being credited with what we have achieved with 27 Squadron, have we?"

So we settled back to carrying out our patrols and harassing Japanese supply lines to the limit of our resources. The battle at that time seemed to be mainly on the Burma/China border where the Japanese were trying to cut the Burma Road to China. It was very mountainous country. Supplies to the Allied Army were carried by a large fleet of American Douglas Dakotas and no praise can be too high for the crews of these unarmed planes. Increasingly bigger, four-engine transports were arriving to help.

All the Japanese supplies had to go by riverboats up the Irrawaddy, or by the single railway line from Moulmein to Rangoon or by trucks up the main highway to Mandalay.

Our constant harassment of these transport routes must have been of great concern to the Japanese, gravely restricting their movement of supplies to the Burma Road front, especially during daylight hours. Each day a Beaufighter or a Mosquito patrolled these transport routes. Rarely were riverboats seen in daylight and very few trains or trucks.

The constant bombing of small bridges must have slowed down rail traffic at night and made truck driving at night very hazardous. Many sorties found little or nothing worth attacking. Our presence was obviously achieving results but it was unglamorous work.

Johnny and I got quite nasty with rail bridge repair gangs. When they had just about finished the repair we would bomb it again, sometimes killing the workers who may have been making too much noise to hear us diving down upon them. We would go a few miles up or down the line and blow another bridge.

Only once, over a two-month period did we get a chance at a real bombing target. This was a Japanese convoy of 11 cargo ships, which set off from Singapore to supply their forces on the Burmese front. Allied submarines sank seven of these ships. The remaining four reached Moulmein. We received orders to bomb them.

The staff told us to fly at 15 000 feet, almost over the top of Rangoon to Moulmein, bomb from that height and return the same way. Obviously, whoever issued these orders didn't know that we had no bombsights to aim with. The route was obviously chosen to save fuel but Moulmein was at the limit of the range of a Mosquito and it gave no thought that Japanese fighters were certain to take off from Rangoon as we flew south and would be waiting for us as we returned. They would also have alerted Moulmein and all the defences would have been sitting on their triggers when we arrived.

I drew up my own plan. Johnny and I carefully worked out the distances on the track we were ordered to fly and our own much safer and effective track to Moulmein. The difference was only 28 miles. We would fly south, at low leve,l out of sight of land until we reached Biesien, on the delta south of Rangoon and opposite Moulmein. We would approach the port at 500 feet over the sea from the east. Flying at a low cruising speed of 250 mph we would save much more fuel than the extra 25 miles and the Japs would have no warning of our coming. We would bomb the ships, one plane per ship, with two 500 pound bombs, attacking at 300 mph and diving slightly with the intention of putting bombs into the engine-room of each ship. Our aim was to start a fire as well as blowing a hole in the side of the ship.

We would then head home on a course that would pass Rangoon 30 miles to the east flying at 100 feet and reducing speed to 285 mph to conserve fuel. This would give us fuel to spare if we needed a short burst of 320 mph if any Jap dived on us. Once 30 miles past Rangoon we would be out of range of their fighters.

Wing Commander Nicholson read it all, grinned and said, "More defiance of orders. More black marks I see, but it is a damned good plan. I'll have a chat with your squadron leader. I'm not sure that he wants to go. I'm sure the Delhi brass don't care what course we fly as long as they enjoy the credit for sinking the ships without loss to us. Anyway I won't mention the track or heights in my report."

After speaking with the wing commander the squadron leader approved the plan and told me to choose the crews and brief them. The raid was on. The two senior officers came to the briefing, after which the wing commander gave a short 'pep talk' and ended by saying, "I'm sure that 'Homer' will bring you all home safely."

We took off at noon and followed our plan of attack. Johnny was spot on with his navigation and we arrived at Moulmein to find three of the ships tied up at a quay, with the other at anchor a short distance away. I dived on the left ship, number two on the one alongside, and number three on the other while number four attacked the one at anchor.

As I dived at the ship I had chosen I kept my sight on a spot on the hull between the waterline and the ship's deck, exactly below the funnel. I let the bombs go and pulled up to miss the mast. Out of the corner of my eyes I could momentarily see people running on the quay. Johnny reported a perfect hit and a big explosion. Then he reported that number two and three had hit and finally number four.

We had bombed in complete surprise. Not a shot had been fired at us. We swung 180 degrees to get a view and photograph of the attacked ship then sped away at 100 feet. Smoke was coming from ships one and two and the third was beginning to list and so was the fourth. I suppressed a desire to go around for another look so we settled on our course for home. Just past Rangoon we saw six Oscar fighters flying at about 3 000 feet a few miles west of us. They saw us and began to dive towards us. We increased speed to 320 mph and at the bottom of their dive they were still about a mile behind. To save fuel we reduced speed to 295 mph. The Oscars did not come within firing range and after 15 minutes turned back and we flew safely home.

Everyone was thrilled with the results although we were only able to claim the four ships bombed and damaged. What we didn't know was that a British submarine, lying submerged off the port, saw us fly over through their periscope. That night they sent a small boat into the harbour and found that the three ships that had been tied to the quay had been sunk and the structures, still above water, were burning fiercely. The fourth ship was lying on its side.

Two days later, when this report was received from Delhi (who had received it from Naval HQ Ceylon) we were really happy with the raid. There was another celebration that night and a few sore heads next day. I had stuck with my couple of shandies.

So we carried on our patrols, harassing the rivers, road and rail routes from Rangoon north.

Only one flight was different. Somehow Group HQ got the idea the Japanese were using the large school at Prome, about 100 miles north of Rangoon, for their Army. We were ordered to attack and destroy it during school hours 'to teach the Burmese a lesson not to help the Japanese'. As if the Burmese had any choice!

I flatly refused to attack the place during school hours. I had seen it on a previous raid and reckoned that only one plane was needed to destroy the L-shaped building. I finally agreed to attack it half an hour before dark; that meant a night landing back at base, but I wasn't really concerned about that.

I had the bombs set to drop one at a time. When I arrived over the school a few people were in the vicinity so I chased them away with a few runs and firing the odd machine-gun burst. I climbed to 500 feet and dropped the first bomb. It hit that part of the building I had aimed at and completely destroyed it. Then I climbed again and dropped the second bomb on the other part of the L shape. It too was blown to pieces. Then we set off for home. I told Johnny just what I thought of 'brass hats' who sent us out to attack schools.

This action had international consequences. The principal of the school was U Thant who in the late 1960s became Secretary-General of the United Nations in New York. If we had followed orders and attacked in school hours, U Thant most likely would have been killed, as well as many children.

Suddenly in mid-May we received orders to cease all Mosquito operations. The Mosquito crews were to proceed by train to Bangalore, inland from Madras in southern India. There we were to form a complete Mosquito Squadron No. 45.

The Monsoon season was due any day. The Monsoon period is when it rains very hard and very frequently over India and Burma, greatly reducing flying operations. The Bengal, Assam and Burma region is the worst area to be in at the time of the Monsoon.

The Japanese had just launched a 100 000 strong attack on two British bases in northern Assam, Imphal and Kohinwe. The British were completely surrounded. This attack finally cost the Japanese their occupation of Burma. The British bases were able to hold out throughout the Monsoon months. They were supplied by air by the heroic efforts of two Dakota (DC3) squadrons. Flying low, through mountainous terrain and terrible weather, and often over the heads of thousands of Japanese troops, these unarmed planes flew in constant supplies to the surrounded British forces. Casualties were suffered but the flights continued. It was possibly the greatest, bravest effort by Allied transport squadrons of World War II.

159

I called on the wing commander to get my log book signed. He wrote across the page "Will make a very good flight commander".

He said, "I hope you get a squadron of your own but I must warn you. There are too many in the 'old boys' club' senior to you, who want the rank of squadron leader in an operational squadron, to have that permanent rank after the war, and remember, you have accumulated a few black marks in Delhi. They have long memories."

I thanked him for his help and advice of recent months and I asked him, "What is going to happen to the Beaufighters?"

He replied, "I've no idea. I would like to see a complete squadron formed and to lead it myself. One thing is certain though. You and I will never again know the freedom of action we have enjoyed here these last few months and we only got that because the 'Delhi Boffins' didn't know anything about operating Beaufighters and Mosquitos over Burma. They let us do all the pioneering work and if we made any mistakes they wouldn't be judged by it. Now we have proved what these planes can do, and they have all our reports to guide them, they will take over and run future operations. I'll have to be very lucky to lead any Beaufighter squadrons that are formed. They will want you and me way down the ranks, just junior officers."

But he wasn't finished yet. "Do you notice? Not a word of acknowledgement of the exceptional results the six Mossies have achieved. Not even a transfer plane to take your crews to Bangalore. I feel we are seeing our version of Keith Park and Hugh Dowding post-Battle of Britain scheming on a much smaller scale. It will be interesting to see what happens to both of us. In the meantime, it has been wonderful working with you, and I wish you every success, despite my gloomy scenario."

So we parted, never to meet again although I heard he had been given command of a full Beaufighter squadron and that he had been awarded the DFC. Sadly he was killed in May 1945 – just a few weeks before the end of the war.

Chapter 13

No. 45 SQUADRON

It took us three days of dreary travelling by train to get to Bangalore via Madras. We had again to fend for ourselves and buy our own food and drinks. Bangalore is 500 feet above sea level. In peacetime it was the place where European businessmen and military officers sent their families during the hot season in Madras.

We found Madras to be an interesting city. It had a wide main street flanked by two and three-storeyed buildings and a city where special hotels, clubs and tennis courts abounded for Europeans and bright bungalows for them to live in. It was quite a 'pukka sahib' place – in fact very snobbish. Most of the town, especially the native quarter where the Indians lived, was out of bounds to officers. We were limited to the palatial Officers' Club that was very expensive to eat and drink in. An airfield had been built close to the city.

Every night everyone deserted the place and went into town. The officers bought a book of tickets for meals and drinks but valid for that day only. The Indian staff handled no cash. Being virtually a non-drinker I didn't find this system very convenient, because I couldn't use up all my 'chitties' in my book although I had to pay the full price for it.

I never did like Bangalore. It was filled with too many staff officers and their hangers-on who never did any fighting in the war. They fought their war with formality and spit and polish and it was far too snobbish for me.

None of our planes from Agartala arrived. They probably all went to Central Maintenance at Allahabad to be examined on how they stood up to operations in Burma.

After the first week the ground staff arrived who were mainly fresh from England and felt the heat dreadfully. Then the flying officers and sergeants arrived. Most of the pilots had not done much flying for a year or so and previously had flown single-engine planes.

I found myself relegated to junior flight lieutenant with two senior flight lieutenants and a squadron leader above me. The latter had flown night fighter Mossies in England. He was pleasant man, easy to work with but knew nothing about operations over Burma.

I was asked to give very basic technical training to the new pilots and took them for flights in the navigator's seat. When the instructors arrived I was given the job of testing all the operational Mosquitos after the tropical modifications had been done.

This was an enjoyable experience. With the first plane I roared down the main street of Bangalore at second-storey height, at 330 mph. With each new plane I came through a bit faster. By the 12th plane I was doing 450 mph. The controls were solid and the plane stable. It was a joy to handle. I lined up at about five miles out at 300 feet and then put the nose down to gather speed. I became known as 'the mad New Zealand test pilot'.

In the last 'beat-up' I reached 465 mph. Regretfully our new CO, an Aussie wing commander, was walking through the town when I came through at 465 mph at second-storey level.

As soon as I landed I was on 'the mat'. The CO was a tall, well-built man, already known for his loud, argumentative ways. He gave me a real ear bashing about dangerous, irresponsible flying and demanded to know what my speed was. I truthfully told him it was 465 mph.

"Bloody lot of rubbish! No Mossie can fly that fast," he roared at me.

"It all depends on how you fly it," I replied. That really seemed to infuriate him.

"And where did you learn to fly like that?" he demanded.

"Fighting the Japs in Burma for the last three and a half months," I replied. That seemed to slow him down a little.

"Well, you won't be doing any more of it here. If I hear a word of you low flying I will have you posted out of here immediately!" What a pity he hadn't asked me about flying a Mossie at that speed. It may have saved his life six weeks later. As a CO he wasn't a patch on Wing Commander Nicholson.

Life got very boring for the four crews who had done operations over Burma. The instructors and flight lieutenants didn't want us mixing with the trainees. They obviously had a training programme based on our Burma combat reports but they lacked actual combat experience to teach others.

Starved of flying, the four operational crews insisted on doing the air-to-ground gunnery and bombing exercise. We only got one flight each but our results were so much more accurate than the trainee crews that it was embarrassing. We could have taught them so many useful things about operations over Burma that would have helped them make successful attacks and to get home safely.

It was just as Wing Commander Nicholson had warned me. We were now securely enmeshed in the RAF India system. We were following a training programme drawn up by 'Delhi-crats' who had no personal experience of Burma operations. In air-to-ground firing for instance, no instruction was given on approaches, height to fly, or length of burst. The flight commander spent a lot of time drawing up graphs for crew exercises and flight times but little else. I longed for an opportunity to share some experience on practical issues such as strafing, bombing, and outwitting Japanese defences. There was so much essential practical information we could have shared but neither the CO nor the flight commanders asked for our input. In fact they seemed anxious to distance us from the whole training programme. I realised again how lucky we had been to have Wing Commander Nicholson as our CO for 27 Squadron and what wonderful freedom of action we enjoyed in the squadron. Our service life in the RAF would never again be the same.

One evening the four operational pilots met an English army major. He told us about his holiday place in the Himalayas, above Delhi. His house was situated beside a big lake nestled in the mountains. His family spent the hot monsoon there. He kindly offered us the use of his house, his servants and runabout for a spot of leave.

Next day we went to the CO and requested two weeks' leave, as there was nothing to do on the squadron and we were entitled to leave after three and a half months of operations. To our surprise he agreed. The four of us left next morning on the long train and bus trip to Naini Tal. It took two nights and days of travelling to get there. At night, we had sleeping cars on a train that was relatively comfortable. Each station had the same great, noisy crowds but being a mainland express no one was allowed to travel on the carriage roof.

We finally left the train and took a rather rough-looking bus for the trip up through the narrow roads into the mountains to the lovely lakeside town of Naini Tal, completely surrounded by mountains and with houses all around the lake.

The house we stayed in was spacious and comfortable. Apart from three servants we had it to ourselves. A man servant looked after our food and meals. Another kept the place clean and did the washing and the third was the general handyman who did all the odd jobs including sailing the Idle-Along yacht. We had all we could ever need for a relaxing leave.

I liked to go sailing. The 'handyman' instructed me and gave me the times when to go out on the lake. When sailing you had to be careful of the sudden gusts off the mountain, which could easily flip the yacht over. The water was very cold coming straight off the mountains. The best idea I found was to sail from the windward end (where we stayed) to the other end of the lake where the 'handyman' would sail it back by tacking all the way. To get back to the house I would catch a local bus. I had five runs in the yacht and enjoyed it immensely.

We were very lucky. There were two girls' schools from Delhi spending the hot season at Naini Tal. All the teachers were Eurasians. The girls were attractive and very good company. There were some very nice social clubs to eat in and to dance with them at night. They obviously enjoyed our company. They weren't only nice-looking girls but very cuddlesome. After a few days the four of us settled down to the one girl each. The girl I was with was 21, with a lovely olive complexion. She was bright, danced well and was excellent company. She came with me on three sailing trips and seemed to enjoy it.

A few days before we left she asked me if I had given any thought to being married. I gently told her I could never mix love with war. The chances of my surviving were not good and if I was married and lost my life there would be another grieving widow. I had seen too much of that to wish on any girl. Tears came to her eyes. I doubt that she had given the war a serious thought until then. When we left she asked me to write to her. I declined as gently as I could. I told her that I had greatly enjoyed her company but there was a terrible, brutal war going on outside this lovely lake-land district and for me it wasn't the right time to make affectionate attachments.

So sadly, but sweetly, she kissed me goodbye. A few days later I was lying injured in a hospital as a result of a bad crash in a Mossie that could easily have been fatal.

Two days after getting back to the squadron the instructors were discussing low-level attacks on bridges. They were instructing the pilots to go in at 50 feet. I commented that in actual attacks we had found two problems in going in so low. One was the bombs hitting something hard and ricocheting back up under the plane, creating a real danger of the Mossie being

165

destroyed when the bomb exploded too close, as very nearly happened to me once. We were just lucky to see it in time to put the Mossie in a steep climb and be safely blown sideways.

The second problem was the 11-second delay of our bombs. Most bridges were so small that our planes had to attack one behind the other, each 20 seconds behind the plane in front, to avoid being blown up by the explosion of his bomb. So as they approached the bridge each pilot must position his plane to be 20 seconds behind the one in front. Because of these problems we had adopted the successful single plane dive from 500 feet.

This was the first chance I had had to share operational experience with the flight crews. Squadron Leader Edwards merely commented that they were teaching the technique set out in the training programme. I didn't debate the matter any further.

When the crews had gone Squadron Leader Edwards asked me to lead a flight of four Mossies on a practice attack on a bridge and give them some idea of how to judge the 20-second interval between the attacking planes. He insisted that the flight fly at 50 feet and said, "Keep it at 50 feet for the last 15 minutes. It will be good low-flying practice for them."

So the programme went on even though we had clearly explained that operationally such tactics had proved impractical and had been abandoned. How often we met cases of senior military ignorance that had not changed since the 'Charge of the Light Brigade' in the Crimean war of the 1850s, of which the great poet Tennyson writing about the subsequent slaughter said "Theirs not to reason why; theirs but to do and die".

I was happy to get a flight together as I was getting little flying at that time. We took off shortly after, Johnny and I leading a formation of two pairs to make a practice run on a bridge 70 miles away – an exercise in low flying and bridge attack. We cruised at 100 feet. Flying at 100 feet reduced pilot stress by 75 percent compared with flying at 50 feet.

We cruised at 280 mph for 10 minutes and then I took them down to 50 feet. Then five minutes out I began to direct them into line astern, at 20-second intervals. This took some concentration as I was looking backwards. When they seemed in correct positions I looked ahead. "Hell!" Dead ahead was a large pre-historic tree stump sticking up some 70 feet. I only had time to heave back on the control column before we struck it. The stump went through the right propeller and sheared off the right rear stabiliser. The controls were jammed right back and only engine and rudder controls remained.

The Mossie shot skywards, almost vertically and I yelled at Johnny to feather the severely vibrating propeller. As the plane climbed steeply I feared we would go right over on our back and spin down to the ground. There was nothing I could do. Speed dropped off quickly and at 1 200 feet the plane stopped climbing and slid into a tail-slide. It actually slid tail first toward the ground. Fortunately all the controls were level when we hit the stump. I yelled to Johnny, who had just completed stopping the right motor, "Unfeather the prop." We needed its power to help keep the plane steady and to pull out of the slide downwards. From the tail-slide the nose dropped and we dived toward the ground. With the control locked full up and speed quickly increasing the nose came back up, went through level and we were swiftly climbing again. I applied full power to gain the most height possible and to steady my nerves. Now I knew how the plane would fly with the locked controls. Relief washed over me as I realised we were not going to die in a fiery crash.

I began to think of getting the plane down. On the way up again I noticed a bend in the river a few miles ahead and thought, "I'll try and put her down on the river. There are no trees to hit."

Going up on the third climb I asked Johnny if he wanted to bail out. "No. No!" He replied, "I could land on top of the jungle

167

and never get to the ground. I could get injured or lost in the jungle." And he lapsed into prayer to every known Catholic saint. Nearing the top of the third climb I reduced power and allowed the stall to lower the nose with a much less dramatic tail-slide. I was by now feeling much more confident in controlling the plane.

You think very fast in such emergencies. We reached 1 050 feet before we stalled and tail-fished again. In all we did eight of these sequences of a near vertical climb, tail-slide and recovery from the dive earthwards.

I knew we would never reach the river. As we came down the eighth time a small clearing in the jungle appeared below. I decided to try to crash-land there. The clearing was a square area in which rice was grown. Between each paddy field was a solid earth walkway. By controlling the power I managed to keep the plane sinking level toward the clearing at 130 mph, getting lower and lower and trying to judge our approach. Just as we approached the edge some people stood up in the paddy field right ahead of me. I had to give an extra burst of power to clear them and then it was all power off and switches off as we tried to land.

I quickly found out that those walls around the paddy fields were as hard as concrete. The Mossie slid into the first one with a terrific crash and tore itself to pieces as it hit one after another. I let go of the control column and wound my arms around the big gun-sight on top of the instrument panel. As the plane crashed into wall after wall the nose crumpled and the wreckage came back on to my legs. Some of it hit my seat and tore it out, driving it under the fuselage. Fortunately the piece of safety wire I had used to hold my straps together failed and let the seat go but I was taken some way with it. With my legs trailing behind me I was being pulled under the fuselage. I hung grimly to the sights and then the plane stopped.

That is, what was left of it stopped. The nose, front guns and the floor of the cockpit were all gone. I let go of the gun-sight and fell to the ground. My trousers had been torn off and I was bruised from my hips to my ankles. My legs were not broken but severely twisted and cut and soon began bleeding freely. Desperately, I dragged myself away from the wreckage.

Johnny, who was seated further back, had only been bruised on one ankle. He helped drag me from the wreckage. I couldn't stand without his help. The Mosquito formation circled for a few minutes and then headed back to base. Our plane was so torn apart that the wreckage was spread over a wide area. Both wings and engines were torn off. The cockpit and two wing-stubs were the only large pieces that were identifiable. Fortunately there had been no fire and we were alive but deep in the jungle and miles from base.

Johnny helped me to the shade of a wing-stub. He then got a parachute, opened it and rolled me into the silk and I found I was able to sit. He got the first aid kit and applied dressings to my bleeding legs.

Indian people quickly arrived on the scene. We knew we were in for a long wait before we were rescued. The crowd got bigger and bigger and Johnny tried to keep them from crowding on to me. I was suffering a great deal of pain from my injuries and not feeling sociable. To keep them away Johnny got them to pick up all the pieces of the plane and pile them around the two engines.

There was a lot of noisy shouting between the various groups and then about three hours after the crash another group arrived with more noise and shouting. The crowd opened to allow a small group of well-dressed Indians to approach. They were obviously the local leaders. They squatted around me and one opened a small bag and took out a dark bottle and made signs he was going to pour it over my cut legs. In a flash the thought struck me, "It's neat iodine!" I struck it from his hands before he could pour it and saw that it was indeed raw iodine.

The shock effect of raw iodine on my raw flesh was too terrible to think about. I was in enough pain as it was.

So the hours dragged on and the blazing sun was merciless. The Indians brought us food and drink but we drank only from our water bottles fearing tummy bug. Johnny became more and more worried that rescue could be hours away. I tried to reassure him that rescue would come but finally, against my advice, he decided to go for help. By this time it was dark and it was the wrong thing for him to do.

It took the rescuers 14 hours to reach the site of the crash (and another four days to find Johnny). By the time they reached me I was just hanging on. They gave me morphine and had to carry me several miles to a jeep and then the jeep travelled 40 miles over tortuous tracks to a waiting ambulance. It was early next morning when I reached hospital. By then I was delirious and knew nothing for three days.

When I came round there was a British Army officer in the same room whose servants were tending to his needs. He didn't appear to be ill or wounded and it wasn't until later that I found out I was in a special hospital, tucked away in the jungle for English officers who had developed VD. The nurses provided the patients with their medication but otherwise kept away from them.

I was the only war casualty they had ever had and although the nurses dressed my wounds they didn't wash me. After four days in that climate, and delirious for a large part of it, I really felt the need for a good wash. It was then that the major's bearer came to my aid with soap and water. He washed me daily and attended to my toilet.

The major said to me, "You must lead a fairly interesting life by the things you have said these last few days when you were unconscious, but your secrets are safe with me." I'm not sure what I said or what possible secrets I could have revealed when unconscious.

The matron was a bright woman, a redhead from England. She was well-spoken and very interested in New Zealand. I heard later that she married a New Zealand pilot and settled in New Zealand after the war.

After five days I was hobbling around and allowed to move about the hospital. All the nurses were open and friendly and willing to talk with me. On the fifth day there, one of the new pilots in the squadron, an Aussie, was admitted. He had an engine give him trouble on a night practice flight. He had no confidence flying on one engine in a Mosquito, so he landed on an American airfield. He came in too fast, overshot the runway and wrecked the plane, although he himself was only slightly injured. We later came to call him 'Pete the Crasher' as he wrecked three Mossies in landing accidents but he was such a nice person he was always given another chance. Over the next four days he and I had a lot of fun together with the nurses.

We both left the hospital on the same day. I went to convalesce in Calcutta while Pete returned to the squadron. The major refused to take any payment for his servant looking after me. He said, "I shall go through this war without firing a shot, and not suffering anything worse than being here. It has been quite an experience for me to be so closely associated with someone really fighting the war and really suffering in doing it."

Aussie Pete's third Mossie prang.

When I got to Calcutta I phoned my bank manager friend and immediately he and his lovely, talented wife came to visit me in the RAF hospital. They offered to have me stay at their home for my convalescence. Naturally I was delighted. They had an elegant home especially set up for a lot of entertaining. It was surrounded by well tended gardens and lawns with servants to cater for everything I needed.

His wife was a talented pianist and had a beautiful singing voice. She was a superb hostess. They only had one child, a lovely, fresh, 17-year-old daughter, who was thrilled to have an injured airman staying in their home.

Life couldn't have been better. I recovered well and spent many hours in the daughter's company, walking through the grounds or seated in the gardens talking about all kind of things. In her company I saw the sights of Calcutta. In the evening there was a beautiful meal often followed by music. The mother would play and everyone join in singing. I noticed the daughter becoming increasingly infatuated with me so I spoke to her parents telling them how determined I was never to mix love and war because of the grief it so often brought. I assured her parents that in no way would I encourage her affection toward me. They both appreciated my frankness but did little to discourage their daughter seeking out my company.

I received notice to call on the air commander of the area regarding my crash. Expecting the worst I was surprised by his friendliness. He had my file open on his desk and asked for details about what had happened. When I had finished he told me that pre-war RAF regulations called for the pilot's logbook to be unfavourably endorsed for losing a plane in training. This was deemed to be a very black mark against a pilot's future but he considered the accident was not the result of carelessness, failure to fly by the regulations, or poor airmanship. In fact he was very complimentary about how I had responded to the crisis. He did not consider what had happened should have any effect on my promotion to squadron leader. In his opinion the RAF book of rules did not apply in my case.

He was frankly amazed that both Johnny and I had come out of the accident alive. "You certainly have a cool head when it comes to emergencies," he said. What he wrote in my logbook was this: "Aircraft severely damaged under exceptional circumstances. Pilot showed commendable courage and skill in controlling such a heavily damaged plane under exceptional circumstances and making a safe crash-landing under very difficult conditions".

"Are you happy with that?" he asked. I expressed my thanks and he wished me well.

A few days later I decided to seek medical clearance to return to 45 Squadron. I made an appointment to see the base medical officer. I used my walking stick to reach his office but left it outside before entering. He welcomed me warmly and asked what injuries I had. I told him I had just twisted and bruised both legs. He lifted them up and tapped the knee of each with his instrument. They both jerked obligingly for him.

"No other problems? Worried about flying again, or things like that?"

"No, I'm very keen to get into flying again."

"Good. Here is your clearance to rejoin 45 Squadron." He wrote it down and shook my hand. I walked out very carefully, picked up my stick and hobbled away.

Next day, after expressing my thanks to my host and hostess for all their kindness to me, I took the train 120 miles south of Calcutta to where 45 Squadron was based. Squadron Leader Edwards met me and I impressed upon him how keen I was to rejoin the squadron. He seemed genuinely pleased to see me and took me to the Aussie wing commander who bluntly demanded, "What are you doing back here?"

I replied, "My injuries have mended sufficiently for me to be cleared for flying. Here is my clearance," and I handed him the medical officer's report.

He scowled, "But you are using a stick?"

I replied, "Bader flew with no legs. I still have both mine."

He turned to Squadron Leader Edwards and said, "If you want him back in your flight you take him up and check if he is fit to fly."

Later in the day I took off with the squadron leader who sat in the navigator's seat. We went through every possible flying requirement and did three landings. He was happy with my performance and welcomed me back into his flight saying, "I really do need you now that we are closer to becoming operational. My other two flight lieutenants have never flown operations in Mossies. You know more about operational flying than any of us."

It was wonderful to be back flying again. I realised that if I had not taken the initiative to ask for a medical clearance I might never have got back to 45 Squadron again.

Shortly after my return the squadron went for a week's exercise with a Mitchell B25 twin-engine light bomber squadron. Our crews were to practise attacks on the bombers and the Mitchell gunners to practise using their turrets on us.

Some ex-Hurricane pilots took our pilots up in Harvard single-engine trainers and flew against other Harvards to learn the tactics of attacking other aircraft using gun-sights. It felt strange flying in a light training plane again. My years of air gunnery had trained me well in the use of gun-sights so I didn't get much flying in the Harvards.

We did our attack runs on the Mitchells at 300 mph. After a while Johnny and I would feather one engine as we closed in and break away with one motor stopped. The Mitchell crews were most impressed.

At midday several Mossie and Mitchell crews were sitting in the shade drinking beer. The CO's wife, a war correspondent, was visiting us. The discussion developed into a debate as to which was the better plane, the Mosquito or the twin-engine American fighter, the P38 Lightning. The Americans of course favoured the Lightning and our crews, who knew nothing about the Lightning, favored the Mosquito.

I noticed the wing commander becoming more and more argumentative and aggressive. Then someone asked me what I thought. I replied that I felt that the argument was on the wrong track. The Mosquito was a composite plane, a fighter-bomber, whereas the Lightning was designed as a fighter to fight other fighters. The Mosquito had special destructive capabilities the Lightning didn't have, but the Lightning was a better fighter only machine than the Mosquito. I told them how on our course at High Ercall we had lost three Mosquitos whose crews were trying to out-fly the Lightning.

To everyone's surprise our Australian commanding officer jumped to his feet, called for his navigator and asserted, "We'll soon show you!" Then they jumped into a jeep and roared off to the Mosquito flight.

A Mosquito took off and came flying low over us and then went into series of aerobatics; rolls, wing tips and loops. Coming out of the bottom of a loop the Mosquito turned into an inside loop. I knew instantly that the plane would crash so got up on a stool behind the CO's wife. The Mosquito flew skywards to the top of the loop and then began the descent. Immediately the speed increased to beyond the 400 mph limits as it hurtled vertically earthwards. By this point the controls would have been unmovable.

Being a big man the pilot obviously heaved back on the controls but the plane plunged into the ground disintegrating on impact. The wings tore off, the tail tore off the fuselage and there seemed nothing left.

I grabbed the CO's wife and held her close saying, "Don't look! They are both dead!" She clung to me in terrible shock. The wreckage hit the ground at the far end of the airfield and exploded into a ball of flame and smoke. Some crew members leapt into jeeps and drove quickly the site. Most of the others sat or stood around in a state of shock at the disaster.

I put my arm around the CO's wife and led her inside the building. In the anteroom was a settee and I laid her on that. She began sobbing uncontrollably. I could only hold her hand and gently stroke her forehead with my other hand. I couldn't think of anything to say but as I sat there I remembered two other widows. I remembered the night trip across London in a taxi in the middle of an air raid with the sobbing, grief-stricken young bride during the battle of Britain and I remembered Mrs Peterson in Canada.

Gradually the sobbing subsided and she opened her tear-filled eyes and looked at me. I'll never forget that look. I just reached forward and gently kissed her forehead. The pressure on my hand increased and she gradually regained self-control. Then she softly thanked me.

She lay there for another 10 minutes then gradually moved into a sitting position. At that moment Squadron Leader Edwards came in and seeing us he turned and walked out again. I told her how sorry I was about what had happened but she didn't reply. We continued sitting there alone for some time. I offered to get her a cup of tea and she accepted. When I returned she was standing up and looking out of the window. "It was going to be such a nice weekend," she said. She told me she had come down with a girlfriend and asked me to contact her. When her friend arrived she left to spend the night with her.

Next morning she phoned to ask me if I would walk with her at her husband's funeral. When she and her friend arrived, the dark shadows under her eyes showed that she had slept little that night. She linked her arm in mine and remained like that for the whole ceremony.

All the air crews paraded. For them it was a sore occasion. We were not accustomed to burying our own dead. They usually just disappeared over enemy territory, or were seen to crash in a ball of flame when shot down. The squadron was rather a sombre place for a few days.

After the funeral the two women stayed for lunch. The widow never left my side. After lunch I asked her what she would like me to do with her husband's personal effects and uniforms. Without hesitation she asked me that they all be sent to her husband's parents. She didn't want to hear about them again. I agreed that I would do this but I did find a useful amount of money among his possessions, which I sent to her.

She told me she intended to continue her job writing war stories for Australian newspapers and radio. When she left she kissed me, thanked me for my help and asked me to call in and see her when I was in Calcutta. I wasn't to see her again until early May 1945.

When we finished our training with the American Mitchells Squadron Leader Edwards asked me to accept the official position of deputy flight commander, as he had so much more to do waiting for a new CO to arrive.

He asked me to take a party and check a possible new airfield. We travelled in a Dakota arriving in the mid-afternoon. Heavy monsoon rain forced us to stay overnight. We found bunks in a new building but it was so hot I slung mine under the eaves and tied one end to a tree alongside. During the night I heard someone, who was sleeping inside, calling "Cliff! Cliff!" When I answered, he softly called through the window opening, "Have you your gun? There is something moving in here."

I replied, "Yes, but keep quiet and don't move." A few minutes later a large black panther moved slowly alongside my bunk. Its head stopped barely a foot away from mine. I let loose the whole six rounds from my revolver as quick as I could pull the trigger. The animal let out a screaming yelp and leapt up into the branches of a tree and then down into the jungle. The shots brought everyone running outside but we made no attempt to look for the panther to see if it was dead or wounded. Next day we flew out and never returned to the place.

The new CO turned out to be another of the 'old boy' network in Delhi and had only flown a few hours in the Mosquito. Before his desk job he had been a light bomber pilot. He was obviously posted to get his six months' service in an operational squadron so he could keep that rank after the war. He was a good administrator but had little knowledge of operations. He often drank until the early hours of the morning and he and I had little in common.

Shortly after his appointment the squadron was moved to northern Assam to take part in a major offensive. General Slim had driven the Japanese back into the mountainous jungle and relieved the twin British bases of Kohima and Imphala, which had been besieged by a large Japanese army during the monsoon season. During the siege the British had been supplied by air.

Late October 1944 saw the final Allied offensive to recapture Burma. The battle had been bogged down since the last Japanese 100 000-strong offensive failed to break through the mountains into Assam. With both Japanese and Allied forces now so well dug into heavy bunkers in the mountainous jungle terrain, neither could dislodge the other. General Slim then came up with the only practical answer. He would move his whole 14th Army over the mountains by air and sweep the Japanese out of Burma before the next monsoon season in May.

This could be done with the large fleet of unarmed Dakota air freighters being used to supply Chinese forces in South China. Such a great airborne invasion was possible only because Allied Beaufighters and Mosquito fighter bombers had completely destroyed the Japanese Air Force in Burma.

Number 45 Squadron was an essential part of the airborne operations. Initially we carefully checked out the landing sites.

Those chosen were two RAF airfields, abandoned in the retreat of 1942. They were still obstructed by poles and wires.

The RAF High Command decided to send in gliders at night. We had found no sign of any Japanese in the area and pleaded that instead of a night landing an early daylight landing be made with an advance party to clear the obstructions and so avoid casualties by gliders smashing into each other in the dark. Our pleas were ignored, however, and the gliders came in at night and suffered very heavy casualties. It was another five days before contact was made with the Japanese.

I flew the first operation when we arrived in Assam. A photo-equipped reconnaissance Mosquito had found a Japanese Oscar twin-engine reconnaissance plane on a small Japanese-held airfield. Flying with a Canadian on his first mission as my number two, we found the airfield and saw the Oscar partially hidden under some trees. I flashed across the field pouring cannon fire into the plane. One wing fell off and it collapsed on its belly but didn't burn. Somehow my number two had lost me as I attacked and wasn't behind me to have a second go at it. When I got him alongside me we continued checking for signs of the Japanese but saw no signs of them.

A young New Zealand pilot arrived and was keen to fly as my number two but unfortunately he hadn't been very well trained. We set up a few dummy ground targets for him to practise his gunnery. On his first run he was too slow in pulling up and crashed into the target. Both he and his navigator were killed. He came from Rakaia in Canterbury and for a short time it was good having another Kiwi in the squadron.

His replacement was older and previously had flown light bombers. He was an ex-band leader and a sociable, extroverted person. Just when he was ready for operations he suddenly developed a mysterious and painful knee condition and he left for Calcutta for treatment. He never flew operationally with the squadron, but I heard later that despite his bad knee he did win a tennis championship in Calcutta.

All flights over Japanese-held territory were now quite dangerous. Units of the Japanese Army were everywhere but so well camouflaged they were hard to find. Often we only knew they were below us when we felt bullets thudding into our planes. To counter this threat I suggested that where Japanese troops were suspected we fly at 295 to 300 mph. Immediately there was a noticeable reduction in bullet damage to our planes. The Japanese ground forces were not used to such high speeds and most of their small arms' fire missed us.

The squadron was given a threefold task: 1) to destroy any road, rail or river supplies; 2) to prevent any Japanese fighters from attacking our Dakota air supply planes; and 3) to bomb any Japanese Army formations that we found.

Our efforts at transport attacks took a heavy toll on Japanese supplies. To keep the fighters away we constantly attacked the Japanese airfields. Meiktila, the main Japanese air base in central Burma, became more and more heavily defended with heavier anti-aircraft guns. These were mainly British AA guns captured at Singapore. We seldom saw any Japanese fighters.

Any Japanese Army formations we found we dive-bombed from 2 000 feet. The Mosquito gained speed so quickly in a dive that we had to take aim, drop the two or four 500-pound bombs and pull out all in a few seconds. Often a horrible curtain of enemy fire rose from the enemy position. A flight commander, a very pleasant, competent Aussie, was the first to die dive-bombing. His plane was seen to dive into a stream of gunfire and just kept going down to crash on to the target in a ball of flame. This was war as we had never seen before – brutally deadly and very dangerous.

Then we lost Squadron Leader Edwards, our B flight commander. He was returning from a patrol and did a low sweep over the field at probably 325 mph and pulled up nicely doing a victory roll. When he reached the top of the roll the Mossie broke apart. The wings and tail parted from the fuselage and everything fell to the ground. Both the pilot and navigator were killed instantly. The wings did not catch fire and when we examined them we found to our horror that the main spar had not been effectively strengthened during the building of the wings. Normal gluing had been done but the line of long screws that gave the wing its strength was missing. Immediately we examined the wings of all the planes and found five more similarly defective. All the defective planes were grounded and used for spare parts. New planes were quickly delivered.

De Havilland, the makers of the Mosquito, sent one of their engineers to India to investigate the problem. He shared my 'basha' and we got on well together. When he had sorted the problem out I tested the new planes with him sitting in the navigator's seat. When we had finished the testing he offered me a job as a test pilot with de Havilland. He told me that the firm intended to be big players in the coming jet age of civilian planes following the war. If I accepted I would be assured of a

Funeral of Squadron Leader Edwards.

lifetime career in aviation. I thought very hard about the offer but finally felt my duty was with the squadron, especially now I had taken over as leader of B flight with the death of Squadron Leader Edwards.

We buried Edwards and his English navigator on the edge of the airfield with a full squadron parade. I made sure all their personal effects were duly checked and sent to their next of kin in England.

Although I accepted full responsibility for B flight operations, the CO didn't appear to make much effort to have me promoted. I had the distinct feeling he was avoiding me and was not too keen on my promotion but I became so involved with the flight I didn't have much time to think about it.

The intensity and pressures of the battle for northern Burma was felt everywhere. New targets, new tactics and constant demands for our support from the army kept me busy. A new forward hospital for army casualties was built on our base. The constant stream of sick and wounded was evidence enough of the cost of the offensive to drive the Japanese out of northern Burma and then the whole of Burma.

The loss of our two flight commanders was a severe blow. They had both been good leaders. Their loss was made worse by the lack of leadership from our wing commander. A strange situation developed. The wing commander took no interest in leading operations but occasionally he took off alone with a sergeant navigator. He flew off toward the enemy and usually returned with most of his ammunition fired but we never heard where he had been or what he had fired at. When he left the squadron after six months' service and his rank assured for post-war service, he was awarded the DSO for leadership.

The pressure of army support operations had one beneficial effect. It put an end to the 'Delhi Old Boys' racket of using 45 Squadron to get promotions for post-war substantive rank. As our flight commanders were lost they had to be replaced by experienced pilots from the squadron. Flight Lieutenant Jack Lawrence became squadron leader of A Flight after I was shot down in November. Flight Lieutenant Duclos took over B Flight. He was actually nine months senior to me but was new to Mosquito operations, which is why Squadron Leader Edwards had made me deputy flight commander when we began operation in northern Burma. Duclos was a drinking friend of our wing commander and was probably his choice to replace Edwards. My loss probably solved a problem for our wing commander. Later I heard that my promotion to squadron leader had come through six days after I was shot down. Being classified as 'missing, believed dead' was sufficient for our wing commander to ignore it. He could just as easily have actioned me with it and still promoted Duclos a couple of weeks later. It was just my bad luck. Both Lawrence and Duclos survived the war.

I also heard that when the wing commander got the radio news that I had been shot down, he immediately rushed into my 'basha' and removed all my personal belongings including the 200 typed pages of my diary covering everything that had happened since I left Britain in October 1943. The diary contained references to the lack of leadership of our CO and the strange business of his 'secret operations'. Although my personal effects were eventually returned after the war there was no trace of my diary or of the miniature scimitar sword exchanged for my silver wings in Bahrein. Regretfully now, 56 years later, I can only recall fragments of the details I wrote in that diary.

Trying to safeguard our Dakota transports from Japanese fighters meant we had to keep a close watch on Japanese airfields, especially Meiktila. In mid-October I led a pair of Mossies on a low-level run over Meiktila and found anti-aircraft fire both heavy and accurate. My plane received many light strikes. A large shell exploded on the left wing between the motor and my side of the fuselage making a hole 20 inches across and destroying the radiators installed there. The shrapnel ripped through the cockpit at stomach level shredding my clothing but only scratching my skin. An inch closer and it would have disemboweled and killed my navigator and me. How lucky can you be?

We dashed home at 300 mph. The cooling system on the left motor soon failed and had to be shut down reducing our speed to 180 mph. This meant that my number two had to go home alone leaving us to chug away on one motor for two and a quarter hours over enemy territory. On the way back we had to climb over the 7 000 feet Chen Mountains to reach our base. Luckily for us there were no Japanese fighters about. The right motor purred away faultlessly but it was a long climb over the mountains and when we finally reached home we found that the undercarriage wheels refused to lower and I had to pancake the plane down on to its belly. It was a good landing but the plane was a write off.

This was my second Mossie lost in India but I was soon provided with another plane – Zombie 3 – and the war ground on.

There were some interesting sidelines. One was our food. Our meat consisted mainly of tinned bully beef. It was dry and

Cliff's Shot Up Zombie 2 Gets Home October 1944

heaven knows how old. We were told it was surplus left over from World War I. It was certainly hard enough, and dry enough, to have been left over from World War I.

Another major item was the soya bean sausages that tasted like sawdust. Vegetables were few and when cooked tasted like no vegetables we knew. The bread was local unleavened bread, a grayish looking material in slabs. The squadron doctor assured us that it was all good food. Both sergeants and officers purchased large quantities of ketchup to make the bully beef and soya sausages edible.

Getting fresh meat was a challenge, usually at the expense of the local natives. They liked to graze their cattle right up to the edge of the airstrip and sometimes right on to it if they were not kept away. Sometimes they were allowed to infringe on the area we used for harmonising the guns and for test firing. When a beast walked accidentally in front of one of the guns there would be a quick burst and down would go one, sometimes even two, straying cattle. The scared native would run off and when they returned the dead animals would have disappeared, skinned and cut up by our airmen cooks. For a few days it was meat three times a day for everyone on the base. Of course the natives complained to the CO and always claimed twice as many cattle as had been killed so we always produced the ears and tails as proof of the number killed. We enjoyed fresh meat every couple of months.

One day an American four-engine transport made a call at our base. They had a small problem that needed fixing and while this was happening it was discovered the plane was loaded with carcasses of Australian mutton for the forces in China. They took off with a lot less than they landed with.

Occasionally we got a few tins of American 'Spam' that consisted of tinned ham, a basic ration for American forces. They hated it, whereas we thought it was a real luxury food.

185

Despite the food, our state of health was good. Sickness was rare and quinine tablets kept malaria at bay even though we became rather jaundiced and yellow-skinned. American air and ground crews objected to quinine tables because of the yellow skin effect and suffered much more from malaria than we did.

Custom in India dictated that officers required Indian servants. I didn't appreciate all the hangers-on so instead of several servants chose just one. He was a bright young man from the Naga tribe, renowned for their fighting qualities, and came from the mountains of northern Assam. I paid him twice as much as was customary and he did everything for me. During the day the locals were afraid of him but at night, if given the chance, would willingly have killed him, so every night he slept across the door of my 'basha'. He was very reliable and most capable.

I didn't like the silly canvas bath used for bathing, so we rigged

up my own shower with three four-gallon petrol tins. One, with holes in the bottom, was fixed in the tree with a ladder to it. When I wanted a shower the bearer would climb the ladder with the other two tins of warm water and pour it through the one fixed in the tree and so I showered. It was much better than sitting hunched up in a canvas bath.

I rigged up my own electrical system with 300 yards of electric cable I acquired. I plugged one

45 Squadron, R A F Assam 1944.
Sleeping Out.

end into the radio trailer and the other end into my quarters, which gave me an electric light for typing my story at night and to use the electric shaver I had bought in America in 1942. It made life just a little more comfortable and was evidence of the usual Kiwi initiative.

When our quarters were unoccupied during the day, snakes would come inside to get out of the hot sun and they would hide in corners and come out again at night. Often I would wake up to see a snake swinging back and forth in front of my face on the other side of the mosquito net we always slept in. Then I would yell 'Snake!' as loudly as I could and everyone would come running to kill it because we had a weekly sweepstake on who killed the most snakes.

I walked with a stick because of the injuries received to my legs, and although I had my own jeep I would often walk to the flight for the exercise. Whenever I saw a snake I would kill it with my stick and leave it there. When I returned I would find that large ants, half an inch long, had stripped away its skin, leaving only the vertebrae, which I would take back and hang outside my 'basha'. The weekly prize for the most snakes killed was always a bottle of Indian gin, which I never drank so I'd think of some competitive game and give it away as a prize. Such small things did much for morale among air crews.

So we reached early November with the battle raging as hard as ever.

The Japanese built concealed gun positions in an attempt to prevent British troops expanding their airborne bridgehead in northern Burma. It was nasty and dangerous work strafing and bombing these many gun positions and our Mossies received a lot of damage but luckily very few casualties.

My luck finally ran out on 9 November on an early morning raid on Meiktila.

I called my Mosquitos 'Zombie', a name going back to Persian mythology. When Aladdin rubbed the magic lantern he

187

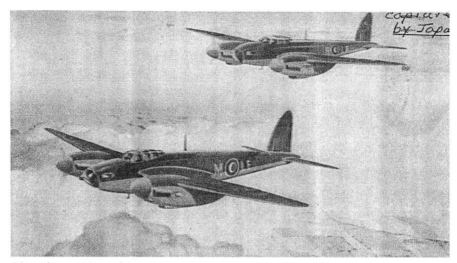

Shot down November 1944, and captured by the Japanese.

found the genie that came out of the spout was named Zombie, the perfect slave. If his master wanted to do nice, kind things Zombie would happily help him but if his master took to being a fierce, killing robber, Zombie would help him do that too. I felt my beloved Mossies were the sons of Zombie. If I merely wanted to fly around and enjoy the thrill of flying peacefully then my Mossie would do that for me. But if I loaded up the Mossie with guns and bombs and went off attacking people and destroying bridges and railroads, my Zombie would do that too.

The name 'Zombie' was painted on my first Mosquito I flew on joining 45 Squadron. Shortly after joining the squadron I crashed this plane when on a training exercise attacking a bridge. Zombie 2 was heavily damaged and written off by ground fire over Meiktila and now I was to be shot down in Zombie 3. I had a painting of Mt Egmont on the door with the words 'Te Kiri' written beneath it. Te Kiri was where I last went to school and the place I called home. Zombie 3 was brand new and flew like a charm.

I carried a special axe in the plane with only a four-inch handle and a three-inch blade to cut my way out if ever I was trapped in the wreckage of a plane. After being trapped in my last crash I knew that the standard axe, with a small blade and 12-inch handle, could not be used effectively in the confined space under the panel to free my legs if they were trapped. I had also prepared a special first aid kit with a looped handle I could grab as I left the plane. I also wore new, but well worked-in boots, in case I came down behind the Japanese lines and had to walk a long way. I wore a pair of special overalls, in the pockets of which were maps, a compass, Burmese money and other things needed to get me back to Allied lines if ever I had to bale out or was shot down over Japanese occupied territory.

I took the possibility of going down seriously and tried to allow for all contingencies. The boys tended to joke about me being round the bend. They never bothered with such precautions themselves, leaving everything to chance or fate. My experience of life made me a little different. I had had to work hard for everything I got in life and for all I wanted to achieve. I suppose I took life, and its possibilities, more seriously than many of my companions.

In the battle for survival over Meiktila on 9 November, all that effort and forethought proved worthwhile and made the vital difference between life and death for Johnny and myself. From that day my world changed dramatically and has never been the same since. What I experienced not only changed my life but also made me different to those who have never shared the terrible experience of being a prisoner of the Japanese.

Seven days after the invasion began, Japanese Oscar fighters suddenly struck in the early morning and shot down some Dakotas. The 45 Squadron was ordered to find and destroy these fighters who must have come down from China. All day Mossies swept known Japanese airfields and then photographic planes checked them again but nothing could be found, so well hidden were the Oscars. They were probably planning another strike at the air freighters next morning.

189

I was pretty sure they were at Meiktila, the main central Burma HQ airfield because the anti-aircraft gunfire was so much greater when we swept over it that day. With this thought in mind I planned a dawn attack on Meiktila with six Mossies from B Flight.

All the Mossies left singly well before dawn. They flew over the Chin Mountains to rendezvous near Meiktila at dawn. Hopefully we would strike at the airfield just as the fighters were taking off. Weather conditions were poor at the rendezvous with patches of low cloud and fog. After 15 minutes I decided to attack with the three other Mossies that had turned up. I was worried that the Japanese fighters might take off before we attacked if we waited any longer. I was also worried about the unarmed Dakotas that might get shot down.

Approaching Meiktila at treetop height the formation opened up to 300 mph. About a mile away I saw a Japanese fighter squadron climbing above the airfield so I radioed confirmation that the fighters were stationed at Meiktila. The Oscars were an improved version of the famous Zero fighter and not to be taken lightly. Soon heavy anti-aircraft shells began bursting above the Mossies as we streaked above the treetops and I knew we were in for a hot reception. I decided to bomb the airfield first and then tackle the fighters already off the ground when we were free of our bombs.

Half a mile from the airfield I radioed the flight to climb to 300 feet so we could clearly see the airfield and spread out and attack worthwhile targets. I could see that some fighters were already beginning their dive on us.

At that moment Zombie 3 was bracketed by exploding anti-aircraft shells. The right motor burst into flames, and the left motor poured out white smoke indicating serious damage to the cooling system. From that moment Zombie 3 was doomed. Johnny successfully stopped the burning motor, put out the fire and feathered the propeller.

I dived at the airfield and before me was an amazing sight. On the other side of the airfield was a huge open underground depot with two Japanese bombers taxiing away from it. It was right in my line of sight. I struck at both bombers with all guns firing, getting a short accurate burst into each of them that destroyed them both. Then I dived straight at the open depot and dropped my bombs into it. The plane missed the trees by inches as it squashed out of its dive in its damaged state. I streaked away at treetop height with light gunfire slamming into the plane. I flashed past one machine-gun emplacement firing at us from barely 50 yards away.

The attack was over in seconds but with one motor stopped and the other damaged, Zombie 3's flying time was definitely limited. There was no hope of escape so I called the others and told them I was heading for the Chan hills and they were to go home. I knew they would have no problem in outrunning the fighters, and would lead them into a trap for other Mosquitos closing in on Meiktila. My flight wasn't the only force out that morning looking for the fighters.

Johnny, looking back, reported a massive explosion from the depot we had bombed and then warned me of two Oscars diving toward Zombie 3. I opened the left motor to full power and the plane steadied to 280 mph. This obviously matched the speed of the fighters as they failed to close the firing range. Unfortunately the left motor instruments showed the first signs of overheating.

I had planned before the flight that if I got badly hit over Meiktila and to have any chance of getting home, I would head for the Chan States about 80 miles from Meiktila. The people in this area were reported to be anti-Japanese. The problem was would Zombie 3 stay together for that distance?

Still flying at treetop level the Mossie ran under some low cloud and I pulled steeply to get into it hoping to hide from the Oscars but it was only morning mist and gave no real cover. I dived to the treetops again. By now my speed was down to 180 mph and the uneven battle between the stricken Mosquito and the two Oscars began. According to the rules of aerial warfare all the odds were heavily stacked against the Mosquito. There was no way such a damaged plane could outmanoeuvre two very nimble Oscar fighters. In reality Zombie 3 had only minutes remaining.

Some months before I had visualised such a situation happening so I carried out experiments with a Hurricane flight commander on ways to reduce the odds of a single-engine Mossie caught in such circumstances. I had worked out tactics that would cause the attacking fighter to waste most of his ammunition and might, just might, allow the damaged Mossie to escape, always assuming the other motor was undamaged. It would be impossible to outmanoeuvre a fighter but not to outwit him. The Hurricane pilot was very surprised at how difficult it proved to get a long, destructive burst of fire into a Mosquito when it was flown very close to the trees. Now was the time to try my theories out in deadly earnest.

Because one engine was stopped the aircraft had extra drag that side and had to be trimmed to keep to a straight course. My theory was to keep so low the fighters had to do a diving turn from above to get at me and come in from the direction of the dead motor. As the fighters entered their diving turn close together, I pushed the control column towards the dead motor, increasing the drag on that side. This caused the plane to slip sideways with the nose still heading forward. I kept the wings level by hard rudder pressure to the left. I was able to side-slip at the right time because Johnny warned me when the attacking pilots were about to open fire. They aimed for the cockpit and along the fuselage without noticing the plane was actually sliding sideways. As a result they only got a very short burst into the cockpit before the fire drifted off along the left wing, and the fighters were forced to break off, climb and come around for another attack.

As the fighters dived firing on Zombie 3 Johnny and I crouched behind our armour-plated shields. Bullets smashed into these and some came through the gap and smashed into the instrument panel. We were both greatly relieved to find the fighters were not equipped with cannon, only machine guns. I switched on my radio to give the others of the flight a running commentary of the battle and perhaps learn from what was happening.

We both could hardly believe we had survived the first attack. Instead of trying to fly away from the Japanese when they climbed to circle for another attack, I followed them around to manoeuvre them into coming in from the direction of the dead motor so I could use my side-slipping tactics again. Again they came diving in; again we crouched behind our protective shields and again the bullets smashed into the shields some finding a way around them. I got better at side-slipping and the next two attacks only got hits on the left wing.

The following two attacks were better aimed. More bullets smashed into the cockpit and made bigger holes in the left wing. I persisted with my tactics, as there was nothing else I could do. The speed was getting lower with each manoeuvre. The question was, what would happen first? Would they manage to set the left motor on fire? Would the motor seize up? Would it stop overheating? Engine heating gauges were already right off the clock. Would the Japs run out of ammunition and allow us to make a crash-landing in the trees? One way or another Zombie 3 was going to stop flying pretty soon.

Johnny was beginning to feel the strain and lapsed into prayer to every saint in Christendom. He pleaded for our survival, constantly interrupted by my demands to know exactly where the Japanese fighters were in their preparations for the next attack.

The sixth attack was by far the worst. Maybe the fighters were coming off to the right to allow for my side-slipping, or maybe the Mossie was getting so slow that it was having the same effect. Both Oscars got a good burst into the cockpit. Streams of bullets poured through the gap between the two sheets of armour-plating, behind which we again crouched for protection. Bullets smashed

193

into the cockpit instruments destroying everything but the air-speed indicator. More ricocheted off the back of the bullet proof windscreen and tore all around the cockpit making many holes in the windows. They made a terrible, frightening noise and seemed to be tearing everything to pieces. One sliced the glove of my right hand slitting my wrist while I was holding the control column hard over to the right to keep the plane side-slipping. Two more hit my legs causing flesh wounds. There was no pain, only the feel of blood running down my legs. Ricocheting incendiary bullets seemed to fill the cockpit, but miraculously we both seemed to have escaped without serious wounds and Zombie kept on flying, but noticeably slower and more sluggish on the controls. We were still at treetop height but this sixth attack had chewed some big holes in the left wing and it didn't seem she could last much longer.

Johnny pleaded with me, "Put her down! Put her down! They are going to kill us. Please put her down!" But I was equally sure that the Oscars would destroy us as we were levelling off to make a crash-landing into the trees or strafe us if we survived the crash. I preferred flying as long as possible in the hope that they would fly out of ammunition.

Then suddenly it all ended. On the seventh attack the left motor burst into flames, either from a hit or from overheating. Speed was down to 120 mph and I had only seconds to prepare for a crash into the trees. I glanced behind to see the Oscars diving on us again with the front one firing and I instinctively knew this was the end. And then, wonder of wonders, behind them was a Mosquito very close, with all guns firing. He must have got some hits on the Oscars because they broke off and fled.

In those seconds Johnny and I prepared for the crash. Johnny jettisoned the door and tried unsuccessfully to put out the engine fire. As the speed dropped off I pulled the nose higher and higher trying to ease the plane down into the trees tail first but just as she sank towards them a big tree appeared right ahead. I slammed the controls toward the left and managed to avoid a head-on collision. The tree slammed into the right wing, which was already on fire and Zombie 3 exploded. It fell through the trees into a swamp below.

I was momentarily knocked out and came to sitting in a blazing inferno with burning shells and bullets exploding everywhere. Johnny had already leapt out but I found my legs trapped by wreckage under the instrument panels. Immediately I followed the drill I had practised just for this emergency. I turned on to full oxygen, breathing only from the oxygen tank. This avoided the super-heated air that would have quickly killed me by shrivelling my lungs, I had seen others die in blazing crashes and I was convinced that it was lack of oxygen rather than the fire that killed them.

I pulled Johnny's parachute over my shoulders to keep the fire off myself and then crouching down in the confined space, got to work with my special axe to clear the wreckage from my trapped legs. I had to use both hands. The heat was terrible. Then I lunged for the door grabbing by its special handle I had fitted to it, the first aid kit.

The blazing wreck of Zombie 3 had fallen into a swamp and the fire has spread over the surrounding water. As I lunged out of the partly submerged door my head and shoulder went under the water. Weakened by the crash I struggled to the surface. Johnny was standing by the edge of the fire, unable to see anything in the cockpit for smoke and flames but now rushed in to the flaming water and dragged me clear. We struggled to a dry spot. I had suffered burns to my shoulders and bleeding wounds to my wrist and legs. Johnny, remarkably, had escaped without any injuries.

I gasped my thanks and after a few more gasps added, "And thanks for your prayers too." Maybe Johnny was too shocked to reply but quickly opening the first aid kit he dressed and bandaged my leg wounds. My frantic slashing at the wreckage with my axe had added a few bleeding cuts to the bullet wounds. Fortunately none were very deep. Later, both my legs were covered with black bruises.

195

After bandaging my cut wrist and plastering my burns with Gentian Violet we both felt he had done a good first aid job. That was the only medical care I received until the capture of Rangoon in early May 1945.

Watching the blazing inferno consuming the wreck of Zombie 3 we were both rather shaken by our narrow escape from a fiery death. Flames were rapidly burning the wooden part of the plane. A large pall of black smoke from the burning fuel, oil and rubber rose up through the trees. Exploding cannon shells and bullets added to the noise of the fire. Johnny commented, "Just as well you had that special first aid kit. We wouldn't have got much from the one on the plane." But I was still wondering who was flying the Mosquito that had arrived so suddenly and driven off the fighters at that critical time. The other pilot would not have been able to speak to us because my radio was on transmit. He would have seen Zombie 3 explode on hitting the trees and had probably reported back that her crew had died in the flames.

Mosquito with engine on fire. Painted by W.G.Laing. Cliff had described to him the battle over Meiktila and from that description Laing painted this scene. Cliff later saw the painting on display at an air show and bought it for $165.

Chapter 14

PRISONERS

For some time we sat there in almost stunned disbelief, then we heard the sound of people yelling nearby. We quickly gathered ourselves together and set off toward the Chan Hills. This was still only about 30 minutes after dawn.

We struggled on through the swamp until midday, when we found a small island covered in bushes. We seemed to have lost our pursuers. Being exhausted we lay down for a rest and were soon sound asleep.

In the mid-afternoon a group of eight Burmese teenagers suddenly rushed us and grabbed our revolvers. We both leapt to our feet and struck out at them with our fists and boots. The kids clung to us like leeches, trying to drag us to the ground. Johnny was six feet two inches and was far too strong for them. I unzipped myself out of my overalls to allow me more freedom to fight harder. Fortunately they knew nothing about firearms. The two eldest were trying to shoot us with our own revolvers from only a couple of feet away. They were pulling frantically at the triggers but the revolvers wouldn't fire because they were set on 'safe'. Finally they fled with their loot comprising our revolvers, my escape suit, first aid kit and my watch, which they had torn from my wrist. Strangely enough it never occurred to either of us to surrender even though the two older boys were jabbing us in the chests with the revolvers and trying to pull the triggers.

We set off again toward the Chan Hills. Just before dark we stumbled on a small Burmese hut with some corn hanging from it. We decided that some of that corn would help us to keep going for several days in the jungle. We hid nearby until it was dark and the four people we had seen around the hut seemed to have gone to sleep. We had just reached for the corn when two dogs rushed at us and within seconds the people came out to see what all the commotion was about.

I acted as friendly as I could. I still had some money hidden in my boots so I offered to buy some corn. The people seemed pleased and offered to cook it for us. They soon had a fire going but it seemed to be taking some time. Suddenly another group of Burmese jumped out of the darkness and quickly overpowered us. They tied our hands behind our backs and then prodding us with spears, we set out with them into the jungle.

There were six men, all armed with spears or long knives. The march began about 9 pm. They seemed to know where they were going and talked all the time between themselves. It was a clear moonlit night and watching the stars I was sure they were talking us back to Meiktila. The track was rough and sometimes swampy and often quite dark because of overhanging trees. As the hours stretched by my injured legs became very painful and both of us were very tired but there was no stopping. They just kept walking on. It was worse when I fell. With my hands tied behind my back it was impossible to get up again. The Burmese would help me up and on we went. The prick of a spear in the back kept me going. Beyond a certain threshold the body becomes almost immune to the pain and sheer willpower takes over. It was a terrible experience. I kept telling myself I was lucky to be alive, so nothing else mattered.

Just at dawn, about 6 am, we reached Thazi, a large village on the railway line not far from Meiktila. Our arrival caused a great stir and English-speaking Burmese immediately untied us and offered us food. I offered them 2000 rupees to be taken to the Allied lines in northern Burma. They agreed to go that night and we felt we were among friends. After our meal of rice and milk we were given mats to sleep on and being thoroughly exhausted were soon asleep.

A few hours later I awoke to find the Burmese standing over us with rifles and we knew we would be handed over to the Japanese. We heard later that the Burmese had to find and hand over the crew of any shot down plane or the Japs would burn every dwelling within five miles of the wreck. They really didn't have much choice.

Around midday there was quite a commotion outside and we saw a troop of Japanese soldiers entering the village and advancing towards us with fixed bayonets. We got up and walked toward them. I was inwardly cursing that Intelligence had not taught us a few words of Japanese. All they did was give each crew member a revolver with six rounds and say, "Five for the Japs and one for yourself. Don't be taken alive." I was thinking 'what armchair idiots' when the Japanese officer spoke in perfect Oxford English, "You are our prisoners. Do you understand?"

I replied, "Yes."

The officer then asked, "Have you any weapons?" I pulled a small knife from my left boot and handed it over, explaining that the Burmese had taken our revolvers back in the bush. Then he noticed my leg and wrist bandages and commented on my being wounded and asked, "Were you shot down yesterday?" I nodded and he commandeered a bullock cart from the Burmese and told us to get aboard. He then held a discussion with the village leaders after which there was a lot of bowing on both sides. Bowing was something we prisoners had to learn the hard way.

The officer, Johnny and I rode on the cart, with the soldiers running alongside. As we left the village I noticed several locomotives hidden under trees on a side line. They all looked heavily damaged and I wondered if some were victims of my own attacks. All rail traffic had stopped over central and northern Burma probably because all the locomotives had been put out of action by air attacks. We reached Meiktila just before dusk and I saw ample evidence of the air attacks made the previous day with many burnt buildings and bomb craters.

About an hour after our arrival we were taken before some senior Japanese officers who tried to question us about the aircraft we flew and our tactics. They had with them the door and one machine gun from Zombie 3. Both of us refused to give any information and I insisted that under the rules of international law prisoners of war could not be compelled to give any more information than their name and rank. They made it plain, however, that they knew I was the leader of the Mosquito formation. They were puzzled that Johnny was called 'Yanoto' and asked him where his parents came from. He replied that his mother was Polish and his father was Czechoslovakian. The general merely shook his head. They also questioned me about the painting of Mt Egmont on the door of Zombie 3. They thought it was Mt Fujiyama and that 'Te Kiri' was an Asian word.

They seemed to accept our refusal to give information and then there followed a long discussion between themselves. The officer who spoke English was called back and given instructions. He took us out and explained that we were to be given a meal and taken elsewhere.

Later that night we left by truck for Rangoon together with the English-speaking officer and 10 soldiers. This officer looked after us well and quickly put a stop to any manhandling by the soldiers. He even made a soldier give back Johnny his watch he had taken from him. He made sure we were well fed and given good sleeping conditions. The truck only travelled at night and all the Japanese seemed terrified of air attacks. At least three times a night they imagined they heard a plane and leapt off the truck in panic leaving us tied up alone. I wasn't particularly worried about air attacks, as I knew none had been scheduled for the area that night.

We arrived in Rangoon after two nights' travelling and were taken to Army Headquarters at the university. Johnny and I decided on a strategy to prevent the Japs playing one of us off against the other in an attempt to get information. We insisted that Johnny, who wore the Canadian Observer Wing 'O' was only just that. As an observer his job was to keep check on where other planes in the formation were and to keep a lookout for enemy fighters. He knew nothing about operations and to our surprise the Japanese accepted this explanation and next day sent Johnny to the Rangoon prison.

I anxiously and rather nervously waited to see what the next day would bring.

Chapter 15

INTERROGATION

An Army major interrogated me whom I will call 'the major' from now on. He was short, stocky with a big head and piercing dark eyes. He shouted a lot and seemed very tough. There was also a quiet, short Japanese clerk, who tried to write notes the whole time. A pleasant, youthful interpreter who spoke good American English, together with several guards led by a corporal were always present.

Officers came and went as the interrogations proceeded over nearly two awful weeks. Called in from time to time were

'Interrogation'.

three karate-trained Japs, big heavily muscled men of whom I have the most unpleasant memories.

The first session began with the major asking a stream of questions: What was the number of my squadron? Where did it operate from? How many Mosquitos did we have? Who was the commanding officer? What was the speed, rate of climb and range of the Mosquitos? What was its armament and bomb load? What were the bombing tactics? Question after question.

I was defensive and felt very vulnerable. Since Squadron Leader Edwards had been killed two months before, I had been acting flight commander, and so took part in briefings on the plans to drive the Japanese out of most of northern and central Burma, and capture Rangoon by 10 May 1945, when the next Monsoon rains were expected to begin. I knew a great deal that would be valuable to the Japanese so decided to refuse to give any answers other than my name, rank and identity number, again invoking the protection of the Geneva War Convention.

Using the interpreter the major read the questions off sheets of paper, all the time getting obviously more annoyed at me as I looked him steadily in the eyes and kept declining to answer each question. Finally he got up from the table, walked around to me and struck me a powerful blow on the face, knocking me off the chair. As soon as I got back on the chair he attacked me again, hitting my face from side to side with his open palms, until I became dizzy and fell off the chair. This time I had difficulty in regaining my seat.

The major returned to his side of the table and began reading out the questions again and I still refused to answer. I concentrated on the thought 'you don't lead men one day and betray them the next no matter what happens'. Soon the major leapt to his feet again and shouted loudly. Immediately three heavily built Japs entered the room. The major shouted at them and they began manhandling me violently, hitting me over the neck, chest and back. They pushed me from one to the other and kicked me with their feet karate-style and picked me up and slammed me to the floor. These painful blows soon reduced me to a state of semi-consciousness and they left me lying on the floor. The major stalked out of the room leaving me there.

I hurt from head to foot and was too weak to get up. The interpreter tried to talk to me but I couldn't respond. Guards were called in and they dragged me into the guardroom next door and propped me against the wall in the corner. They brought in some water and washed my blood-covered face and gave me a drink. Later in the day they gave me some rice to eat. Next day bruises had appeared all over my body and it was very painful to move.

The questioning began all over again. I decided I would vaguely answer some of the least important questions. This seemed to infuriate the major even more. When he demanded to know how I shot down Japanese fighters I answered, "Just dived down behind them and opened fire." He leapt to his feet and screamed, "You lie! you lie!" In rushed the karate trio again and the same terrible violence of the day before was repeated reducing me again to unconsciousness. Again I was dragged to the guardroom and assisted by the guards. My body ached so badly that night sleep came only with complete exhaustion.

Next day the questioning began again. I felt so sore I could hardly sit in the chair opposite the major. As the questions were read out I just shook my head and leaned painfully on the table. The major became very frustrated. Finally he got up, removed his revolver from his holster and leaned across the table pointing it at me and speaking to the interpreter. The interpreter translated, "If you do not agree to answer all questions he will shoot you at the count of five!"

The major placed the end of the revolver between my eyes and began to count, with the interpreter translating the numbers.

The open end of the pistol began to grow immensely in size in front of my face and I noticed the trigger finger of the major gradually squeezing. At the count of two I forcibly switched my gaze to look directly into the Japanese officer's eyes and a dull feeling enveloped my body. I vaguely heard the numbers four and five and then there was silence.

I became aware the major had withdrawn his revolver from between my eyes and returned it to his holster. Without another word he got up and left the room. Gradually my mind cleared from the effect of the shock and I dragged my hurting body back to the guardroom. Every movement was very painful.

That evening a young American pilot was brought in. His Thunderbolt fighter had been shot down by ground fire while he was strafing Japanese troops. He had suffered a nasty head injury in the crash. His head was bandaged and he looked weak and tired. In the night he was semi-delirious and held his head in pain. I was sitting uncomfortably against the wall and he laid his head on my upper leg. This must have somehow eased the pain for he was soon asleep. My leg became numb with the weight of his head and it certainly didn't help the pain of my bruises. In the morning the American looked much better. During the day the Japs took him away and I didn't see him again until they moved the prisoners from the cell-block to No. 8 compound two months later. He survived the war.

For two days there were no interrogations. Then the major returned to the fray and began reading the same list of questions. Again I refused to answer them. Suddenly his annoyance seemed to quieten down. He became cool and started issuing orders to the guards. Then two of the guards dragged me, one by each arm, out of the guardroom to where a group of four other guards were lined up with the major alongside them.

Still dragging me, the whole group set off past a large building and then turned and faced the wall behind it. The two guards holding me by the arms walked me to the wall and turned me to face the group. The major shouted some orders and the guards lined up about 15 feet away, took aim, and I suddenly realised that I was facing a firing squad. I stared at the rifles and that terrible shocked feeling of impending death swept over me again. My mind seemed to be set on one thought only, 'No one will ever know!'. I forced myself to look away from the menacing rifles to the major who had raised his sword above his head. Down came the sword. I saw his lips move and then there was nothing.

I did not see the flashes or hear the roar of the rifles as they fired. I must have collapsed and fainted with shock. The first thing I knew was my two guards holding me up. My body felt like a rag doll; my head wobbled around my shoulders; my arms hung limp and my legs buckled under my weight. They were trying to make me stand but I couldn't. The major came forward and slapped my face but my head merely rolled from side to side. I was alive but my nervous system was not functioning because of shock. A terrible pain engulfed my stomach and left chest and I could only breathe with deep gasps. The two guards dragged me back to the guardroom and dumped my limp body on the floor.

It was some time before I gradually began to realise what had happened. It was several hours before the dreadful pain in my stomach and chest subsided. I realised I had survived an execution. Obviously the major hadn't meant to kill me. They must have either fired blanks or fired over my head. They all couldn't possibly have missed me from only 15 feet away.

Once again the major had failed. His treatment had so severely affected me that coherent interrogation was impossible. He persisted, however, and two days later he repeated the mock firing squad treatment with the same terrible effects. Then after two more days he did it again. This time I felt angry and watched the rifles. I may have seen the flash as they fired and heard a

206

little of their noise, but again I collapsed with the shock. Each time the recovery was the same painful experience. How much more stress could the body and nervous system stand?

Next day the major and I were back in the interrogation room. He'd only just started reading the list of questions when another officer entered and began speaking sternly to him. The major seemed quite subdued. Then the visitor left and the major followed him. I asked the interpreter for an explanation. He replied, "It is good for you. He is not allowed to hurt you any more. You are Samurai now. If you die it will be by Samurai code." Then he too left and I returned to the guardroom.

That afternoon the major returned. He began to shout orders and a post was hastily erected on the bit of lawn in front of the guardroom. I was roughly manhandled out to the post and my wrists were tied behind it. Another rope was tied to my collarbone and another just below my knees. I assumed that the major was planning to break me by keeping me tied there day and night without food and water until I collapsed. In the blazing heat of the sun and the cool of the night flies and other insects constantly tormented me.

The first night was terrible but I found I could actually rest on the ropes if completely relaxed. The worst pain was from my wrists tied behind the post but after a few hours they just became numb and the pain became bearable.

Next morning small groups of officers stopped to look at me and chattered away amongst themselves. I would try to stand as firm as I could and stare back at them. I would relax when they had gone. I could feel the blazing sun burning my face and I began to suffer from extreme thirst. The night was a welcome relief. The next day was terrible. I could feel myself weakening. Perhaps I didn't look so defiant when the Japanese officers stopped to look and chatter as they passed. I hadn't shaved since I had been shot down and perhaps my growing beard was helping to protect my face from the sun.

On the second night I was feeling far from well and was afraid I wouldn't see the morning, when a passing soldier pushed some food into my mouth. It was some kind of pastry with what tasted like a date in the centre. I was so dehydrated I had difficulty in producing enough saliva to swallow. Then a second soldier did the same. Then a third soldier, looking furtively about in the darkness, raised his water bottle and gave me a good drink from it. Another later gave me some more food. It was much easier to swallow the food after I had drunk. I wondered if these were the same soldiers who had been part of the fake firing squads. At that stage most Japanese soldiers looked alike to me and it was dark when they helped me.

The effect of such help was to greatly raise my spirits and determination to last another day of heat and suffering. Probably much to the major's surprise and to the surprise of the group of officers that stood talking around me next morning, I was not only alive but looked a little refreshed. But that was a terribly hard day and by night I was close to collapsing again. Again the guards did the same as they had done the night before. Shortly after midnight, when there was no moon, the guard NCO untied me and helped me stagger into the guardroom and laid me down on a bamboo couch. One gave me a good drink and signed to me to sleep, which I did very easily. An hour or so later they woke me up, gave me some rice to eat and another drink and then took me out and tied me up again.

I was amazed at this treatment. The relief on my tortured body was considerable. I felt wonderfully refreshed. Soon the dawn came and I decided I could stick it out for another day and see what would happen. Again the major and the other officers came to check me out. Again I looked at them defiantly. That night the same thing happened, the guards giving me food, water and rest so that next morning I was still there. Even the major seemed puzzled by my endurance. By this time the sun had blistered my face and I must have looked almost like a skeleton.

That day I began to think beyond defiance. I became concerned that the major could easily break my resistance and obtain from me the information of how the Allies planned to drive the Japanese out of Burma. I began to think seriously about how the major interrogated me – he always read the list of questions the same way in the same order – and how he reacted when I answered correctly about attacking behind a plane to shoot it down. Gradually it dawned upon me that the major knew absolutely nothing about aviation, Mosquitos or aerial warfare. Maybe he just had a list of questions that had to be answered but he wouldn't know if the answers were right or wrong. Thinking about the questions and the answers I would give made the day go quickly.

That night I decided to give in and engage in a battle of wits with the major. When I saw the NCO coming toward me later that night I feigned collapse and hung over the ropes with my eyes closed. He immediately untied me and helped me into the guardroom. After a drink I appeared to come to and by sign language indicated that I was finished with resisting. The Japanese NCO disappeared and returned with a meal of rice and vegetables and helped me to eat it. He then laid me down to rest and I slept until dawn. When I woke up I felt quite refreshed and ready to face the major.

He had apparently been informed and arrived at the interrogation looking more relaxed than I had ever seen him. He began by asking me if I would answer the questions. When I replied that I would, he proceeded to read them out. Nearly every answer I gave was false and of no value to the Japanese whatever. Dutifully the interpreter translated both question and answer and the clerk wrote them down. I found the whole proceedings quite unbelievable. I had been right. The major was quite satisfied and hadn't the slightest idea if the answer was right or wrong. I was careful to give answers that seemed relevant. For instance when I was asked, "Where was I based?" I named a small emergency airstrip 200 miles from my base. I gave false names for commanding officers and false figures on the number of planes, and exaggerated their performance, speed, armament and bomb loads. Now and again I made some complimentary remark about Japanese planes, their pilots and Japanese troops, which the major seemed noticeably to enjoy.

The interrogation lasted for about three hours. In the end he actually smiled and offered me a small cigar and lit it for me. I wasn't a smoker but I took it and bowed slightly. The major bowed back and left the room. He must have spoken to the guard NCO for soon afterwards some rice and water were brought in to me.

What a change! I was amazed and secretly cursed my stupidity for not judging the Japs better. But what had I to judge by? My intelligence officers at the base had emphasised the sheer brutality of the Japanese towards their prisoners. As I have already mentioned air crews were given a Smith and Wesson revolver with the advice 'Five shots for the Japanese and one for yourself. Don't be taken alive'. What idiotic advice! They knew nothing about the Japanese. But my suffering may not have been in vain. Possibly it may have so earned the respect of the Japanese for my courage and sense of humour that they now believed anything I said. Possibly my co-operation in finally answering the questions was very much a face-saving situation for the major that fully justified the brutal methods he used to get his answers. I could only speculate on these things.

I now found the interpreter willing to talk about himself and discovered he was 25 years old and had been born in America and was caught by the Pearl Harbour attack when visiting his grandparents in Japan. He was conscripted into the army as an interpreter and finished up in Rangoon six months before I arrived. He was delighted to know that the Allies were definitely winning the war with Japan and apologised for the brutal treatment I had received.

I was kept in the guard cells for the next two weeks. Three times I was taken out and interviewed by Jap officers. They couldn't be called 'interrogations' because they were quite peaceful occasions. The officers wanted to hear news of the war in Europe and the Pacific. I told them about Allied victories in both theatres. With some senior officers quite a discussion developed over treatment of prisoners of war. I argued the Christian view-point about Allied forces, that they were fighting to defend freedom, not for conquest and plunder like the Japanese, and that when a serviceman lost his weapon or surrendered, he was entitled to be treated as a peaceful human being. The Japanese on the other hand insisted that an officer should never surrender. He must always die fighting and prisoners were slaves and should be treated as such. I assured them that the Allies would win the war, but that officers could surrender with honour and would be sent back to Japan again to take up their lives.

Alone in my cell, whenever I recalled my brutal interrogation treatment, the severe pain returned to my stomach and left chest. I finally decided I must never think or speak about those awful experiences again. This was the only way to escape from such horrors. Not until recently has anyone heard a word of what I suffered during my interrogation. I simply could not control my subconscious mind. For years after the war I experienced terrible, vivid dreams of these horrors. Damage to my stomach nerves greatly affected the digestion of food all those years. Only in the last 20 years, by means of natural healthcare and a milk-food diet, has the nightmare diminished and my digestion improved.

The severe sun burning experienced when tied to the stake, has caused skin cancer problems over the forehead and to my face. Twice medical professionals have advised drastic surgery and radiation treatment, but fortunately my understanding of natural healthcare has enabled me to avoid such treatment.

Chapter 16

HELL ON EARTH

Sometime later I was taken to the Rangoon prison; the former British prison in the centre of Rangoon. I was still heavily bruised and shocked by the brutality of the beatings I had received during my interrogation. I had no idea what was in front of me or what would happen next, but nothing could have prepared me for the sight of what I experienced when I entered that place.

As we walked in I passed haggard men, just skin and bone, dressed only in a loincloth hanging to them by a string. The sight of them, cowed, bent and stealing only a brief stricken glance at us, created an atmosphere of awful terror filling that place. What had happened to these men to cause them to be like this? Whatever I felt about my own condition, the pitiful state of these men meant that even greater suffering was ahead. I found out later that these were the prisoners too ill to work. Their loincloths were all they had to wear. As a prisoner's clothes rotted off him the Japanese refused to replace them.

We entered a big, two-storeyed building in the centre of the compound and climbed to the upper storey. This place contained cells with barred windows. As we walked through, the occupants were standing in the centre of their cells, two or three to a cell, and all seemed to be bowing and looking at the floor. Only an occasional one stole a glance at us as we went past. The only sound was the sound of our boots on the floor. Eventually we came to an empty cell and I was pushed into it. The door slammed and I found myself in a cell about eight feet long and six feet wide. The floor was bare except for a slightly raised board about six feet long and twenty inches wide along the right wall and an empty ammunition box on the left. The barred windows looked down on a yard across to the bare walls of another prison block. The sun was shining through the cell window.

I hadn't been there long before a Japanese guard came to the door carrying a pick handle. He yelled and gesticulated at me. I just looked back at him. He opened the door and rushed in, swinging the club and striking me around the shoulders. I kept trying to dodge his blows and then he left. About an hour later he returned and repeated the same performance. Later in the afternoon some Chinese came through the prison with rice in a container and water in another. They paused briefly outside my cell and then moved on. I suddenly realised that I had nothing to collect food and water in. Then darkness fell and the guards seemed to leave the building.

After a while a whispering voice came from the next cell, "Hello, hello."

I answered, "Yes," and the voice spoke a little louder and asked who I was and where I came from. I gave him my name, rank and service number and told the voice, "I am a New Zealander." A joyful reply welcomed me and the voice began to tell me why I was being beaten. All prisoners had to stand in the middle of the cell every time the guard came past, usually about once an hour. The prisoners must keep their heads bowed and their eyes looking at the Jap's feet otherwise they would get a beating. The ammunition box was a toilet box. Each morning I would have to carry it out and empty it in the barrels just outside the building. I must not speak to any other prisoner while doing this or I would be beaten. The Japs, I was told, would not give me anything to put food or water in, but the Ghurka who swept the corridor floor twice daily would push a piece of tin under the door and I would have to make a container out of that.

213

The voice then wanted to know news of the war. He wanted to know what was happening in Europe, the Middle East, the Pacific and Burma. I was able to tell him the Allies were winning everywhere and that the 14th Army hoped to reach Rangoon by May before the Monsoon broke. He was delighted with the news and asked to be free to tell the others. For hours excited whispering voices on that floor passed the news around. It must have been wonderful for them to hear how well the Allies were doing and especially that the 14th Army was on its way to rescue them, but May would seem a long way away. I realised later that many feared they would never live to see May.

Eventually from sheer exhaustion I lay down on the board to sleep, but the painful bruises and the horror of my interrogation and the horror of where I now found myself made sleep difficult.

It was obvious the Japanese couldn't have cared less whether we survived or not. Our lives meant nothing to them,

Rangoon Central Jail. Entrance seen here in Commission Road, Rangoon. This prison was condemned by the British in 1938. It had no sanitation, no water, and no lighting.

so I devoted myself to survival. I knew that the 14th Army was due to enter Rangoon on 10 May so all I had to do was to survive until then.

My first problem was to get food and water. For two days I watched the Chinese food suppliers come and go without giving me anything. On the third day I pushed my boots through the bars and they put rice in one and water in the other. My boots had splashed through miles of Burmese mud after we had been captured but right then that didn't matter. I had to get something to get my rations in or I would die of starvation or thirst. For 14 days I ate my food out of my boots using my fingers to get the rice out. I noticed that the Chinese gave me an extra half scoop the first day. Maybe they sensed my desperation.

Using my handkerchief I washed my wounds with my drinking water. When the sun was shining through my window, and the guards were not passing, I exposed my wounds to the sun.

On the first morning I was let out with all the other prisoners on my side to empty my toilet box. Now I knew what the smell was when I first entered the prison. It came from all those open ammunition boxes. We trooped outside to a row of barrels. The box had its opening in the middle and it was impossible to empty it completely. There was no way of washing it clean and the unpleasant stink remained with the prisoner day and night in his cell. Just try to imagine the smell in cells with three or four prisoners sharing the one box. If even one had dysentery it was almost overpowering.

On the fourth day we were taken out to have a wash in a big circular tank in the centre of the prison. I noticed many of the men, as they scrambled over the wall of the tub, were suffering from large ulcers. The thought struck me that I must never get into that water with my open wounds or they would become infected and soon I too would have pus-oozing wounds like these men. I played the idiot and kept falling over as if I couldn't get into the tank. I got whacked a few times but then I found a prisoner so weak that he couldn't get in and I took to splashing water on his face and body. He looked at me so gratefully; we managed a smile. How he must have been suffering as his life slipped away. Helping him used up my time and all I did was wash my face. The Japs left me alone when they saw me helping this man.

I never did get into that water and my wounds did not become infected. Each time I would look for a prisoner too weak to climb into the tub and I would use my time helping him to wash. The guards seemed quite happy allowing me do this and no longer beat me for not getting into the tub. This was just another example of my concentrating on survival.

A few days later I found a small nail sticking out of my board bed. I set to work to loosen it and to pull it out. It was to prove a useful tool for my survival. On the 10th day of my imprisonment, the Ghurka sweeping outside my door suddenly crouched and pushed a small piece of tin under my door. I pounced on it and shoved it under my bed board. Now I had the means of making a container for my food and water.

I thought about it all day and decided I needed a double container, one for rice and the other for water, so I could use the water to clean my wounds. Between the times the guard went past my door I drew designs on the side of the tin with my nail and finally worked out how to make a double container from a ten-inch square of tin.

Next day I began tapping the tin with the heel of my boot on the corner of my bed board. It took me four days to finish the job; I had to work in the intervals when the guard was not passing my cell. I carefully counted how long it took him to pass my cell and return. Remember I had to be standing in the middle of the cell and bowing to him each time he passed. If he had caught me making my container I would have been beaten and my tin taken from me. I was thrilled when I had finished it. It was quite an important victory on the road to survival.

My next task was to use the nail that I had sharpened by rubbing on the concrete wall. Its first job was to prise off two slivers of wood from the bed board to use as chop sticks so I wouldn't have to use my fingers to eat my rice. It took me two days to achieve this but what a thrill it was to succeed. I felt I had made a real step toward being a civilised human being again.

Then came a dramatic event when I took a great risk and surprisingly got away with it. There was a lot of noise as the guards half pushed and half dragged a prisoner past my cell. While bowing I stole a glimpse at the prisoner and noticed the 'New Zealand' flash on his battledress. It was obvious that he had a broken ankle and was dragging that leg. A few minutes after he passed the commandant appeared. I leapt to the door and cried out, "The new prisoner is my cousin. Can he come into my cell? I am a doctor and can help his broken ankle."

The commandant stopped and tried to say, "Cousin? Cousin?"

So I went one better and called out, "He is my brother, my brother."

The commandant replied, "Aye, brother! brother!" and walked away. A few minutes later he returned with the guards dragging the prisoner. They opened my cell door and pushed him in. He fell to the floor and I pleaded with the commandant that he be excused from standing all day. "Aye, aye," he answered and spoke to the guards. I bowed and there was much "hi, hi-ing" until he turned and strode away.

So Craig Edwards came into my cell and his life was saved. I helped him on to the bed board and he was almost unconscious with the pain. Carefully I felt his leg and found the break just above the ankle, which badly needed setting and support. We took off our shirts, and using my nail, I cut strips from the shirts and used them to bind the break in place and greatly

217

relieve the pain he was suffering. I had done a first aid course while attending the Territorial Army Camp in Trentham in 1938 and what I had learnt in that basic course was now proving invaluable. It was great to see poor Craig relieved of some of his pain. He had crashed his Thunderbolt fighter 10 days before over Japanese territory and he must have suffered terribly as the Japs moved him about.

We really needed a splint to hold the leg rigid so I resorted to the nail again. The guards bought in a bed board and food container for Craig and I got to work to prise four strips of wood from his bed. The timber was softer than mine, so easier to work. Craig couldn't help for more than a few minutes, he didn't have the strength. It took four days to prise apart the strips we needed. We cut another couple of strips from our shirts and found we could bind his leg firmly.

For three weeks he didn't move from his bed except to use the toilet box, which I placed beside him. Then he carefully tried to stand and found the break had healed although for another week he moved very cautiously and slowly. Four weeks after he came in he could stand on his leg although we didn't let the Japs know that.

So I got to know Craig. There couldn't have been two more different people stuck in a cell together. Craig was the only son of a dentist in Wanganui. He had been raised wanting for nothing. He had attended Wanganui Collegiate and had a wide circle of friends from his own background and in his teen years enjoyed a lifestyle that was completely unknown to me. He had a bright personality with a boisterous sense of fun that often led him into trouble.

He had joined the Air Force and trained as a pilot. He flew Hurricanes in England but was always in trouble for low flying and low aerobatics. Finally he was transferred to India to fly Thunderbolts over Burma. On one of his first operational flights over Burma his plane was hit by ground fire. He was too low to bale out so he attempted a crash-landing and broke his leg. His plane was destroyed by fire and his comrades flying overhead were sure he had died in the flames.

There is no doubt that if he had just been thrown into a cell when reaching the prison he would have died. It was good for me to have another New Zealander for company. We talked for hours about home and the life we had lived and what we intended to do after the war.

Life settled down to a very limited routine. Twice daily we were fed rice and given water, each day we emptied our toilet box and once or twice a week we would go out for a wash. I never once got into the water of that tub. I attended to my own injuries and tried to keep healthy. Both Craig and I were lucky that neither of us got dysentery.

I was taken out three times to be questioned by senior Japanese officers about the war. The first time this happened there were four officers present who wanted to know about the war in Europe and in the Pacific. Maybe my resistance to their tortures caused them to seek out information from me. After a little questioning I got the distinct impression they knew very little about the war outside Burma. They seemed to know only the propaganda put out by the authorities.

On a world map I showed them how the Allies had driven the Germans out of North Africa, had invaded Italy and successfully invaded Europe. I pointed out the Russian victories of Stalingrad and how the Germans were on the retreat in Russia, the American victories of Midway, Guadalcanal and the Philippines and the recapture of the Aleutian Islands. Everywhere the Axis powers were losing the war. The war could be over everywhere within 12 months. They listened in silence until I had finished, asked a few questions and then left.

The next time there were nine officers present. They wanted me to go over it all again. They asked a few more questions and left. The next time there were 21, including some very senior officers.

219

Once again I was asked to cover the whole ground, but this time there were many more questions. They wanted to know about the food supplies in Britain, and how many Allied ships had been sunk. I was able to tell them how the Navy and Airforce had won the Battle of the Atlantic and how great liners were bringing 20 000 troops safely from America each trip. Very few ships were being attacked now and the German submarines were suffering heavy losses.

Huge RAF and American bomber fleets were bombing German cities and factories around the clock. The Americans were bombing by day and the British by night. The war in Europe would be over by mid-1945 and those huge Allied armies would be moved to the Far East.

The questions this time went on for three hours. Finally a discussion on prisoners of war took place. I tried to explain that our armies had a different philosophy to the Japanese about prisoners of war. We did not believe that if a man had fought honourably and then been captured that he was forever disgraced and deserving of humiliation and even death. Life for a prisoner wasn't easy, but a prisoner was treated as a human being. If wounded he would be taken to a hospital and treated, as our own soldiers would be. If not wounded, he would be confined to a camp and well treated and fed. Officers could surrender and would also be well treated and cared for. When the war ceased they would be taken back to Japan and released to take to take up their lives again.

Some argued hotly that Japanese officers should never surrender. If they were not killed in the fighting they must kill themselves. Others argued that prisoners of war were really slaves and should be treated as slaves and that captured airmen should be executed for their crimes in killing women and children. I noticed that the senior officers took no part in this debate. Then there was a great deal of talking among the Japanese.

Finally one came forward, bowed to me and told me in English that I had been sentenced to be beheaded by the samurai sword before a military parade. He bowed again and retired.

There was a strange sound of hissing as he walked away. The prospect didn't impress me. The thought of it gave me a painful feeling in the stomach. Many times later, when the commandant came into the compound with solders, I worried they were coming for me and that this would be my last day on earth, and the feeling in the stomach returned. I was told some time later the reason my execution was not carried out was that authority for such a ceremonial event had to be obtained from the Emperor. Papers must be sent to Japan for the Emperor to sign and the papers returned to the prison.

A few days later we watched the army and navy prisoners from a neighbouring compound line up to go out to work. Suddenly two guards rushed into the group, dragged a man out and assisted by another guard beat this man to the ground with their clubs; they went on beating him without mercy as he lay writhing at their feet. Four times he raised himself to his knees only to be beaten back until he lay still and the guards marched off leaving him there. He lay there not moving. A while later four prisoners came and carried him away. We didn't know if he was dead or alive, nor did we know why he had been attacked but it was a graphic reminder of the danger we all lived under.

Soon after I arrived in the compound one of the boys found a rusty safety blade and a corroded teaspoon, which he brought to me. What would seem like rubbish to most people was very valuable in a prisoner of war camp. I sharpened the razor blade by rubbing it on a concrete wall and it was perfect for cutting strips off shirt-tails to make bandages. It was much better for this purpose than my nail. When the spoon was cleaned up it was just what we needed to feed the ill and those too weak to feed themselves.

221

Ken, a very sick man, was being fed at that time. I found it too difficult to feed him with my chopsticks and so I had to use my fingers. It was much easier to feed him with the spoon. We kept poor Ken alive until three days before we took over the prison. He just died in his sleep. The razor blade became especially useful, as I will shortly explain.

My 25th birthday on 11 January fell on a day when the guards were being particularly vicious and beating anyone at whim. I thought back to my 24th birthday when I did my first raid over Burma and to my 23rd when I was so kindly treated by the family in Boston, USA. It made me realise how war can cause a man to launch from such heights of joy as in Boston in May 1943 to the depths of hell, which we were experiencing in Rangoon in 1945.

Those strange people who think war is a great adventure and highly glamorous need to experience what we were experiencing in Rangoon. There is nothing adventurous or glamorous about being a prisoner of war. On the other hand there are those useless political leaders, who do nothing to stop the useless slaughter of a war when it could have been prevented by a strong stand at the beginning. I wonder how far Hitler would dared have gone if he had been faced with strong resolution, and forces to back up that resolution, instead of appeasement. Irresolute politicians perhaps also need to experience the horror and hopelessness of a POW camp as we did.

Roll call was a daily ritual of prison life. Sometimes there would be several each day. My first experience of roll call came shortly after I was transferred from the cells to the compound. We were preparing our first meal of the day when three guards came bursting into the compound yelling, "Tenko! Tenko! Tenko!" I had never heard this before but rightly presumed it meant a roll call. Quickly, those that could helped all those who found it difficult to stand and to line up. The others, too weak to stand,

Tenko – roll call – held first thing in the morning and last thing at night.

had been put in the sick room at the far end of the building, away from the entrance gate of the compound. I stood outside the door of the sick room. Two of the men who were able to walk tried to indicate where the missing prisoners were. They bowed to the guards and said, "Billi man" (that we understood meant 'sick man') and then they pointed to where I stood. We were about to learn a painful lesson.

The guards counted the men present and finding some missing began to yell at Wing Commander Hill. He was the senior officer on our floor but he was so ill he had to be held up by two other prisoners. Not understanding Japanese he could not answer the guards. They attacked the two prisoners holding him up and knocked them away from him. He fell to the ground where upon the guards attacked him with their clubs. Another prisoner stepped between the wing commander and the Japs, bowed and said, "Billi man" and pointed to where I stood about 80 yards away. Yelling and shouting the guards beat him to the ground. Another prisoner stepped forward trying to protect Hill, but he too was attacked and knocked down.

Then the guards rushed down to where I stood. I bowed and said, "Billi man" and pointed to the door of the sick room and tried to tell them how many were there by holding up five fingers. They yelled at me in Japanese and let me have it with their clubs until I too was knocked to the ground. They walked over me on their way into the sick room, counted the men inside and came out. I had dragged myself back to my feet and was leaning painfully against the wall. Each guard as he came out slapped me on the face as he walked by.

This brutality continued twice daily for six days. To save Wing Commander Hill from further attacks he was placed in the sick room. Those of us in the line-up continued to be beaten. We tried to think of some system of communicating to the guards where the missing men were but they simply beat anyone at random. They then took to beating anyone in the line-up who was assisted by another prisoner.

The worst cases of those unable to stand unassisted were put in the sick room. Men trying to help those unable to stand in the line-up were getting very sore and bruised but we persisted. We hoped that before long the commandant would come and we would be able to explain the situation to him.

He came on the sixth day and asked for Wing Commander Hill. John took him to the sick room and on the way explained to him what was happening. The commandant immediately lined up the guards before the parade and began to punish them. He spoke sternly to each in turn and then slapped them hard across the face. He then came back to us and told us we had his permission to leave sick men off the 'Tenko' and to use the sick room.

He was still under the illusion that I was a doctor and spoke to me as such. I thanked him and asked him if we could have some medical supplies especially for bad ulcer cases. "I will see. I will see" and he strode out.

A week later a medical orderly and an interpreter came to the compound and brought some ointment and bandages for the ulcers. Regretfully it was only enough for a few cases. Periodically they would appear with a little more ointment and a few more bandages. It was only a fraction of what we needed but at least it was something. The 'Tenko' took on a more humane operation and only occasionally was anyone beaten.

The soldiers were paid every two weeks and on pay day a few would get drunk on saki. They would come into the compound at about midnight and start chasing the prisoners around. Cook, John and I, and later Wing Commander Hudson, would keep together in a group and so we were never attacked. They would occasionally gather around us, yelling and waving their clubs but they never touched us. We would walk around the compound keeping out of their way but if we saw them beating a fellow prisoner we would intervene, saying "Billi man" and waving them away. Surprisingly they always responded and stopped beating that prisoner.

By this time Pilot Officer Eric Osboldstone, a fellow New Zealander, had come into the prison. He was a Beaufighter pilot and had been shot down by ground fire and regretfully his navigator had been killed in the crash. Ozzie had a very happy and pleasant personality and got on well with all of us.

Christmas 1944 arrived. The Army and Navy prisoners, who worked for the Japanese, got paid. They bought some small Burmese cigars and gave them to us airmen in the cell block. The commandant visited the cell block on the morning of Christmas Day. The guards with him handed to each prisoner a small cigar. Another guard followed and gave each prisoner a light so he could begin smoking. When this formality was completed the commandant called out in English, "You can now sing for one hour."

A great gabble of voices broke out as prisoners suggested what we should sing. Suddenly a wonderful Irish voice broke out singing: "I will take you home again Kathleen, to where your heart has always been. Across the ocean deep and wide, since you were my blushing bride." When he finished his song everyone cheered. The singer was an American airman called McClusky. I never hear that song, even to this present day, without it reminding me how wonderfully McClusky sang it in that awful place. So for a couple of hours that silent, terrible place, with all its suffering humanity, rang with the sound of prisoners singing their hearts out. Finally the guards returned and ordered everyone to be silent again. That was a great break for us and we all enjoyed being able to use our voices again.

So the routine continued. Wing Commander Bill Hudson, CO of the new 110 Mosquito Squadron, joined us. As the offensive continued more and more airmen prisoners arrived. There were some Dakota crews and a few Beaufighter pilots who had been shot down. The big influx came, however, when three of the huge US Super-fortresses came down during a raid on Rangoon. They were flying at 25 000 feet, too high for anti-aircraft fire to reach them, and at that height they were too fast for fighters to do much harm, but someone had mixed up the bomb load of the leading formation. All high-altitude bombs were meant to have delayed fuses but someone had put some instant exploding fuses into the mix. The huge bombers were racing along at 350 mph so that the next formation of three planes was passing overhead when the bombs with instant fuses exploded and brought them down. I actually saw from my window the flaming wreckage coming down and then the parachutes beginning to open. Because they were so high most of the crews were able to bale out. Fifty-six new prisoners joined us and this caused severe overcrowding in many cells. In several cells the Japs took the bed boards out so that the cell could sleep four on the floor.

Within a week the prisoners were reorganised. Some Indian prisoners had joined a pro-Japanese force leaving the compound empty. Over 100 airmen were moved from the cell block into the compound.

It was a terrible night when the transfer took place. More than half of these 100 airmen couldn't walk more than a few steps. Most were extremely thin and many had large, weeping ulcers on their arms and legs. It was an effort to get them downstairs and across to the compound, especially with the Japs yelling at us and sometimes striking a sick man with their clubs. Nothing I can write can adequately describe the scene. Many of these poor men were close to death.

I decided to put all the sick men into one of the ground-floor rooms where there were bamboo frames about a foot off the ground to sleep on. Those of us fit enough also had to bring down their toilet boxes and eating containers. The smell of carrying those boxes was awful. I noticed from the boxes that several were suffering from dysentery.

Wing Commander Hill, an Englishman, was the highest-ranking officer, but was so ill he was incapable of giving any leadership. I decided to take upon myself the responsibility for the sick. An American offered to be the cook and he turned out to be a treasure. (I can't remember his name now so I will simply call him 'Cook'.) He had lived outdoors all his life and wasn't afraid of hard work. An English army officer also offered to help and he too was a great help and a good friend. (Again I can only remember that this man's Christian name was John.)

The Japs supplied us with wood, water and rice. We had to cook our own food with what they gave us, mainly white rice. Occasionally we got a few pieces of meat that Cook would cut up into smaller pieces with the axe used for chopping wood. He wielded that big axe like a sharp knife as he tried to cut the meat small enough to give each man a piece, no matter how small. Sometimes we got an eggplant and a few leafy vegetables. With amazing accuracy Cook cut it all up so everyone got the same share. He had lived most of his life with his father outdoors. We were most fortunate to have him with us. Supplies of wood and water were not consistent. Sometimes we would have nearly enough, at other times we had not nearly enough. There was always plenty of rice. We tried to have two meals a day but sometimes there was barely enough wood to cook one meal. To solve the problem we tore down all the boards around the divide between the two floors. Although the Japs had a security post looking down on the compound they never caught us taking the boards. We had a great system of lookouts and watched the Japs so closely we knew exactly when their attention was distracted. The axe would fly, down would come a board and just as quickly disappear. We also took every second rafter out of the roof of the top storey. After we got the first one out we organised diversions on the ground so the guards were busy looking at the ground rather than where the action was. Some men were caught and got a few whacks for their trouble but the food was cooked. Our goal was to get out before the Monsoon broke, when it was likely that the roof might blow off with so many missing rafters.

The cooking was done in a lean-to beside the bottom rooms. For our liking it was too near the toilet with no handy water. The toilets were larger ammunition boxes that we squatted over and were emptied daily into drums for disposal. There was a permanent and terrible smell. In the compound was a big tree. It kept us supplied with leaves to use instead of toilet paper. The ration was two leaves per day per man.

Dysentery was the main cause of death through illness in prisoner of war camps. We had no medicine to treat this illness and could get none from the Japs. Dysentery could reduce a man to extreme weakness in a matter of days. It simply seemed to strip the flesh from a man's frame leaving him literally skin and bone.

The only practical treatment available to us was to starve the sufferer for four to five days, by which time his pulse would begin to falter. To continue to feed him only prolonged his suffering. As the food was digested it simply increased the stress and strain on his digestive system. After five days we would start feeding him rice that had been cooked to a jelly condition. After a few days of this, if we had any eggs (or other special food), we would gradually feed him some to help build him up again. Crude though it seems the system worked and by this treatment we never lost another man to dysentery. When you consider how ill some of the men were when they came over from the cell block it is understandable why we felt such a sense of achievement.

We tried to keep the illness under control. Three times daily I checked the toilets and if I saw any trace of dysentery we tracked down the sufferer and put him on the treatment.

Flies spread dysentery, so we began 'anti-fly duty'. No one liked it, but it was absolutely necessary if we were to prevent the disease spreading. Prisoners who were fit and strong enough each stood for two hours over the open toilets keeping the flies away by swishing a branch backwards and forwards. The nauseating smell caused you to want to vomit or gag. More often than not you did. It certainly was unpleasant work but every fit person, no matter his rank, took his turn. More importantly, it seemed to work.

Our next big problem was beri-beri, caused by lack of vitamins in the diet. It caused swelling of the body tissue, starting from around the shins and gradually spreading upwards. In extreme cases it would spread right to the chest. It was probably a form of water retention. We had no idea what caused it or how to treat it. We had no access to medical knowledge whatever.

I noticed that I showed no signs of beri-beri whereas most of the other prisoners had at least a mild form of it. I began to ask myself what was I doing that the others weren't. Then I stumbled on the difference. Because of extreme perspiration in the tropics the Japs gave each prisoner a daily ration of salt. I didn't take any of the salt, because I used most of my water ration to wash my wounds, which although clean would not heal through lack of sustaining food. The other prisoners took all the salt they could, especially those suffering from bad beri-beri. So all salt was removed from serious beri-beri cases, and salt rations reduced drastically to those only slightly affected. It was not a popular decision because salt added flavour to the tasteless rice diet we were eating twice a day. We compromised on a two-week trial. Water rations were also cut to severe cases. One American absolutely refused to co-operate. In fact he increased his ration of salt and stole water from others. He was the worst case we were trying to treat and the least co-operative so I gave him the choice to either co-operate or leave the sick room. We were giving him all our small supply of extra food to try to save him. He decided to leave the sick room and died five days later. This man (I think his name was King) was the only patient who came into the sick room that we lost. His body was carried out of the compound in a rough wooden coffin and all who could stand formed a guard of honour and saluted as he was carried by.

His death was a salutary lesson to all the prisoners and we never had further trouble through lack of co-operation. When men were ill they were desperate for help and as time went by our system proved helpful in keeping them alive. Most prisoners accepted my directions, which were always worked out after a great deal of discussion with Cook and John and Wing Commander Hudson, who arrived in the compound later.

Our beri-beri experiment was successful. By the end of the two-week trial all the bad cases showed signs of improvement and the milder one showed no signs of getting any worse, so we kept it going.

Fever was another problem. It usually lasted about four days. The Chinese delivered the rice to the Japs in big sacks. We stole four of these sacks, kept them well out of sight of the Japs and made good use of them. We would wash the fever patient with warm water and then cover him with a sack causing him to sweat. He was given no food for three days and only boiled water to drink. The fever was literally sweated out of him.

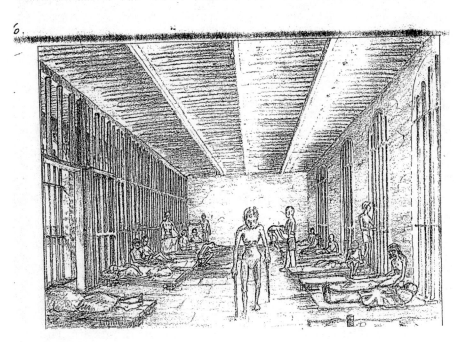

The Sick Room.

The biggest problem was the awful ulcers. For some time we had to rely on the irregular visits of the Japanese medical orderly who brought some kind of ointment to treat them. We tried to keep the ulcers covered and most of the patients lost their shirt-tails to make bandages that we boiled daily. I eventually solved the problem when I remembered how on the farms I worked as a lad, a product called Condy's Crystals was used to cure foot-rot in sheep and cows. By this time we had established contact with an Indian doctor and we got a message to him asking for some. A few days later a little bag of it was flung over the wall as a work party marched by.

I took it and diluted it with water until I could bear the pain on my own open wounds. Then I applied it to the ulcers of the patients in the sick room. It was very painful when first applied, but within a short time the pus stopped and the incessant pain was greatly reduced. Many of these ulcers had eaten right into the bone and were crippling to those suffering from them. Everyone was thrilled how quickly they cleared up with the application of Condy's Crystals. What we used obviously killed the bugs eating into the flesh. Regretfully our diet was so poor that new flesh couldn't grow. After that all we could do was keep the wounds clean.

I enquired how prisoners got ulcers in the first place. Some originated from wounds but most admitted scratching insect bites and once the skin was broken it became infected probably from the bathing water. The ulcers just got bigger and more painful. The obvious remedy was not to scratch, so we instituted an 'anti-scratching' campaign. When a prisoner met another in the course of the day he would say, "Don't scratch. Don't scratch." Fewer new ulcers appeared so it must have worked.

The bamboo bed frames were lousy with lice and other bugs that came out at night to feed on the sleeping prisoners. During the day we mostly wore our underwear but as the temperatures dropped at night, and as protection against the bugs, we put more clothing on when we went to bed. Our hair was full of lice so every couple of weeks we paired off and methodically cleaned the lice from the other's head as monkeys do in the jungle. For most of the boys it filled in the time with something to do but it is most unpleasant with a head of hair filled with lice.

Four men succumbed to scratching their scrotum when bitten by lice. They soon had an infection and their scrotum swelled to the size of a tennis ball. The problem was solved by our safety razor. Working on a farm I had had experience of castrating piglets and lambs and I felt the answer to this problem was to slit the lower part of the scrotum with the safety razor. When I first suggested it to the four patients they were far from happy and pleaded that we approach the Japs and try and get a doctor from another compound. When the Japanese 'medic' saw the swollen scrotums he just laughed, so the poor fellows just had to trust me. I assured them that the piglets never complained and they lost their testicles whereas they would keep theirs. Their quick reply was 'but they didn't speak English'. I assured them that there would be little bleeding but that they would have to squeeze the pus out three times daily until it stopped. They were really scared of this 'op', especially as it was to be done with a rusty old razor blade. The blade was well boiled and it turned out that because the scrotum was so swollen there was no pain when the slit was made. I carefully checked the position of their testicles and made an inch slit at the lowest point of the scrotum. The pus simply shot out under pressure and it drained effectively without much squeezing. Within 24 hours their scrotum was back to normal size. The wound was dressed for a week by which time it had healed. Keeping the dressing in place was quite a challenge. I was told years later that all four had married and had children. I hate to imagine what they would have suffered without my farming experience.

Wing Commander Bill Hudson of 110 Mosquito Squadron was transferred from the cell block to the compound at the end of January. By then Cook, John and I had all our systems organised. Bill had flown too low down the Irrawaddy River, dipped the props in the water and survived the high-speed crash that followed. Both he and his navigator suffered injuries to the knees. I found out later he had not bothered to read our 27 Squadron combat reports, which advised never to fly low down the rivers where the smooth surface makes it very difficult to judge heights. We advised always to cross rivers at right angles, unless attacking, and any patrols should be done at 300 feet to have any chance of seeing a target and effectively attacking it. When he crashed Bill was not even on a definite operational flight but just having a joy ride over Burma.

He was a newspaper reporter in civilian life, quite a good talker, and always pushing himself forward. He was able to take over from poor Wing Commander Hill as the compound's senior officer. Cook, John and I were more than happy leaving him to deal with the Japs while we concentrated on keeping the men alive and easing their suffering. Bill seemed to enjoy his role as commandant of the compound and dealing with them. He wrote a book about being 'Rats of Rangoon' some years after the war. It was well written but about Bill Hudson. Few of the details I am speaking about now are mentioned in his book. Other than a couple of slaps, and perhaps one beating, he never suffered any real violence in the compound. He was a very fortunate and lucky man.

Then some of the B-29 bomber crews were transferred from the cells to the compound. The number in the compound went up to 127. Most of the Americans had gone straight from college or university into the Air Force. Few had worked before entering the Air Force and it must have been a terrible shock to them to have landed in this Rangoon prison. A small group of them became very religious. They took to praying three or four times a day, pleading with God to save them. They obviously didn't appreciate how painfully we had developed the practical systems, which kept people alive in our primitive and dangerous world. This group never volunteered for any jobs around the compound and obviously objected to our disciplined and responsible system.

The Americans had their share of health problems, especially malaria. None of them had taken the anti-malaria pills because it yellowed the face. We had big problems with the 'prayer group' boys when they got ill. They seemed to lack strength of character and just wanted to lie down and die. They would refuse food but wanted a lot of water and salt. We had to force feed a few of them for some days until they got over the worst of their fever. They were always pleading, almost insisting, that Bill, John or I ask the guards for permission for them to hold prayer meetings for all prisoners twice daily. We declined their constant demands and suggested to them that they step out of line and ask the Japs themselves. We were quite certain they would not be interested in such demands even if they understood them and equally certain that anyone who asked would more than likely be beaten.

They never did step out of that line on Tenko parades but kept insisting that they must be allowed to hold prayer meetings in the sick room. They were very critical of me depriving them of their rights to worship their God and to ask for his help. Whenever they asked I declined saying, "The real Christians are the ones who come and offer to help. When I see you offering to help I will be happy to consider a prayer meeting." They never did offer to help but became sullen and withdrawn as fewer and fewer prisoners took any notice of them. Bill, Cook, John and I would all have happily called ourselves 'Christians' but we preferred to spend our time and thoughts in practical ways by helping others to keep healthy and trying to help those who were sick

The four of us had made our own way in the world at a young age and three of us had to fend for ourselves in the depths of the Great Depression. John, the son of an aristocratic English family, was sent off to boarding school when he was seven years old and he too learnt to look after himself at an early age. It was interesting to note the background of the men with strength of character and independence in Rangoon. Those that had been 'spoilt' and 'coddled' in childhood found it much more difficult to survive than those who hadn't.

We felt that our prison situation called for a strong practical Christianity rather than the vague trappings of religion. While Bill concentrated on getting help from the Japs in the form of visits by the medical orderlies and supplies, Cook, John and I kept trying to improve our systems to keep the prisoners healthy and alive. The combination of both worked.

Apart from this small handful most of the other Americans got on very well with the rest of us. Several volunteered to help with the cooking and with other jobs that had to be done.

Finally I found the factor that did more than anything to improve our health. For some time I had been concerned that there must be something wrong with our rice. It was very white but didn't seem to provide much real food. We had a good ration of rice for the compound. One day I asked the interpreter, "How do you get the rice so white?"

He answered, "We grind the husks off it."

"And what do you do with the husks?" I asked.

"Throw it away by the sackful," he answered.

"Could we have a couple of bags of the husks?" I asked.

"I'm sure the Chinese will be happy to give it to you. I will tell them you want some."

Next day two large sacks of husks came with our supplies. They tasted a little bitter so we gradually introduced them with the rice. Soon everyone, except the prayer group, was happy to get all they could. It added a little taste to the bland rice. Within a week we began to see an improvement in general health. Within two weeks I could see the beri-beri declining in the bad cases. We were thrilled. At last we had found the missing health factor. The real food was in the husks that the Chinese were busy grinding off. The Japanese and Burmese had vegetables to eat with their ground rice but with only rice we had lacked real nutrition. From then on we got all the rice husks we asked for and our chance of survival was assured. It was a great feeling to realise that we had passed the worst but regretfully that was not true for everyone.

On a very hot day one of our sick decided to go to the toilet alone. His sight was poor and usually someone went with him. As he came out of the door he failed too see the guard standing outside the compound fence and he failed to bow. The guard yelled at him and called him to the fence and made this man, ill with fever, stand in the hot sun. I noticed him becoming unsteady on his feet so took a hat and placed it on his head.

The guard yelled at me and indicated that I stand there too. Then he and two other guards rushed into the compound yelling and striking me with their clubs with all the force they could muster. There was no opportunity to tell them why the man needed a hat. They seemed possessed with a brutal madness. Desperately I tried to dodge their blows and parry them with my arms but several struck home on my shoulders and head. I suddenly had a vision of the man we had seen beaten to death and feared they meant to do the same to me. I started to back toward the door when two blows hit me very hard against my right jaw and mouth. I turned around and sprinted for the door. They got in a few more blows on my back and were still yelling at me when I rushed through the door into the arms of Cook and John.

They had watched the whole scene but there was nothing they could do to help me. Fortunately the guards stopped outside the door and we moved away from it and after some more yelling they too left.

My mouth was full of blood from three broken teeth and the pain in my right jaw was acute. Two broken teeth were in the right upper jaw and one in the right lower jaw. I was in severe pain. Cook brought me some cold wet clothes and placed them on the injured jaw but what I really needed was ice, which of course was out of the question. Later heavy and painful bruising appeared across my shoulders. I am quite certain that had I not fled inside they would have clubbed me to the ground and continued to club me until I was either unconscious or dead.

I was in severe pain for a month. The top broken teeth recovered in about 10 days after severe toothache but the lower broken tooth developed an abscess and gave me hell for a month. Because it couldn't drain, it oozed pus for over three weeks. The severity of the toothache day and night was terrible. At night the discharge would go down into my stomach and cause severe stomach pain. I would spend hours at night walking up and down in the dark side of the building. Sleep only came with complete exhaustion.

It was 10 days before I could eat ordinary cooked rice. Mine was cooked to a gluey substance that I could swallow without chewing. Cook insisted I should have first call on the 'special food' to keep me going. Two weeks after the attack I could tell my jaw was not broken but it was very painful to touch for another six weeks. Then I got a dose of fever. My eyes were so sore I could not turn them. If I wanted to look around I closed my eyes, turned my head and then opened them again. Four weeks after the attack the abscess had drained and the toothache was beginning to ease. It had been a very bad and dangerous time for me.

When I was at my lowest ebb an amazing thing happened to save me from becoming one of the sick in the sick room. The commandant offered to buy a good wristwatch the Japs had taken from an American fighter pilot. A junior Jap officer who spoke a little English did the bargaining. The commandant finally agreed to pay 300 rupees for the watch. The American pilot generously gave the 300 rupees to Cook, who despite my protests was determined to spend the money buying eggs and chunks of milk powder to feed me on. For 10 days I had eaten nothing but overcooked rice and I was very weak when hit by the fever. Fed two eggs a day with milk powder not only helped me to get over the fever but also helped me recover from the terrible toothache and the nightly stomach pain and the lack of sleep that I was suffering from. The 'special food' kept me on my feet and with John's wonderful help, the sick room operation continued on as before. John was one step ahead of me with everything. He never waited to be told what needed to be done. By the time I thought of something that needed doing John had done it.

Sick men continued to come into the sick room, were looked after and left during those awful three weeks, without me having to think or do a thing for them. Once the fever subsided and with the help of nutritional food I gradually regained my strength. After four weeks the worst of the pain was behind me and life was livable again.

By this time it was the end of March and the Japs seemed to have sensed the danger of losing the war. An offer was made to buy all the watches and pens taken from the prisoners. We were surprised as the Japs already had them so why think of buying them? We happily agreed to accept the 6 400 rupees they offered and the money was used to buy extra food in the form of eggs, milk powder and vegetables. The milk powder was probably old British stock left behind when they retreated. The vegetables were mostly onions and eggplant. The eggplant had very good food value being full of easily digested oil.

Our rice and bran rations were increased. Each compound must have been treated in the same way because the Indian compound next to ours began tossing some food and tobacco over the wall at night. Then the Japs began to bring bullock cart loads of wood into the compound followed by cart loads of more rice. We wondered if they were stockpiling essentials in the prison thinking the Allies would not attack it. Maybe the supplies were for them? Maybe they were planning a last ditch stand in the prison? Rumours spread around the prison like fever. Daily we were hearing that the British Army was getting closer to Rangoon. From the beginning of April food, water and wood supplies were no longer a problem.

239

It was getting very hot and there was not enough water to wash with. With all the dirt and insects and heat, skin troubles began to reappear. The only answer was to wear less clothing during the day and let the sun help to keep our bodies resistant to infection. The majority of prisoners just wore a jockstrap during the day and the compound took on the appearance of a nudist colony. The 'no scratching' comment became a vital safety factor. We looked a pitiful bunch with everyone so thin and practically naked.

For some time I had been sleeping outside the building to get away from the lice and bedbugs. Now that it was very hot another 50 also took to sleeping outside. The Japs didn't seem to mind. Then one night after they had been drinking, they came into the compound at about midnight and began kicking and beating everyone they found sleeping outside. I was a light sleeper and woke up as soon as they arrived. I slipped into a deep hole and hid there. From then on I always slept in a dark spot and was never troubled.

Many others suffered terribly in that camp. One of the B-29 crew had a badly damaged hand and wrist. It became infected and eventually gangrenous. Bill sent a letter to the commandant, via the interpreter, urgently requesting that a doctor in the army group remove the hand and wrist. The pain was dreadful and the smell as bad. The commandant came and looked at it and arranged for an army surgeon to operate. There was no anaesthetic and his arm was sawn off five inches below the elbow and the skin carefully draped over the stump. The Japs provided twice-weekly dressings and things went well for him. He was a brave, uncomplaining patient and we all admired his quiet courage.

In the meantime we all continued to make slow progress toward better health. We started a daily discussion session when someone would give a talk about himself; where he lived, where he went to school and some information about his family, occupation and religion. There were two Reformed Jews among us. A Reformed Jew rejected the orthodox Jewish teaching that the Jews were God's chosen people and everyone else were Gentiles, to be lived among but not fraternised with nor married to. Reformed Jews believed more in Christianity and that everyone on earth should live in peace and harmony. These sessions were not only educational but also did wonders to get one's mind off food and our dangerous existence. We found it easier to exercise longer on the rice bran too.

We developed a good means of communication with the army and navy prisoners in the neighbouring compound. Standing with our back to their compound and writing in the air with our arms the reader received our words straight and he answered by writing in the air backwards and we received his message in the same way. In this way we kept up with the rumours of the fighting in Burma. There was one upstairs window in our building opposite a similar one in the next compound and both were out of sight of the Japs. This is where a great deal of signalling went back and forth between the two compounds.

We also conducted our own quiet prayer meetings around the bathing tank. We confused the Japs by facing outwards and mumbling out of the side of our mouths. It may have just been the reflective time we spent together, or the deep desires of our heart that we tried to express in words, but I always left those gatherings feeling renewed and encouraged.

And so we reached April, which was to prove a month of activity and change in the prison. Easter was late in 1945. Bill Hudson asked permission to hold an Easter religious service. Easter came and went with no reply from the commandant so a service was held inside the compound with the hymns sung in whispers. The service was attended by about 70 of the prisoners. The prayer group was naturally thrilled. They were convinced that God was coming to our rescue. I told them I had greater faith in the courage of the 14th Army and the Air Force squadrons to get us safely out of Burma. It was their casualties that would pay the price for our freedom and it was them that I would eventually thank. They made no comment and I couldn't help thinking that too much religion and not enough human feeling can so easily blind the simple and thoughtless from feeling grateful for the terrible cost their fellows pay for their freedom to worship as they do. So often the prayers at ANZAC Day services ignore those who paid with their lives for our religious freedom. Significantly, later in April, the Japs allowed the occasional religious service.

From late March, air raids on Rangoon built up to almost daily attacks with low-level strafing and high level bombing by formations of US Liberators and B-29 bombers. Anti-aircraft defences were completely ineffective against these high attacks. We made a big show of being afraid of these attacks hoping to persuade the Japs from using the prison as refuge from air attacks. We pleaded, and got permission, to dig trenches and foxholes for shelter against the bombing.

The Japanese brought in extra troops to guard us during these raids. They seemed much tougher and better armed than our guards. When the sirens sounded they spread out through the prison. Some occasionally entered our compound and took shelter in our foxholes. One day I looked over the top of the foxhole I was in and looked right into the eyes of a Jap soldier only a couple of feet away. His eyes had the look of deep fear in them. Maybe he knew that they had lost the war and could only look forward to fighting to the death. These soldiers showed none of the contempt and brutality towards prisoners that our guards had and did.

Some of the bombing was quite close to the prison. We were thrilled to see the Japs being bombed but were careful to keep our delight hidden. Although conditions continued to improve, the danger from attacks by our guards still existed. We still had to be careful in their presence. Prisoners were still being beaten for the slightest excuse. Possibly their leaders were worried by the approaching Allied Forces and were trying to get us in better condition before they arrived. Some guards, however, seemed incapable of changing their ways. We noticed they were drinking more often and even our quiet 'medic' got horribly drunk one night. At midnight there was much yelling in the circle of the prison and we saw our 'medic' being held down by three men who were slapping and kicking him in an effort to keep him quiet. They eventually carried him away no doubt to wake next morning with a sore head and hurting from the bruises where he was kicked.

All the time we felt that the 14th Army was getting closer and closer. I knew the original plan was that Rangoon would be freed by 10 May. By mid-April fighter and bomber attacks on Rangoon clearly indicated preparations for an advancing army. We watched the Japs carefully. 23 April saw the first change. Some new guards appeared around the prison and they looked a very sorry lot. All wore glasses and all walked clumsily with no military bearing whatever. Their rank stars seemed very new and the uniforms ill fitting. When we saw them spending an hour 'bowing' we figured they must be newly recruited guards straight from 'civilian street'. We were right. They were our new guards.

Then the news came from the Japanese that President Roosevelt had died. The Americans were visibly shocked. Then we saw our old guards had new uniforms. Everything indicated some drastic changes were taking place among the Japs and the prison was alive with rumours. Then we saw all the regular soldiers marched out of the prison gates. Unbelievable!

An even more dramatic event followed the next day, 24 April, when we saw Japs running out of the main office with armfuls of paper and making a big fire with them. All day they continued to feed the fire. A whispered voice along the wall told us they were

243

leaving and destroying all their records. That day we received a heap of celery with our rations. Late in the afternoon we watched elderly Japanese soldiers leaving the barracks carrying heavy kit and tottering out through the main gate. Surely this must be an evacuation of some kind. Could it be the Japs were fleeing from Rangoon? We were afraid to believe such a thing could be happening. It seemed too good to be true.

Another important event early in April was the murder of a prisoner, a Chinese general, the brother-in-law of General Chiang Kai-shek, of China. It seems the Japanese supplied a Chinese prisoner with a knife and paid him to stalk and murder the general. For a couple of hours that night there was yelling and shouting from the Chinese compound nearby as the murderer stalked the general and stabbed him several times. He lived through the night but died next day. For us it was a gruesome experience.

On 25 April, there was a junior NCO to take 'Tenko'. He was dressed in brand new clothes and obviously feeling very important so we were careful to do everything right.

As the day went by all sorts of strange things happened. A score of water buffalos was driven into the prison, then a large number of pigs, followed by a herd of cows, some with calves at foot. Why was all this livestock coming into the prison? Where were they going to keep all these animals? Most of them were herded into the damaged section of the prison and left there. Soldiers, all with new uniforms, kept scampering about the place. Much of this activity continued into the night with lanterns seeming to be everywhere. Many of the guards were flinging unwanted clothes and other discarded things into heaps. It was obvious they were preparing to go somewhere. We waited impatiently to see what was to happen to the prisoners. We heard heavy traffic far into the night.

Chapter 17

CHANGING THE GUARD

As we watched and waited everyone was guessing what was going on. I stuck to my view that the Japs were retreating from Rangoon; otherwise the advancing 14th Army would surround them. I guessed they were moving south to the port of Moulmein where they had a sea supply route and the railway from Bangkok. To me this seemed a wise military decision. No one else shared my views, not even Bill Hudson. I felt that they would take the walking fit prisoners and leave the sick behind. That seemed to me to be the only reason for the new civilian guards.

News reached us that prisoners in 63 Compound were being given new Jap clothing and were loading rice and meat carcasses of beef and pigs into carts.

At mid-morning there was a call for Wing Commander Hudson 'at the gate'. We all watched Bill walk to the gate. Standing there was a Jap who spoke a little English. We called him the 'Ape' (because he looked like one) and with him was another man. The Ape produced a list of all those in our compound and demanded to know who could walk. Bill Hudson called for his deputy commander, Captain Hunt, an American pilot and myself. He then instructed us to check all prisoners and decide who could walk and who couldn't.

I went straight to the sick room and told everyone there that they must make up their own minds if they wanted to join, what seemed to me, to be a plan to walk to Moulmein. The Japs only wanted those who could walk so obviously planned to leave those who couldn't walk here at Rangoon. A chorus of questions arose. What will happen to those who remain? And are you going? I admitted I had no idea what would happen to those left behind but the new guards seemed more decent than the old ones and there was plenty of food. I also told them that some would not be able to go and I would stay behind to care for them if the Japs would let me. I urged those who did not want to go to make sure they had a bandage on their leg and to start limping and those who wanted to go to walk briskly to the gate with me.

The Ape seemed to be becoming more and more impatient so I quickly got all those who were going to leave in two lines and took them off to the gate. I showed the Ape those who could walk and those who couldn't. He checked those who could walk and marked them off on his list. The others he directed to wait in a group. Sixty percent of the sick decided to stay. The Ape agreed I could stay with them. Personally I would have preferred to go but I had no choice as I felt I could not abandon the sick.

New clothes and Japanese rubber-soled canvas boots were issued to the walkers. The boots didn't look the best for walking in so those who stayed behind gave up their boots in exchange for the Japanese boots. It was rather a crazy sight to see these men being dressed in Japanese uniforms as they were so thin and only the smaller sizes of uniforms fitted them. There was great mirth at the transformation. Some of those going actually kidded themselves the Japs were going to take them to the British Army. Bill Hudson was quite disappointed that the Ape wouldn't take him because, 'he was a trouble maker'. Actually Bill was lucky to be left behind. In the end 49 men decided to stay although some could walk quite well. Sixteen from the cells remained with them.

Captain Hunt was to be in charge of the walkers and they would leave at 4 pm. Our cooks not only cooked a special meal for them but gave them another in buckets to take with them. The commandant told the leaders of each group that they were going 'because of the war' but nothing else.

When they were about to go it began to rain heavily. The Monsoon was two weeks early in 1945. The walkers stood in the pouring rain while the Japs bustled around. Bill and I walked among our own group saying our goodbyes. We suggested to them that if low-flying planes looked like strafing them they should all take their hats off and wave them wildly about. Dressed in Japanese uniforms it would be very hard for an attacking pilot to know they were POWs especially as their guards carried weapons.

We watched them parade out of the prison from our top storey. We were sad at heart watching them go but those leaving the prison were surprisingly cheery especially as they were marching into the unknown.

They were led out by an advance party of Japs followed by a large army group led by a colonel. The procession was chivvied along by Japs at intervals armed with machine guns or rifles with fixed bayonets. Each group was followed by a handcart pushed or pulled by six to eight men. Then came the airmen led by Captain Hunt and then a brigadier who marched erect and soldierly ahead of his men who had been in captivity more than three years. The entire group numbered more than 400 British and American prisoners. In comparison with the cheerful attitude of the prisoners the Japanese looked like serious little boy scouts.

Our own air force group looked a motley crew, dressed in a mixture of Japanese Army, British and American Air Force clothing. They marched briskly, almost like a ceremonial goose-step. No one cheered or waved. I think we were all deeply concerned about what would happen to them. Some were carrying bags while others were pulling handcarts. I worried about those who wouldn't be able to keep up and what would happen to the stragglers. If they were already wet with the pouring rain before they left on the march, how would they cope with the cold at night out in the open? I also knew that they would have to march 15 miles towards the 14th Army lines before turning south towards Moulmein.

There was little talk at supper that night. Just before dusk a Beaufighter flew low over the prison and then headed towards where the column had gone. We saw the flashes of his rockets and heard his canon firing and we fervently hoped that he wasn't attacking the column. We felt the greatest danger they faced was being strafed by our own planes. We all slept poorly that night and many of us just wandered about for hours.

Next day we realised the changed world we were in. Bill and I walked out of our building first. The guard seemed shocked to see us so we quickly took the initiative and walked to the gate, opened it, and walked off to the next compound. We didn't bow or pay any attention to the guard.

The British contingent of prisoners was led out by Brigadier Clive Hopson who had been captured at the fall of Singapore in 1942. After three years of imprisonment he was the only one of the 'marchers' killed when Hurricanes strafed the column a few hours after the Japanese guards had deserted them.

Once in the next compound we discussed what we should do and decided to move actively around the prison as if that was what we normally did. It was obvious the old guards had not told the new guards much about how to run the prison and it was equally obvious that the new guards were raw recruits and, being recently civilians, had no malice toward us and were unaccustomed to violence. As we walked about and talked to the inmates of other compounds the guards merely walked about with us. There was no bowing or pressure to do anything. We immediately took back to our compound enough wood for a week. Then we opened an upstairs room we were previously not allowed to use, which gave us a good view over the prison.

It was great to be able to talk to other prisoners. There were still over 600 Allied servicemen of several different nationalities left in the prison – Indians, Gurkhas, British, Chinese, Americans, Anglo-Burmese, two New Zealanders, one Australian and one Canadian.

Wing Commander Hudson, the senior officer, took command. Practically all the European prisoners were weak and ill but the Indians and Gurkhas were fit and fiercely loyal, and had resisted all Japanese efforts to recruit them. Language difficulties prevented us having much contact with the Chinese.

In the city of Rangoon many fires were burning and large explosions rocked the prison. The Japanese were burning as much of their military supplies as they could. For five days these fires and explosions erupted all over the city. The Japs must have built up a huge supply of war materials but now they had no means of getting them away. We were delighted to see the fires because it showed the Japs were really abandoning the city and Rangoon would be spared street-to-street fighting. We could hear a lot of rifle fire and some machine-gun fire and came to the conclusion the Japs were trying to stop Burmese looters. We stayed put in the safety of the prison.

249

We found that an Indian had been put in charge of supplies and there seemed no limit on how much each compound got. There was plenty of the usual rice as well as things we hadn't seen in months. There were all kinds of vegetables, fish and beef and all the wood needed to cook it with.

We presented a list of what we wanted for the week and got it. The small guard, who looked about 14, told us to come and get some more if we were short of anything. It seemed amazing that the Japs had brought into the prison so much food and wood when a few days before there was a great shortage of everything. Our cooks really enjoyed themselves cooking attractive meals for us.

Our Tenko parades were very different and almost enjoyable under the new regime. Only the fittest attended and the others just reported in from the sick room. There was always a Jap on parade who spoke English and through him we asked for medical supplies, but they never came as the retreating Japanese had taken all the medical supplies with them.

During our first 'free' afternoon Major McCleod, a British medical officer from one of the army compounds, came to see us. He was very impressed with what we had achieved. Fifty very sick prisoners, plus the six men we had carried out of the cell block in mid-January, had been treated in the sick room and out of that number we had lost only two. Major McCleod commented on how well we had done with the deaths of only two men. He told us that prison doctors, who saw the movement from our cell block, expected half to die. He examined all the sick and told us he would be back as soon as possible with some medical supplies. He was unable to get any medicines but even without the medicine some of our sick began to show a marked improvement because of the better and greater variety of food they were receiving.

The new commandant was a heavily built man who spoke good English but looked nothing like a soldier. His new uniform was entirely the wrong shape for a man of his build.

After the second day of the 'new guard', 27 April, our gate was closed again. Our new commandant must have read about airmen prisoners being classified in Tokyo as 'criminals' but in every other way we were well treated. The Chinese were ordered to do all the carrying for the sick and our workload was reduced considerably.

So we slipped back into the routine of prison living but how different to the routine of just a few days before under a frightening, unpredictable regime. Now too there was much more to take an interest in. During the day formations of bombers came over and started fires in Rangoon. Single Beaufighters and Mosquitos made sweeps and fired at targets. The Japanese started more fires to burn their papers on, and the fires grew bigger and more numerous. At night the fires lit up the great gold Pagoda. The Japs had stolen all the gold off it and replaced it with gold paint but it still looked impressive.

The only thing we worried about was the possibility of the 14th Army pushing the Japs back into Rangoon and we would get caught up in the fierce fighting.

On 30 April everything seemed the same. Fires were raging everywhere in the city. That night one of the guards said, "Sleep well." A guard wishing the prisoners a good night's sleep was unheard of and was an indication of a marked change of attitude.

As the day ended I was sitting high on the compound steps looking out over the walls to the city beyond where numerous fires could be seen. I was in the company of Karnig Thomasian, a young American who had come down when 'friendly bombs' had exploded beneath his B-29 (Karnig and I remain good friends to this day). I remember it as a clear, moonlit night and as well as the fires we could hear explosions all over the city. Suddenly we realised that we had seen nothing of the guards on their nightly rounds. We waited a few minutes longer, moved carefully and quietly down the steps and over to the Jap storeroom in the

251

corner of our compound. If we went into the small building we would be able to get a clear view of the front gate. After some minutes of waiting to hear any noise made by the guards, we opened the door and went to the window. We could see clearly through the prison entrance and beyond that to the city street. The large teakwood doors were wide open. After standing there for some time to make sure there was nobody about we hurried back and told Bill Hudson of what we had found. We all got the impression that the Japs had gone.

Without too much thought we heaved each other over the nine-foot inner wall and into the lane that led to the main gate. We approached the building as quietly as we could and kept to the shadows. There had always been a light on in the gatehouse at night but now there was no sign of life. Very quietly we pushed open the door. There was no one inside.

We looked outside and saw the road was empty. We banged the big gate shut and locked ourselves in and then we saw the note. It read: "Rangoon, 29 April, 1945. To the whole captured persons of Rangoon Gaol. According to Nippon military order, we hereby give you liberty and admit to leave this place at your own will. Regarding the food, and other materials left in the compound, we give you permission to consume them as far as your necessity is concerned.

We hope that we shall have the opportunity to meet you again at the battlefield of somewhere.

We shall continue our war effort eternally, in order to get the reunification of all Asiatic races.

Signed: Horuo Ito, Chief Officer, Rangoon Gaol."

We read this note in the light of a fire in the street and we all let out a great yell of joy. We were free and safe at last.

We rushed through the buildings and found the keys to the compounds. Then we ran through all the compounds to tell everyone the Japs had gone and we were free. Everyone was soon up and mingling together throughout the prison. The Chinese were the only ones who stayed in their compound.

To me it seemed the greatest moment of my life. At no time have I felt so deeply moved or affected as at that moment. Never before or since have I felt anything like it. The arrival of the British troops a few days later was merely an enjoyable event in comparison to what I felt that night. Very few of us went back to sleep.

Next day we found another note. This is exactly as it was typed:

"To: Gentlemen,

Bravely you have come here opening prison. We have gone. Keeping your prisoners safely with Nipponese Knightship.

Afterwards we may meet again at the front somewhere. Then let us fight bravely each other.

Nipponese Army

(We have kept the gate keys at the gate room.)"

By dawn Bill Hudson had got some army officers together and formed a pretence of military leadership. We raised the British flag on the flagstaff as soon as it was light. Immediately the Burmese going past the prison stopped to stare at it. Bill called out from the second floor window that a thousand British troops had arrived in the prison overnight and demanded that the Burmese bring some Rangoon leaders to the prison.

The first to arrive were some officers of the Burma Defence Army as they called themselves. They were the officers of some of the thousands of Burmese the Japs had recruited, equipped and trained. Now they had changed sides by giving themselves a new name and planned to take over the Government of Burma.

Our guards escorted them to Bill's office and the game of bluff began. Bill made them wait as he and John (our army friend) made out they were studying a map. He didn't sit himself so they too had to keep standing. One told Bill that he had 500 troops and 200 police, all armed, dispersed throughout Rangoon and he was in command of the only civil or military force in Rangoon. Bill sternly told him that he was a traitor to Burma by joining the Japanese. He told him very convincingly he had 1000 troops in the prison and that the Burmese were to co-operate with the British forces. We needed some more weapons for our force and we expected him to supply them. The supply of weapons and his co-operation would decide his future in Rangoon. Bill also told him he must be ready to help defend the city against any Japanese who might be forced back there by advancing British forces.

Within an hour the Burmese commander had supplied 17 rifles, 430 bullets and 12 hand grenades. I scratched my name on one of these rifles and still have it. He later supplied more weapons which were distributed among some of the European and Gurkha prisoners. The Gurkhas immediately began training how to use them and without being told began patrolling the top of the prison walls with sticks and brooms over their shoulders to give the impression to those outside that a well-armed force was in control. I took a German sporting rifle with a magazine that held six bullets.

The senior officer of the local Indian Army arrived at noon. He commanded former British Indian soldiers who were captured when the Japanese took Burma in 1942. They had been left behind to fight a rearguard action but had been surrounded and captured. The Japanese had recruited them as a force to help when India was invaded and surrendered. I guess they had little choice but to do what the Japanese demanded of them. There were 2 000 of them spread across the city but they only possessed 150 rifles and not much ammunition. It was decided that they would be used as a military police force to stop looting in the city. The Burmese Defence Force was to be ready to stop armed Japs re-entering the city. The prisoners would be held as a reserve.

The Indian officer told us there were 500 Japs just south of the city and about a 1 000 at the Mingaladon airfield, north of the city. He also told us that the 14th Army was at Pegu, 40 miles north and that there was a force of 10 000 Japs between Rangoon and Pegu. We considered his report much more reliable than the Burmese Defence Forces' report. In fact his report turned out to be accurate.

What we didn't know was that the British expected the Japanese to make a last ditch stand in Rangoon and had no idea the Japs had in fact left the city. Nor did we know then that Lord Mountbatten had left Ceylon with an invasion force to recapture Rangoon.

After the first day, and seeing nothing of our advancing armies, we decided to paint a message on the roof of our compound buildings; 'Japs gone' and 'British here'. Just as it was finished a Beaufighter came over low, circled and then waggled his wings. We all waved our arms and cheered.

We went to sleep that night feeling that at last the advancing troops must now know the Japs had gone and that our own forces would be in Rangoon very soon. What we didn't know was that the Japs had blown up three bridges between Pegu and Rangoon, that the rivers were running in full flood from the heavy Monsoon rains and that Slim's 14th Army was prevented from reaching Rangoon. Each week General Slim took to the air in a small spotter plane trying to get a clear idea what was happening around Rangoon. On his last flight, a burst of anti-aircraft fire straddled his plane severely wounding one of the crew and an unexploded shell embedded itself in the radio. Without doubt Slim was one of the great generals of World War II and never received the public recognition he richly deserved.

On 2 May we added another word to our signal on the roof; 'Extract digit' which in military terms means 'Pull your finger out!' or 'Do something!'.

A Mossie pilot must have taken us at our word because he suddenly swung around and threw a 500-pound bomb at the prison wall just behind number 6 Compound. The wall was blasted and flying bricks hurt several prisoners. Fortunately no one was killed but some very uncomplimentary remarks were made about RAF pilots. No one could guess why he bombed the wall because our message on the roof clearly stated: 'Japs gone. British here.'

An English and an Indian doctor had now taken over the sick patients in our compound. They both expressed praise for the way we had looked after and cared for patients but neither asked how we had done it. So I left the sick room glad to be relieved of the responsibility.

Rangoon Prison – 'Japs Gone'.

Chapter 18

THE WORLD OUTSIDE OUR PRISON

I was part of the first patrol that ventured out of the prison on 2 May. What a shambles everything was! Fires had burnt out whole streets and there were gutted buildings everywhere, and piles of rubbish where explosions had shattered Rangoon.

It must have been a lovely city under the British, with its wide streets lined with two and three-storeyed buildings that now were just burnt-out shells. Most of the bombing we had seen from prison must have been on the port and other military targets.

Despite the wreckage there were many Burmese people on the streets. The Burmese had sacked the city in 1942 after the British left and before the Japanese arrived. The looting Burmese killed and robbed Indians, Chinese and Eurasians. We saw none of these nationalities on the streets and it seemed that few, if any, were left in Rangoon. We were quite happy to get back to the relative undamaged security of our prison.

I led another patrol out that afternoon. We rounded a corner and came upon a bazaar and I saw a man shaving another. I stopped the truck and went up to the pair and when he had finished shaving his friend I sat in the chair and said, "Take it off. Take off the beard and give me a good hair cut." The barber nodded and went to work. When he had finished my face was clean and soft and my hair closely cut. I felt a different man without my itchy beard and unkempt hair. When we got back to the prison it was some time before many of the prisoners recognised me. Soon the only one of us left with a beard was Bill Hudson. Some of us who knew Bill felt he was leaving it on for the impression it would make on reporters and photographers who were bound to interview him as senior British officer.

He called a conference of Burmese and Indian leaders to direct the security of Rangoon. They both arrived well dressed and readily agreed that the prison headquarters should be in overall charge. It was agreed the Indians would patrol the city while the better-armed Burmese would position themselves to prevent any Japanese from entering Rangoon.

From somewhere news came through the British had reported finding the column of prisoners that had been marched out of the prison. Strafing had killed only one and tragically that was the brigadier who had endured several years of brutal imprisonment only to be killed by friendly fire within sight of freedom. We also heard that General Slim was just 36 miles south of Rangoon and that Hitler was dead.

Then two well-dressed, clean-shaven RAF officers appeared. They were Wing Commander Saunders and his navigator. Saunders had taken over 110 Mosquito Squadron when Bill Hudson had crashed his plane. They had seen our roof messages and taking it literally thought they should comply. They had checked out the airfield just north of Rangoon and seeing no sign of the Japanese, attempted to land between the bomb craters. They almost made it when a wheel broke and they couldn't take off again. They had then made their way to the prison. We were all glad to see them and to get their up-to-date news.

We sent another radio broadcast out that Wing Commander Saunders had landed in Rangoon but despite sending the message several times we received no reply.

Saunders told us a parachute force had landed near the mouth of the river the day before and a big force was coming ashore the next day to be preceded by a huge bombardment from naval forces and the Air Force. He was really concerned and urged us to help him find a boat so that he could go downstream and intercept the landing. He feared a lot of people would be killed needlessly in the bombardment.

The local Indian forces found him a large sampan but pleaded with him not to go because the sea was becoming stormy and rough. We later heard what happened.

A real storm blew up causing the fleet to stand 30 miles out to sea. It was raining heavily and blowing almost gale force. Despite the storm the landings were planned to go ahead early in the morning. The first few landing craft actually left the fleet and one of them struck a mine dropped earlier from the air. The landing craft was sunk with no survivors.

Just when things looked really bad for the other landing craft a large sampan appeared among them, with a man standing in the bow calling "Ahoy there Oracula!" (the code name for the invasion). When he boarded one of the boats he quickly told them there were no Japanese left in Rangoon and there was no need for them to land. All they need do was to wait for daylight and sail up the river to the city. The assault craft sent a signal back to the fleet and the invasion was called off. Saunders was taken out to meet Mountbatten and explained the situation to him.

Mountbatten claimed all the credit for capturing the city and he and his senior officers were decorated for something they never fired a shot over. Mountbatten became 'Lord Mountbatten of Burma' whereas General Slim, whose nine months of heavy fighting and fast approach to Pegu caused the Japanese to abandon Rangoon, received little recognition and was in fact removed from command of the 14th Army.

There is some argument as to who actually relieved Slim of his command, either Mountbatten or his second in command, but Slim was not the kind of man to take lying down this kind of underhand military politics. He appealed directly to the British High Command in London and the matter was quickly put right. He was reinstated as Commander-in-Chief of the 14th Army and not recalled to London.

I subsequently met Mountbatten when the POW party I was with arrived in Calcutta by air. He came to see us while we were in hospital and emphasised the importance of keeping all the details of the part we had played in the recapture of Rangoon airfield secret. If the Japanese heard about the part prisoners had played they might begin to kill off the 300 000 Allied prisoners they still held captive. He told us he had released information about a major battle to recapture Rangoon to deceive the Japanese. He assured us as soon as the war with Japan was over he would personally ensure that the part we had played, particularly at the airfield, would receive full recognition. We believed him and were careful not to reveal any details of what really happened but Mountbatten failed to keep his promise. I can only assume he had ambitions that didn't allow for the true facts to come out.

A few hours after dawn we watched a formation of naval men marching toward the prison. Its leader, wearing a red sash across his uniform and waving his sword above his head, was obviously feeling very proud of being the first liberator into Rangoon. He banged his sword several times on the gate of the prison shouting, "The Navy is here! The Navy is here!"

Bill Hudson, a bit peeved with all this showing off, leaned out the upstairs window and shouted back, "F... off! The press was here hours ago!" The naval officer was not impressed. After a few minutes we opened the gate and they marched in and our boys gave them a warm welcome. The Navy complained bitterly there wasn't a single Jap to have a shot at.

We showed them around the compounds and the sick room but they remained put out that there was to be no action. The silly fools. They didn't realise how lucky they were not to have to fight the Japanese. No doubt some of them would have been killed or wounded.

Next morning, Bill Hudson, and the New Zealander Eric Osboldstone, together with a force of Indians and myself, set out for the Mingaladon airfield. We took with us some spades, shovels and some rifles but not much ammunition. We found the airfield deserted but the Burmese told us that Japanese troops marched along the road on the other side of the airfield every night.

The Mosquito had been pulled out of the bomb crater by locals and parked near the wrecked buildings and was guarded by a few Indian troops.

We organised hundreds of Burmese to dig soil and cart it in baskets on their heads to fill in the bomb craters on the runway. While they were doing this I cleared the airfield of mines. When we arrived we found tripwires, about two feet off the ground, stretched at intervals across the runways. Only the part along which the Mosquito had landed was free of them. The Japanese must have left before they mined that end of the runway.

I dug a trench at the end of the wire, got into the trench and reaching up cut the wire. Nothing happened so I followed the wire to the other end and cut it again and again there was no explosion. I had with me two Indians with spades. I took one of the spades and began to dig when about a foot below ground level I hit something metallic. I gently cleared the earth around it and found it to be a bomb. It was probably about 200 pounds. We gently lifted it out of the hole, fearing that it might explode. We had brought some sacks to sleep on and very carefully rolled the bomb on to one of the sacks and carried it to the side of the runway. I assumed the bomb wasn't armed.

We followed the same procedure at the end of each wire and dug out 30 bombs and heaped them together with the first one we had dug out. By late afternoon 700 yards of one runway was cleared. I later talked to some bomb disposal people in India and they were certain the bombs would have been armed. They thought they would have been armed to explode by the shock

Bill Hudson (with samurai sword) hamming it up at Mingaladon Airfield watched by Cliff Emeny and Eric Osboldstone. On the left is Lieutenant John Kerr of Glamorgan Wales. (He is probably the one Cliff refers to as 'John' the one who helped him in the 'sick room'). A Dakota aircraft, possibly the one they flew out of Rangoon in, is behind them

Same four deciding on a plan of action.

of an aircraft or vehicle hitting the wire at some speed. Because we simply cut the wires there was no shock for them to explode. They still thought we were 'mad amateurs who deserved to have been blown to Hades'.

At nightfall Bill Hudson took one of the trucks back to the prison while we organised some way to cook our rice. We slept in some trenches near the bombed out buildings just in case some Japs missed the road at night and stumbled on us.

By noon the next day we had one runway ready for landings. By this time we had nearly 1 000 Burmese digging and carrying soil. Ozzie Osboldstone organised them into groups of 100 with a leader for each group. The leader signed for his group when it began and when it finished working. Ossie did all the paperwork. He was a very cheery personality. He laughed and smacked the leaders on the back and kept them in good spirits. There were long lines of people streaming across the airfield and they filled the bomb craters one after another with baskets of soil carried on their heads. It was an amazing sight to see and it worked. By the end of day two we had two thirds of the second runway re-paved and by midday of day three it was ready. To consolidate the fill every one who dropped a basket of soil into the crater had to walk around inside it and tramp it down. Big problems had to be solved by simple means.

At the end of each day every leader got a signed note saying his group had worked that day and the Burmese were quite happy about this. Pre-war the British had widely used 'chitties' or written notes to pay for most things. The Burmese could cash their chitties in shops or in banks. The British did not carry money because of the danger of being robbed or mugged. The Burmese, we were told, preferred stealing to work. It was said that in pre-war Burma there were the British administrators and military authorities, Chinese merchants, Korean farmers, Indian coolies who did a lot of the manual work, and Burmese bandits.

In the mid-afternoon, a Dakota, piloted by a group captain, landed. He irresponsibly swung off the runway and put one wheel in a newly filled bomb crater and was stuck fast.

I had put full RAF landing instructions out for him to see but he ignored them. We rushed over to his plane and his first question was, "Where are the Japs?"

I answered, "They will be marching along that road over there after dark. There are lots of them north of here but they are not interested in retaking the airfield, we hope!"

His second question was, "Who is in charge?" I told him I was but I don't think he was very impressed that someone dressed in just a loincloth could be in charge. To make it clear that I was in charge I asked him why he hadn't followed our clearly laid out landing instructions. Probably this was the first time someone dressed in a loincloth had told him politely to obey landing instructions.

We got some planks and with lots of human labour we soon got his wheel out of the hole and he seemed quite impressed with our efficiency. Apparently he thought he was coming to rescue the Mosquito crew, Wing Commander Saunders and his navigator.

Meanwhile in the city the invasion soldiers and sailors were pouring in and all busy trying to get the best shelter in the ruined buildings. The prisoners were all taken out to a hospital ship and treated wonderfully. The ship sailed for Calcutta where they got a great reception.

The day after the Dakota landed part of the army that had landed at Rangoon arrived at the airport, but on the way they got lost and reached the airfield just after dark. As they came across the airfield they were deployed in attack mode, running a few yards and then going to ground. When they were halfway across the airfield we sighted them and fearing they were Japs, we took to our trenches. I was armed with the Very signal gun from the Mossie, as well as my rifle with six bullets in it. There were 12 other rifles, with a few bullets each, among our group. I gave the order, "No one fire until I fire the signal gun." In the darkness we could see them getting ever closer. There were about 30 of them. If they were Japs our only hope was to wait until they were right on the edge of our trench and then hope to kill most of them with a surprise volley.

They went down about 200 yards out and then made another dash. I still couldn't identify them and whispered along the trench, "Don't fire! Don't fire!" They went to ground again about 50 yards out but one must have accidentally hit another because he was sworn at in English. I then realised it was the British Army. I let fly with a stream of oaths, "You stupid pack of Pommies, coming here after dark when we expected Japs."

Someone replied, and with a sneer in his voice asked, "And who may you be?" We eventually established who was who but it had been a very close thing. If they had got up again we would have opened fire, so tragedy was averted by a stroke of luck. It could have turned out quite differently if someone hadn't been accidentally hurt and started to swear loudly enough for us to hear him. When we had all settled down they got on their radio and reported in and then ordered food for all of us for the next day.

Next day two Dakotas arrived filled with personnel to tape the airfield and then later in the morning Bill Hudson and the last few officers from the prison arrived. One of the Dakotas was to take us to Calcutta.

I grabbed one of the trucks and raced back to the prison to get my diary, in which I had kept a record of all the sick prisoners and their condition, their home addresses and how they got into Rangoon. When I looked where I had hidden it, the diary had gone. Only two men knew where it was hidden – Johnny Yanoto and Bill Hudson. I thought Johnny might have taken it out with him but he hadn't. By that time Bill Hudson had gone. He had disappeared into senior rank circles in India and

I never got a chance to ask him if he had it. The information it contained would have been invaluable to him. He made a name for himself after the war writing about the happenings in the Rangoon prison, but sad as I was to lose it I have to give him the benefit of the doubt that he hadn't taken it without telling me.

The RAF took some interesting photographs of us at Mingaladon and kindly sent some home to me after the war.

Leaving Rangoon. Cliff and Eric's last task before leaving Rangoon – folding up the flag.

Chapter 19

LEAVING RANGOON BEHIND

We flew out of Mingaladon on 7 May 1945 and so ended my experience of being a Japanese prisoner of war. This experience shaped my life for the rest of my days. What I experienced was so extreme in human brutality and hardship that I personally felt the impact of war in a way that is impossible for those who have never been through it personally to understand. The horrifying, frightening thought is that millions of other human beings suffered not only under Japanese aggression but also the horrors of enslavement and slaughter by the Nazis in Europe and the Russians under Stalin.

While in the prison compound four of us spent hours walking up and down at night talking about the war, why and how it happened and how we happened to be in Rangoon prison. We reached the conclusion that war was not really between the peoples of the world. It was really between ambitious, brutal and criminal leaders and politicians, generals, powerful financial people and business people who made immense profits from the war.

The populations of these countries were actually sucked into war by too much power in the hands of bad leaders. We made a solemn vow that we would make the study of the causes of war and the defence of human freedom our interest and life's work. Regretfully I have to say that only one of us has kept that vow. Keeping that vow has been the major interest of my life since 1945.

That evening our Dakota arrived at an airfield on the Arakan Front where it was refuelled and where we spent the night.

267

Incredibly whom should I find stationed there but 45 Mosquito Squadron and I found myself back with my old friends. They could hardly believe their eyes when they saw me. I found Flight Lieutenant Duclo had taken over B Flight to replace me. The wing commander had left at the end of his six-month tour of duty and Duclo had been promoted wing commander in charge of the Squadron. The previous wing commander had been awarded the DSO for leadership. It was a case of the 'Old Boy's Network' in action again. He got the credit for all the operations that 45 Squadron had done. He had contributed little or nothing to actual operational flying. Duclo seemed cool and indifferent in his welcome to me. Everyone else was overflowing with warmth and enthusiasm in their welcome.

My roommate still had the same servant but when the servant saw me he just froze with fright thinking he was seeing a ghost. My mates tried to get him to prepare a bath for me but he just stood there with his eyes wide open with fear and quite speechless. Eventually they persuaded him to get the water and I had my first bath since 9 November 1944 when I was shot down. He brought several buckets to the bath and poured them over me and it was wonderful.

After dinner the whole squadron assembled on the slope of a small hill and I told them as much as I could what it was like being a prisoner of the Japs. Everyone listened in absolute silence for three hours. Only Bill Hudson and Duclo were missing. They were drinking in the bar where no doubt Bill was telling Duclos his version of the Jap experience – all about Bill.

My friend John was still squadron leader of A Flight and he filled me in with many details. He told me how the then wing commander had taken all my personal effects even before all the Mossies had returned from the raid on which I was shot down. Included in those personal belongings was my prized diary and the priceless scimitar sword given to me by the sheik's son.

He told me the only raid the wing commander ever led was a flight of 10 Mosquitos against five small bamboo buildings. The raid was a shambles from start to finish. The wing commander claimed the buildings housed a vital Japanese headquarters. Although all the buildings were destroyed there was not one shot fired at them from the ground and not a sign of any people or military supplies.

John also told me that my promotion to squadron leader had come through six days after I was shot down. It could easily have been credited to me because I had been listed as 'Missing, believed killed'. The CO hadn't bothered to action it. No doubt he would have been very annoyed to read in my diary the comments about his lone 'raids' and his lack of operational leadership. No wonder the diary was never seen again.

Next day John took me up in a Mosquito and even although I couldn't fly it I did enjoy it. This was to be my last flight in a Mosquito.

Later, everyone in the squadron began to celebrate the end of the war in Europe, but we took off for Calcutta arriving there mid-afternoon. Few people were about as most were celebrating. No transport had been arranged and all our attempts to raise RAF HQ failed. No one was answering the telephones. Not even Bill could get through. Then someone noticed an Indian bus standing empty with the driver on board. We bought a bottle of Indian gin and began offering him sips and we all became very chummy. He was obviously enjoying himself until he slumped to the floor unaware of what was happening. We laid him down on the back seat and I drove it off into the city.

We found RAF Headquarters full of drunks. When we eventually found the orderly officer he too was drunk. He looked up Standing Orders to see what it had to say about POWs. It was obviously written for the Army on the North West Frontier of India in the 19th Century. It stated, 'If not wounded or sick,

Arriving in Calcutta on the 5th May 1945– Cliff (centre of doorway), Eric Osboldstone and Bill Hudson. On left of doorway and facing Hudson is John Kerr. Sgt Norman Davis (RAF) is standing on bottom step. American crew members share in the good cheer.

to be placed under military police control. If wounded to be sent to detention hospital.' So he got an ambulance and had us conveyed to a detention hospital.

When we arrived at the door of the hospital it burst open and three very loud-mouthed NCOs shouted at us, "Get out of the door at the double!" Not the welcome we had been expecting. We jumped at them. Bill was swishing his Jap sword around their heads with great flourishes. I attacked them with the butt of my rifle and then jabbed the barrel in their chests. In moments we had them backed up against the wall. Bill then pulled his rank on them and demanded, "What the hell do you think you are doing? Who the hell do you think you are speaking to?" Obviously very scared they explained that the hospital was for wounded 'bad guys' and they were very apologetic.

We took the ambulance and drove up town to get some clothes. We stopped at a big store and demanded to see the manager. When he came I got him to phone my bank manager friend at his home. I had an account with his bank and he guaranteed to pay for anything we bought. We all bought light, tropical shirts and trousers and new underwear and felt new men.

Bill phoned someone of importance and disappeared. The rest of us were concerned to find a good hotel. Unfortunately most of our party felt duty bound to do a little celebrating themselves and far too much alcohol was drunk and without exception we were all very ill. We had kept the ambulance for emergencies. The hotel management simply phoned the hospital and we all finished up back there, where we had to stay for two days before we could get the RAF Headquarters to put us into a normal hospital.

In the hospital they found everything possible wrong with us, especially bugs, so we were kept there for 10 days to be cleaned up. In my case they were very concerned because my X-rays showed some marks on my lungs. These marks were diagnosed as TB and I was put in isolation. My bank manager friend and his wife came to visit me but were not allowed to take me away. It was a terrible experience. Receiving good food and good care, I felt much better but I was allowed only an occasional walk in the grounds. The rest of the POWs left and I was alone. After all I had been through I felt that I was being literally imprisoned by the medical profession.

The wife of the wing commander, who killed himself in that terrible plane crash at Ranchi, heard I was in town and came to see me. She tried to get the authorities to give me leave to have lunch with her but they bluntly refused. They did allow us to walk in the grounds, however, and we just walked out of the hospital.

We had a great time for five days. We stayed in a hotel and I enjoyed a sense of freedom that I hadn't had in months. She wrote an article that was published in all New Zealand papers called, 'Back from the Dead'. This article was directly responsible for deciding my future life in New Zealand. She organised an interview for Ozzie and me with another journalist that was printed widely in POW literature. In those five days I enjoyed the sense of freedom and enjoyment we had all longed for in prison. I will be forever deeply grateful for her help and company.

According to the military doctors I had transferable TB and it was this wrong diagnosis that destroyed any chance I had of continuing a career in aviation. It also caused a host of other problems for me when I returned to New Zealand.

I personally felt that being trapped in a blazing Mosquito and breathing in very hot air had caused the scarring but the doctors refused to give such an explanation any credence. Their attitude was that they were doctors who knew far more than I did.

I pleaded with them to look more seriously at my condition. I had none of the symptoms of TB. I experienced no shortage of breath, no personal sickness, no weight loss (my weight in fact was steadily increasing from the six stone ten pounds when I was liberated from the Jap prison). My energy levels were good. I had no pulmonary discharge, no night sweats, no coughing and I was recovering faster than most of the other prisoners. None of the other prisoners showed any signs of TB. How could I possibly be the only one with the disease? The only evidence the doctors had was the X-ray shadows on my lungs. Surely there could be another explanation for these shadows.

The doctors, however, refused to consider any of my suggestions and insisted I was a health risk to those who came in contact with me and should be left in isolation. They had the authority and the power to impose these conditions on me despite all the other evidence of my constantly improving health. My whole life was to be blighted by their flawed diagnosis and there appeared absolutely nothing I could do about it. This was the stupidity of the bureaucratic military in its worst form and in no way would they be held personally responsible for the blighting of my future life.

After five days of 'liberty' the RAF medical bureaucracy caught up with me, certain that I was spreading TB germs everywhere I went. I insisted that in hospital I be allowed to have visitors and they reluctantly agreed. I told them that I had just come out of one prison and refused to go into another.

After two days it was decided to move all New Zealand and Australian POW patients to a hospital in Bombay, a huge city on the eastern coast, on the other side of the continent from Calcutta. I insisted we go by air and no doubt my TB rating helped to get us there by Dakota. From Bombay we were supposed to catch a ship home to New Zealand and Australia.

In the last few weeks in the prison in Rangoon I had lost touch with Johnny Yanoto. (We of course had seen a lot of each other in the Rangoon prison.) He had left Rangoon by the hospital ship. After I had been a week in Bombay Johnny phoned to say that he was leaving by air for England and then home to

Canada but the medical authorities refused permission for him to come and visit me in hospital. He and I had shared so much together and I had the greatest regard for him as a navigator and an even greater respect and affection for him as a man. We have kept in touch each Christmas and my wife and I have visited him twice in Canada – in 1973 and 1991.

It was then that I began to think seriously of how to get back to New Zealand. I heard there was an Australian flying service from Ceylon to Perth. I made plans to leave the hospital in Bombay and fly by Air India to Ceylon. I got hold of an Air India schedule and decided on the day of my escape. Each day I was allowed to go for a walk for a few hours. When the day came for me to escape from RAF medical imprisonment, I quietly got my things down to the exit floor and walked out. I hired a taxi and set off for the civilian airport. En route I wrapped a bandage around my head, put my arm in a sling and bought a walking stick. I looked every bit a medical 'repat'.

When I presented myself at the airline booking office I was asked for my papers. I feigned surprise and said that they had already been sent to the airline and would surely arrive in a day or so. I stressed how important it was to leave Bombay that day to keep arrangements to fly to Perth. I offered to pay for the fare and they accepted token payment of 500 rupees and put me on a plane flying south to Madras with tickets to fly on to Ceylon. I suppose they simply pocketed my payment. There is something to be said for the system of bribery.

On the DC3 I could hardly believe how easy it had been. To avoid any search for me I had arranged with my New Zealand friend Ozzie to tell the hospital I had been ordered to see the New Zealand Indian office in Delhi. That worked too. No one looked for me.

I stayed overnight in Madras and next day flew to Ceylon where I installed myself in the RAF Officers' mess. The Australian service to Perth flew the American Liberator, a large four-engine plane with a great range. The pilots were operational sea reconnaissance aircrew. I introduced myself to them and told them about flying Mosquitos and being a Jap POW in Rangoon. They invited me to lunch in their mess and introduced me to their CO. He had heard a rumour of the prisoners taking over the Rangoon airfield and was keen to get the real facts. By the time lunch was over he assured me that they would get me to Perth within a week. I was very keen to get away from Ceylon in case the RAF medical authorities caught up with me again.

Within five days I was on the plane to Perth. Before leaving I asked the CO if they could do the same for Ozzie. He agreed, so I wrote to Ozzie telling him how to get to Ceylon and who to meet there.

It was a beautiful trip to Australia. I occupied the many hours writing about the sunrise before we left and the beauty of the cloud masses en route. I was so happy to be free of the terrible treatment of the arrogant, domineering regimental RAF doctors. At last I really felt free. This was late in June.

When I got to Perth I phoned Peter Ewing's home. (Pete was the Aussie pilot who came into the hospital after my terrible training crash when I hit the tree. Pete 'the Crasher' had himself crashed four Mosquitos. He was awarded the DFC for going into Meiktila after I was shot down and although badly wounded got home safely.)

His family was thrilled to hear that I was in Perth and made me very welcome as I waited there for Ozzie to catch up with me. He and I were together again in eight days. It was wonderful being in a European city again especially without blackouts or wartime restrictions. A new song had just come out 'Don't Fence Me In'. It so suited my lovely feeling of real freedom and I walked the streets of the suburb Pete lived in singing it.

I remember Perth as a city very much like Wellington with a good port, lots of nice, clean houses and buildings. It was the nearest thing to being home and I was so happy.

275

When Ozzie arrived we went up to Army Headquarters and introduced ourselves as medical 'repats' from Burma. They had seen photographs and read reports of the suffering of prisoners at the hands of the Japanese and they readily agreed to our flying on to Sydney. We left three days later with a stopover at Adelaide. When we reached Sydney we found the New Zealand Services' Office and were assured we would be flown on to New Zealand as soon as possible.

While we waited we settled down to enjoy Sydney. That night we went to a dance and I met a rather nice girl who asked me what I was doing in Sydney. When I told her that we were ex-Japanese prisoners of war she became very interested in me. She kept asking me to have the next dance with her and as she was a good dancer I was happy to oblige. When the dance finished she asked me to go home on the bus with her. I assumed she lived with her parents but found she lived in a flat. When I saw the photograph of an airman on the mantelpiece I asked her who it was. She told me that it was her fiancée who had been a prisoner of the Japanese since the fall of Singapore.

Now I knew why she was so attentive and had invited me to her home. She wanted to find out what it was like to be a prisoner of the Japanese. What could I possibly tell her that would not make her life miserable and unhappy? If still alive he would have been a prisoner for three years and from what I had seen in Rangoon he would be very lucky to have survived. If he had survived he would be in poor health and a very different man to the one she had become engaged to on his final leave. I could not have found myself in a worse situation. We talked for hours. She felt obliged to remain faithful to him in the hope that he would survive and find her still waiting for him. I didn't sleep too well that night.

Next day we had dinner together and went to the movies that night. Then an RAF medical officer noticed Ozzie and I had

276

bugs beneath the skin of our hands and we were put into isolation for five days while sulpha drugs were used to get rid of them. We took the opportunity to get a medical clearance for our health.

The nice girl I had met at the dance came to visit me every lunchtime. She told me she just hoped and prayed her fiancée would come back such a well, happy person as I was. She was clinging desperately to the hope that her life would be on track again when he returned. I could only suggest to her that it might take a while for him to recover from the hardship he had suffered and wish her well. When we left she was at the airport to see me off. She kissed me very sweetly and thanked me for being so helpful and kind.

So we left by flying boat to Auckland. It was mid-July and I can still vividly remember the wonderful sight of Auckland as we came in to land. There was no welcoming group. We were just two more passengers.

No one in the RNZAF seemed to know about us but we did get a month's pay given to us. The problem was we had no papers from RAF India. We blamed the people there for not sending them on. The adjutant we dealt with was most upset at our lack of papers and told us we would be confined to the RNZAF base in Auckland until we could prove who we claimed to be. Finally he got word from RNZAF Wellington that we really had been Japanese prisoners of war but he still wasn't happy because he had no proper service records.

We finally got permission to go off and meet with our families and Ozzie and I parted to go our separate ways to start a new chapter in our lives after four and a half years of warfare.

(A few months later Cliff wrote a letter to Eugene and Barbara Skinner. Eugene was one of the American electronic engineers who had installed radar in 409 Squadron's Beaufighters late in 1941. He and Cliff became close friends. By the end of the war Eugene had attained the rank of Colonel in the USAAF.

In 1973 Joan and Cliff visited Barbara in San Antonio. Eugene had died some years before. Barbara gave to Joan the following letter.)

F/Lt. Cliff Emeny. RNZAF. NZ 40204

Air. Dept. E Wellington.N.Z.

DATE. 18th. Aug. 1945.

Dear Gene and Barbara,

I've received your grand letters and cable. It sure was good to hear from you again. Reckon you must be a Major now Gene. Well there won't be any competition this time. I've had it. Just can't make the grade no how. But we can't be worried. Figure when it is all sorted out that I got far more out of the experience than I lost by going down at that time. Now it's all over I wouldn't have missed it for anything in the world.

Gosh your letters were wonderful to read. Am I thankful for the fate that brought us together. It's so comforting to know that a man has friends like you folk. Reckon I'll be keeping those letters for the rest of my life. Had a grand one from Norma Jean too. She sounds to have a really super husband. No matter what happens in the future or what the world comes to I'll always think of America as you people and things will certainly have to go pretty bad to spoil the respect and affection I've developed for your country. But I won't be coming to live there Gene. For all its beauty and its grandeur this is my country and here I will make my livelihood in the days to come. The most wonderful thing about America is that it makes me homesick for N.Z. so you can see just how deeply this feeling goes. N.Z. is what I fought for and it is what I live for now. Without such a paramount influence a man couldn't have even thought of enduring what victory cost us. That was my major war aim. To preserve N.Z. and have the chance of developing it to the highest standards even dreamed of by mere man. Now the threat to our existence is over I reckon it's time to take on the developing side of the ideal. They should supply a man with all the excitement and interest he needs for the rest of his life. In my ideals there's more to living than just existing and running the farm. There's the little matter of public service to the community and that should be enough to keep me going.

Thanks all the same for your invitation to come to America Gene. I'd like to do the trip alright but doubt if it will be for a long while. Maybe I'd better tell you why eh? ... Boy and am I going to enjoy it too.... I'm in LOVE Gene.. As Norma Jean once said "starry eyed, walking on air and everything else you imagine" and/or should know. It's great, worth anything I've ever been through to get back to this. She's the daughter of a family who were my closest friends before leaving N.Z. and has been in the army for the last couple of years. Could be said she's much like Jean Watson to look at, fair, sort of grey-brown eyes, about 5ft1, pleasant features, good figure and is 21. To sum it up she has everything. Personality, good looks, experience, a heart of gold and she knows me – and she loves me. Oh. Boy do I feel good .... Her name's Joan McDonell. She was just a 16 year old college girl when they saw me off but she is one real grown up lady now. I'm glad that things never became serious overseas for this has something an overseas romance would lack. Joan knows my background, knows our life here and knows what I'm talking about when I voice my hopes for the future. She belongs to – in fact is – New Zealand, so there won't be any business of having to settle down to a strange existence. Apparently her family reckon the sun rises and sets on me by the reception they give, that's a help. But we're not rushing things. I've still a spot of hospitalisation to do and we figure on letting things run until around Xmas. Then we'll either go all the way or not as we happen to feel. But if the present is any indication my single days are numbered, and I like the idea of it too.

Just to give cupid a break I've got me a journalist's job in RNZA F H.Q. Wellington. Joan is stationed nearby and we can have weekends and odd nights together this way. Have bypassed the hospital for a month. It is time that's valuable so I reckon things can wait for this. Another month around will make a big difference to the way we know each other. The work's interesting for I've always had a bit of a kink for writing and this is a chance to try my hand. While I'm on the subject – you can do what you like with that letter you have Gene. There's not a lot to it but the war is over now so it doesn't matter. All Jap prisoners should be home soon. If you do get anything for it don't bother to send it in cash. I've a case of things at your place. Maybe it will help pay for their transport back. Could you arrange for them to be sent one of these days Gene please? Let's know the expense and I'll send it to you. Though I'm afraid the Communist touch has crept into N.Z. affairs these days and reckon there'll be some bother sending money out of the country, I would like to get you to send me some film for my cameras, have a wizard 1237 and a 120 but films are no more here. These are great days and one's that would be good recorded in snaps. I'd give anything for a movie camera actually. It shouldn't be long before they come back on the market though. It all depends on America I reckon. You should lead the field in those things.

I cabled and wrote Jean Watson as soon as free. Have had a letter from her. She was pretty sad about me going alright. Jean and I have known each other so long, since before the war. Her letter was lovely to read, especially when one knew she meant every word of it. She was engaged a week or two before getting the news but he's a grand fellow. Has been putting in some hard work for that result for years. I often wonder what the situation really was between us but reckon it has worked out for the best. I never felt about Jean the way I do Joan so am happy now. Jean sure was great, someone really fine, but she belonged to her own people and would have found N.Z. hard.

My own people gave me a wonderful welcome home. Country folk are the same the world over. They came in hundreds to attend an official welcome. Then we had a great party in the district hall that night. I never felt so happy and stirred emotionally in my life. Their words were like music and just the sight of the joy and pleasure on their faces worth more than any material thing in the world. I tried to tell them how much it mean to be back among them but the women present started to cry so I had to give up. There was so much I wanted to say but never was anything so hard to put into words. I'll remember that day and night as long as I live. It can never happen again.

It's spring here now. The Victory celebrations are all over and everyone is wondering what to do with themselves in the future. Our folk took great heart at the news of final victory. I was here in the city and they mobbed any of us servicemen they found on the street as the news came over. For a few hours that went on until I was just about ready to drop. Am far from fit yet. However contacted Joan and we lit out for her home some 76 miles away. Went to a victory dance and sat up before a warm fire until dawn. One just couldn't sleep a moment of that day. Next saw a very pleasant scene of victory parades and sports in the small town nearby. Most of N.Z. was having terrible weather but Joan lives in a valley nestled in the mountains and it was brilliant sunshine there. I tell you – the whole world shines on us. We took an extra day's holiday but the Powers That Be just overlooked it.

My family moved just before I returned so I've not got a home address anymore. However the Dept will always send on my mail so you can use it. My folks sold our farm just before they got the news of my safety. They are looking for another one but that's no easy job now. But I'm hoping to get out of my own when I'm fit enough to go chase one up. Didn't exactly waste all my pay overseas so have something to start on. But I'm afraid the country isn't what it was when we left. N.Z. used to be the most outstanding example of moderation in socialism but today it almost smells of Communism. I'm terribly afraid that the death of our early war leaders has allowed into power men who cannot appreciate the spirit of we who went to the war. We believe in developing our own traditions and institutions, not copying them from some other country. It was to ensure that freedom of enterprise that we fought but right now it doesn't exist. However I'm hoping that they will realise the seriousness of catering for the spiritual ideals of the servicemen and the country as a whole and drop the innumerable bureaucratic powers in force today and treat them as essentially wartime measures. If they don't we shall have to take control from their hands for they will, by allowing rule through sectional interests, defeat the very principles for which we fought. I am not content to work, think, or plan on lines laid down by a central power. My future is my own and I ask only to be allowed to work it out for myself. If I wanted to live like Russians I would go there but as I chose to live here then I demand the right to develop the country on lines in keeping with our own constitution. We have an election in a year. They either give us freedom as we know it or we shall remove them from office. Honestly Gene – I just couldn't believe it for the first few weeks. It didn't seem possible that a people could allow such totalitarian rule as has developed here. We're all the same, every serviceman whose (sic) been back a little while is still dumfounded. Well we're a quiet people and will settle the issue in a quiet decent way – but we won't be any the less sincere for our quietness.

Give my regards to all the family Gene. Tell Jean I'll write her later. I hope you're all getting on fine. Thanks for all your grand letters. Here's wishing you, every one of you, all the very best of good times in the future.

KIA ORA..

POSTSCRIPT

Cliff Emeny's war service covered a period of five years. In that period he served in two very different theatres of war. The first was over England beginning with the Battle of Britain, through the Blitz, until mid-June 1942 when the great air battles over England were over. During that time he flew over a 100 missions. The second theatre of operations was in India/ Burma against the Japanese. It was in this period that Cliff made several long and lasting friendships and he made them in one of the most horrible places on earth – the Rangoon prison. The British authorities had condemned this dreadful place in 1938 but it was here that he survived the last six months of his war. He was shot down on 9 November 1944 and the Japanese evacuated Rangoon on 28 April 1945. In the months of his captivity he, along with the other prisoners, suffered appallingly. His sole goal was personal survival and yet he devoted his time and energy to help over 40 other prisoners, worse off than he was, to survive those dreadful last few months of captivity.

When I thought back to the people he told me about in his story particularly those he was imprisoned with I found myself asking: **I wonder what happened to?**

Flying Officer Johnny Yanoto

Johnny Yanoto was Cliff's Canadian navigator and was with him in the Rangoon prison. He remembers Cliff as 'a very good pilot, steady and reliable and popular with the other airmen'.

Johnny remembers too some of the stories that Cliff relates but has only has a hazy memory of others. For instance he remembers flying up to the Syrian/Lebanese border to find Cliff's brother Bert. He can remember also, but not with the same detail, the few days' leave spent in Calcutta but has little recall of the train being stopped by Indian nationalists on the way back to Argartala.

It was Johnny who pulled Cliff clear of the burning wreck of the Mosquito when they were shot down on 9 November 1944 and spent the last months of the war incarcerated with him in the dreadful Rangoon prison.

After the war Johnny worked for the Canadian Postal Service. He and his wife Helen live in Glenmore, Blairmore, Alberta, close to the Rocky Mountains. He enjoyed the hunting and fishing of that region and watching ice hockey. He is far less mobile these days with 'legs that won't support him as they once did'. He and his wife Helen 'have been blessed with seven children'.

Cliff and Joan Emeny named their eldest son, who was born in March 1947, 'John' after Johnny Yanoto. Cliff held a very high opinion of Johnny both as a navigator ('one of the best') and as a man. Several times when speaking of his former navigator Cliff's voice became filled with emotion. He regarded him as one of his cherished friends who had literally shared life and death experiences with him. He and Joan have twice visited Johnny and his family in Canada.

Flying Officer Craig Howard Edwards

Craig Edwards was born and educated in Wanganui. His father was a well-known dental surgeon and his mother was matron of the Wanganui Hospital. He enlisted and was trained as a pilot in Canada and flew Hurricanes and Spitfires in England and then P-47 Thunderbolts in the battle over India/Burma. His wife Sylvia kindly sent me the following account of how he was shot down and his subsequent imprisonment.

Craig was on a ground attack mission when his plane was hit while he was strafing the Japanese. The plane crashed and he was thrown from it into swampy ground before the crashed Thunderbolt caught fire and was burnt out. Craig suffered a severely injured foot and was taken prisoner by the Japanese ground forces. On his departure from base on the day of the crash, his rank was that of Pilot Officer. Very soon after, the Air Ministry promoted him to the rank of Flying Officer. His P-47 Thunderbolt was the first of that type to be shot down over the Burma/Japanese war zone. The Japanese sought information from him concerning essential details about the Thunderbolt. He exaggerated the armaments and power of the P-47. He told them the P-47 carried four or five times the armaments that it had and that it was far more effective than it was, with the idea of making it appear far more formidable to fight against. The P-47 was in actual fact the largest and heaviest single seat piston fighter ever produced by the United States and used by the US Army Air Force. A few days later another P-47 was shot down in the same area but did not sustain serious damage. The Japanese were able to examine the wreckage and establish that Craig had lied about the exaggerated armament of the P-47. He was again interrogated about its performance and armaments. As soon as he became hesitant or reluctant to answer the question of the intelligence officer he was buffeted and cuffed with an open hand around the face. Sometimes he was punched with a closed fist. Each time this happened he felt the jar to his foot and back through his whole body. Finally his guards dragged him from the interrogation room and through the gates into the prison. By this time he was almost insensible with the pain and shock. They manhandled him up some stairs and it was there that Cliff Emeny entered the life of Craig Edwards.

Somehow Cliff persuaded the guards and the Commandant to allow him to treat Craig in his own cell. Craig often said with conviction that Cliff saved his life that day. Apart from the beating the Japanese had given him, his injured foot had received no medical treatment and by the time he met Cliff his foot was severely swollen, inflamed and infected and was turned 90 degrees from the normal position. At times he would say, "Cliff I am never going to survive this!" Cliff would reply, "What about your fiancée and what about your mother and sister in New Zealand? For their sake you have to snap out of this." He did not and would not allow Craig to give up. Their association became a great friendship that lasted until Craig's death.

At the time of his crash Craig was engaged to Sylvia Cole in Ranikhet, India. Sylvia had been brought up in India where her father served in the Indian Army. Sylvia herself served for two and a half years in the Women's Volunteer Service. She first met her fiancé when she was on duty in the orderly room of the air station on which he was based at that time. They became engaged in July 1944.

The leader of Craig's section saw him go down. He circled over the crash site for some time and it seemed to him very unlikely that Craig had survived the crash and the burnout of his plane. He telephoned Sylvia to tell her that Craig had been shot down and was listed as 'missing in combat, presumed dead'.

Craig and Sylvia returned to New Zealand six months after they were married in India in July 1945. Craig underwent orthopaedic surgery to treat and realign his damaged foot. The couple lived in Wanganui for a time before settling in Wellington. Craig obtained a flying job with the then Public Works Department. His work entailed flying Public Works' engineers around New Zealand. It was on a return flight (March 1951) from the South Island that the Gemini aircraft he was piloting crashed near Rakaia, Canterbury, killing him and his passengers and leaving his wife with three pre-school children.

Cliff Emeny named his second son 'Craig' (born 28 February 1956) after the friend he first met in such traumatic circumstances.

Pilot Officer Eric (Ozzie) Osboldstone

Back in New Zealand at the beginning of August 1945, Eric married his fiancée, Betty, on VJ Day. He was unable to get his old job back as a customs and shipping clerk for Hardwick and Robertson Ltd, so he bought a small grocery business. He prospered and eventually owned two supermarkets in Karori, Wellington.

He and Betty are now retired in Waikanae, Wellington, blessed with good health and lead active lives.

Eric and Cliff had much in common. Both spent their late teenage years in Wellington. Both ended up in England and then separately made the long flight to India where Eric joined No. 27 Squadron flying Beaufighters. Within a month of each other they were shot down, to meet in the infamous Rangoon jail. Like Cliff, Eric began his military service in the prewar Territorial Army. On 7 September 1939 he was posted to the 22nd Anti Aircraft Battery of the New Zealand Artillery. He was trained as a sound locator operator based on Mount Victoria in Wellington. He confirms Cliff's description (Chapter 7) of the antique nature of this equipment for the detection of enemy aeroplanes.

(From the papers of Eric Osboldstone printed in *P.O.W. The Untold Stories of New Zealanders as Prisoners of War* David McGill, Mills publications.)

"These Sound Locator Units were used to detect approaching aircraft, and would hopefully give an early warning of an incoming enemy. This was of course before the development of radar systems, which provided a more accurate and reliable system of aircraft location. Radar scanned the whole area of sky automatically, but the sound locating apparatus had to be manually operated to scan sections of the sky. Sound Location used two devices something like giant ear trumpets mounted on a frame, which could be rotated and also tilted up and down. As the two 'ear trumpets' were mounted some distance apart, slightly different sounds could be heard from each, and by using stereophonic effect, the device could be moved until the same sound was heard from both units. At this stage the unit would

287

be pointing at an aircraft, in ideal situations, up to 40 miles distant. The anti-aircraft guns known, as "ack-ack" would be aimed toward the area indicated by the Sound Locator, ready to fire at the aircraft should it be one of the enemy's. Fortunately no enemy aircraft were detected, and units also managed not to shoot at any friendly aircraft."

Eric served in the Army until 26 February 1941 when he was discharged from service with the Royal New Zealand Air Force. He trained as a pilot and embarked in April 1942 for England. After further training Eric and his navigator, Sergeant Alick Shaw, set out in a brand new Beaufighter Mark 10 on 10 December on the start of their delivery journey to India. The 6 000 miles journey took 20 days.

Eric was posted to No 27 Squadron RAF based in India flying Beaufighters. Twenty-nine days after Cliff was shot down Eric was to meet the same fate. On 14 December on his ninth operational sortie he took off at dawn with Flight Sergeant Blundon as navigator to attack the Thazi-Mandalay railway. Machine gun fire hit his plane. He attempted a crash-landing but the aircraft was wrecked and Flight Sergeant Blundon, was killed. Eric was captured and two days later found himself in the Rangoon Central Prison – the prisoner of war camp.

To quote from *The New Zealand Official History - Prisoners of War* "A number of New Zealand airmen captured in operations over Burma were confined in the former British civilian jail at Rangoon. Treatment of prisoners in this camp, more especially of the air crew in 1944 and 1945, was bad and at some times inhuman. In 1943 it was possible to buy eggs, tomatoes, and sugar fairly regularly; but as time went on this became impossible, and men had to exist on little else than an inadequate rice ration and vegetables grown in the camp garden. Medical care was hampered by lack of supplies and sometimes by obstruction on the part of the Japanese. It was only after some time that books were allowed into the camp, and a ban on all gatherings made it impossible to carry out any organised recreation, to set up educational classes, or to hold religious services. It was exceptional for a day to pass without someone receiving a beating with bamboo, steel golf clubs or other weapons, and beatings into unconsciousness were not uncommon. Air crew received worse treatment still. They were kept sometimes five to a filthy cell measuring five yards by three, were given no bedding, except old sacks, received half the rations of the other prisoners, and were beaten if caught conversing with one another. Those who came in wounded were almost without exception denied the services of a medical officer. Some of the inmates of the cells were in time moved to another part of the camp and were able to improvise some kind of medical treatment for their sick and wounded comrades. In the last week or two before liberation some prisoners noticed a slight improvement in the general treatment, but some record that some of the guards were 'nastier than ever'. Over the whole period of its existence the camp had a death toll of more than 40 percent of its strength. Perhaps in this camp more than in any other prisoners had good grounds for wondering whether they would survive until liberation came. As British forces approached Rangoon the Japanese attempted to transfer fit prisoners to Moulmein (by a forced march), but the rapidity of the British advance compelled them to release most of their prisoners while on the move. Thus on 25 April about half the prisoners in the Rangoon area were marched off towards Pegu, and two days later they were abandoned by their guards.

The last Japanese abandoned the Rangoon jail on the night of 28–29th April; leaving behind them a message informing the prisoners that they could regard themselves as free and saying that they hoped to meet again on the battlefield. Four days later units of the British Army marched into Rangoon, and liberated prisoners were sent by air or by hospital ship to Calcutta."

On the 11 May 1945 a radio reporter interviewed Cliff and Ozzie in Calcutta a few days after their arrival from Rangoon. The introduction to this interview begins: "Flight Lieutenant Cliff Emeny and Pilot Officer Eric Osboldstone tell their tough story with that offhand, stiff upper lip modesty of the British airmen and also with a certain Kiwi directness. They make a great team".

Emeny: I'll remember November 9 1944 for the rest of my life. Just after I'd had a go at an aircraft parked on an aerodrome, I was hit in both motors by ack-ack, then a fighter got on my tail; after several attacks, he set us on fire. I felt like the captain of a damaged tramp steamer being attacked by a destroyer. I'll always be thankful to the two Aussies who chased him off my tail and gave me a chance to crash-land. I had the laugh on the boys there. They'd always been joking about that little personal axe I carried everywhere. I couldn't get out of the cockpit when I landed, but I knocked out the side with that little axe, freed my trapped feet and dived straight into the mud. I was suffering badly from shock, but my Canadian navigator pulled me away from the burning Mosquito and helped me to a Burmese village. The Japs picked us up there next morning.

Osboldstone: When our troops were putting pressure on Mandalay, I was strafing railway traffic on the line leading into town and I was hit by 'ack-ack' on my starboard engine. I made the best of a crash-landing, but my navigator was killed. I'm sure the prayers of my people at home saved me. I knew I had a lot to live for as I was waiting to get home to be married. My fiancée was right there all the time. It wasn't long before the Japs picked me up. By the way Cliff, for a long time we were in solitary confinement, did the Japs put the heat on you too, to make you talk?

Emeny: Heat's hardly the word. They left me without food or water for four nights and three days, and then they gave

290

up and took us to Rangoon jail. I started off with a couple of months' solitary. You know how grim that was.

Osboldstone: You're not telling me a thing. The Japanese had started a reign of terror, treating us captured airmen as criminal prisoners. Those months in the cells without sunlight knocked us all around. Practically all of the boys contracted some skin disease or other. It was just like heaven when they moved us out into the compound in January.

Emeny: It was great to see the way the sun worked wonders with the fellows' skin after they had been shut up for so long. Sun and fresh air made all the difference to men who had been suffering from scabies, ulcers and other horrible skin diseases.

Osboldstone: The Japs didn't think us criminal airmen deserved medical attention, so we had to do our own doctoring.

Emeny: I don't know why you picked on me. I didn't know anything about doctoring, except what I had picked up on the Taranaki farm and in spells in hospital after various crashes. I just had to work by trial and error.

Osboldstone: There wasn't much error about it. More than one man owes his life to you. You used to keep written case histories as though you were a pukka doctor. It seems to the rest of us that you reached each man's stomach individually.

Emeny: I had to, there wasn't much food, as the Japs kept all the air crew on half rations. I had to learn what each man could digest. Food was one of the worst things about prison. Rice day after day with a few vegetables occasionally, and once a week a 100 of us would share what would be one family's small weekend meat ration at home.

Osboldstone: Lack of water was another problem. The Japs denied air crew the privilege of washing and shaving. The only way we could manage was by saving a little of our drinking water, and even that meant going for two or three weeks without a wash. That was another of the difficulties in the hospital. You seemed to manage all right with the advice and medicine that Indian doctor used to smuggle over the wall from the other compound.

Emeny: Yes, a lot of us would have died if it wasn't for the help a lot of the other prisoners gave us. They used to steal food from the Japs for us. They even gave us some of their own because they knew we were in such a bad way. Remember the time they smuggled in a 1 000 cigars in the middle of some rice? Remember how we used to pounce on every newcomer and then pass the latest news from man to man in sign language? We had a pretty good idea all the time of just how the war was going. But the few things that really kept our pecker up were the secret prayer meetings and concerts.

Osboldstone: Yes, I think everyone of us got a lot of comfort out of those prayer meetings, yet the Japs never suspected. We used to escape notice by sitting round the water trough facing different directions and apparently talking no notice of each other.

Emeny: Well, we couldn't afford to be caught out otherwise the guards would have made our lives hell by kicking and punching us. You know that well enough.

Osboldstone: The nights when the Japs got their monthly saki rations were the worst. We had to be especially careful when they came round to taunt us, otherwise we were in for a beating. We all had our share of these beatings. Remember when the Jap doctor beat up Wing Commander Bill Hudson, the Aussie in charge of our compound?

Emeny: Yes. All because the wingco asked that two men suffering from beri-beri, malnutrition and dysentery be sent to hospital. The Jap doctor claimed the wingco wasn't qualified to tell whether a man was sick, so he beat him up. But both those patients were dead 10 days later.

Well, it's hard to realise that it is over now. Remember how strangely quiet it was the night the Japs pulled out. It's almost like a fairy tale, the way the wingco and the Indian doctor crept

292

out to the front gate and found it open, with a note from the Japs saying we were free and they hoped we'd meet again on the battlefield, as they put it. I'd like to meet them on the battlefield somewhere all right. But looking back on it, it does seem a bit fantastic, the way the wingco put his foot outside the gate, just to test, to taste freedom, and then came back and locked us all in. He certainly did a good job the way he managed us both when the Japs were there and when he became uncrowned king of Rangoon from the time they left until the arrival of the 15th Indian Corps. It was easy to see why he rose from sergeant to wing commander in the record time of two years and one month."

Osboldstone: Yes, he pulled a gigantic bluff when he took control of the fortress the Japs had raised in Burma, and set them to the task of protecting the city. It is not every wing commander who has the experience of hearing a major general say to him, 'I surrender to you'.

Emeny: He didn't waste any time preparing Rangoon for the coming of our troops. The morning after the Japs had gone he advised our headquarters the position by painting on the roof the sign: 'Japs Gone, British here'.

Osboldstone: That's nothing to the rude but urgent sign he put there the next day.

Emeny: And he didn't waste any time making me station commander of the aerodrome.

Osboldstone: You did a pretty good job there Cliff, getting the strip ready for our aircraft to land.

Emeny: Oh, I only supervised. You fellows did all the hard work.

Osboldstone: Oh, yes, maybe, but we'd something to work for as the rest of the boys had been evacuated by hospital ship. The eight of us remaining were flown out by the first aircraft to land.

Emeny: And isn't it good to see civilisation again? I think the best night of the lot was the one back on my old squadron, when the boys gave me the good news that I'd destroyed the Jap I attacked six months ago. I was too busy too look back then.

Osboldstone: That makes another for your bag. You destroyed a couple of Jerries when you were a gunner early in the war. Your folks will be glad to see you after all these years, and they will be surprised to find you in such good condition after a spell in a Jap prison.

Emeny: Yes, it's all over now. Here's hoping it won't be long before the rest of the boys in Japanese jails are free like us.

Wing Commander Lionel Hudson

Lionel (Bill) Hudson returned home to Australia and took up his former occupation of journalist.

In 1988 his book *The Rats of Rangoon* was published. The flyleaf reads 'the inside story of the fiasco that took place at the end of the war in Burma'. Hudson confirms Cliff's account of what happened in the four days when the Japanese evacuated Rangoon and before the city was recaptured by Mountbatten. He also confirms Cliff's 'medical work' and together with Flying Officer Eric Osboldstone the part they played in retaking the airfield, restoring it and making it operational before the 'invasion' forces arrived.

In December 1988 Emeny's wife Joan received a copy of Lionel Hudson's book with a note that read:

"Joan,

 Please stick this on the title page of your copy of "The Rats" before Cliff rips it up.

What I neglect to say on page 187 is that I recommended in my report that the three who went out to Mingaladon airfield should be awarded gongs!! They deserved it. However, it seems that the brass thought it better to gloss over what happened in Rangoon before the British forces "captured" it.

Lionel Hudson

Sydney, June 29, 1988."

Staff Sergeant Karnig Thomasian USAAF

Karnig Thomasian was a member of the crew of a B-29 tragically brought down over Rangoon on 14 December 1944. He was 18 when he enlisted in the United States Air Force and celebrated his 21st birthday on 8 April 1945 in the Rangoon prison. When he was released he was taken by hospital ship to Calcutta and then home to the United States by plane.

After his discharge from the Air Force he attended art school in New York. After graduation he worked in advertising agencies and a graphic design firm for the next 44 years. He joined the ex-Prisoner of War Association in 1989. When he retired from business at 71 in 1995 he devoted his full attention to help ex-POW veterans to get their disability compensations.

It was Karnig who was with Cliff on the evening of 29 April 1945. They were sitting on the compound steps looking out over the walls of the prison to the city beyond when they suddenly realised there were no guards around. "From that moment," wrote Karnig, "events unfolded quickly and dramatically."

In one of his letters to myself, Tom Woods, he wrote:

"Cliff was an amazing source of logic and pulse of history. He was an egghead to be sure but a humorous one. When he and Joan visited us for a couple of weeks they were loaded with their herbal pills expounding on all the wrong things we ate, and all the wrong pills we took, and of course our diet. They themselves looked the pictures of health but Cliff always looked gaunt especially in his last years. When we visited them they were in the pink and took us all over the North Island and then gave us a wonderful itinerary to follow with a bus tour of the South Island. Joan is such a bundle of positive bubbles. She is an amazing lady with so many wonderful gifts. We met the entire family and kids and their spouses and their children. Quite overwhelming to be sure."

Twice he wrote with encouragement to write Cliff's story: "The more people know accurate history the less others can distort it like the Japs themselves and other opinionated writers."

He himself has recently written and had published a book entitled *Then There Were Six* – the story of the Rangoon disaster when only one of 11 B-29s returned to its home base. Eighteen men were killed and the Japanese captured 29. He tells the story of the suffering of these 29 and how after the war the American authorities tracked down 23 Japanese army officers and prison guards who had beaten and murdered American POWs. When captured they were put on trial and several paid for their crimes against humanity with their own lives.

Joan McDonell

Cliff makes no secret of the fact that during his war service he met several young women whom he was attracted to and they to him. He was an excellent dancer, a good mixer and looked the part in his uniform so it is not surprising that women found him attractive. Although he obviously enjoyed the company and companionship of girls he wouldn't allow himself to become emotionally involved.

The one he was to give his heart to was the 16-year-old girl he had met before going overseas when he had just turned 20. He first met her at a dance arranged by the Women's Division for servicemen at Levin. He met her family at dinner the following Sunday, and saw and spoke to her briefly on the train between Palmerston North and Levin when he was returning to Ohakea from his final leave. They exchanged a few letters in 1940–41and then nothing more for nearly four years.

He returned to New Zealand in July 1945 and after a period of leave worked at Air Headquarters, Wellington advising on the treatment of Air Force prisoners repatriated from Japanese prisoner of war camps.

He and Joan met soon after he returned to New Zealand. Joan's mother had read the following newspaper column in one of the Wellington daily papers and suggested to her that she get in touch with the young airman she had met and danced with five years ago. The article the mother and daughter read in the newspaper had been written by the widow of the Australian Wing Commander (CO No. 45 Squadron) killed in the air accident at Ranchi. She was an Australian war correspondent and visited Cliff when he was in hospital in Calcutta and they went off to spend five days together in Calcutta. The article reads:

"Missing Pilot Lives To Tell Of Good Luck
Te Kiri airman found in Rangoon jail.

R.N.Z.A.F Official News Service.

Eastern Air Command, May 9.

Flight Lieutenant Clifford S Emeny, Te Kiri, who was posted missing, believed killed, in November last year, was found alive and well in a jail at Rangoon and has now reached Calcutta.

Flight Lieutenant Emeny must have had one of the most remarkable careers of any man in the Royal New Zealand Air Force. When he was shot down near Meiktila by Japanese fighters last November he astounded the other crews of his squadron by calmly giving a running broadcast description as his Mosquito crashed.

The aircraft hit the ground with such force that it burst into flames immediately and Flight Lieutenant Emeny and his Canadian navigator were both reported missing believed killed, for it was considered most improbable that they could have survived.

Escape from Aircraft

Flight Lieutenant Emeny states that he owes his life to his 'little tomahawk,' which he always carried with him and which was long regarded as a squadron joke. He cut himself out of the aircraft and the navigator dragged him clear.

The two men crawled to a village, where the Burmese robbed them, and later Burmese police arrived and held them till the Japanese came. Flight Lieutenant Emeny and his navigator were kept standing for three days and four nights without food to try to make them divulge information, but the Japanese finally gave up and moved them to Rangoon.

Though he had the skin torn off his leg and suffered burns about the head in the crash, the Japanese did not give Flight Lieutenant Emeny any treatment. He was able to use his own first aid kit. In the Rangoon jail he took charge of the airmen's hospital, though the Japanese provided no facilities.

Strict Doctor

By his cast-iron discipline Flight Lieutenant Emeny forced his patients to maintain the will to live. During his term as doctor he treated 41 patients only three of whom died, in spite of complete Japanese indifference toward the sick. He carefully kept a diary with the case histories of every patient.

'I was thankful for the time I spent in hospital after several 'prangs'.

Flight Lieutenant Emeny stated in an interview. 'The knowledge I gained there proved invaluable while in prison. Providing adequate nutrition was my main difficulty. The diet mainly consisted of rice with a few vegetables. Once a week we got as much meat as the normal New Zealand family eats in the weekend. That had to be shared among 100 men.

'Later the Japanese gave us our money back and we pooled it to buy food. The rest of the boys gave me half of it, and I managed to buy enough eggs to keep the worst cases of malnutrition alive.'

Flight Lieutenant Emeny has been overseas since March 1940 and has refused three opportunities of returning home. He did his first tour as an air gunner in Defiants and scored two kills. Later he became a radar observer and finally he was trained as pilot."

After reading the article and thinking about it for some time Joan wrote to Cliff's parents. A few days later she met with them in Wellington. Cliff's mother encouraged her son to "get on the phone and ring that nice girl". Joan received a phone call from Cliff at Army Headquarters, Trentham and they arranged to meet at the Wellington Railway Station.

There is no doubt, reading from his diary, that he was soon head over heels in love. After two and a half years service, Corporal Joan McDonell (816438) received her discharge from the Women's Auxiliary Army Corps on 5 October 1945 and in the same month became engaged to Flight Lieutenant Cliff Emeny.

They were married on 6 March 1946 in the Levin Presbyterian Church and spent a wonderful month honeymooning in the South Island. On the return from his honeymoon the first thing he did was to have removed the tonsils that had plagued him overseas. Significantly he was still not strong enough for a general anaesthetic and so had his tonsils removed by a 'local'.

Joan shared 54 years of her life with Cliff and these 54 years provide material enough for another book. It wasn't always easy sharing her life with such a single-minded, resolute and indomitable person who was a character often larger than life and who invariably became the centre of attention, no matter the company. Nowhere is this better illustrated than at the 25th anniversary of the Battle of Britain. The following is from a London newspaper of that time. Unfortunately the name of paper is not included.

"Friday, September 24, 1965

CITY PAYS HOMAGE TO THE FEW IN SPLENDID FASHION

....After the pomp and ceremony of the reception itself, with a guest list that included Mr. Harold Wilson, Mr. Edward Heath, Gp.Capt. Douglas Bader and no less than seven Marshals of the Royal Air Force, the 1500 men and women settled down to enjoy themselves....... the Lord Mayor, Sir James Miller said before leaving the reception: 'It's been a wonderful evening, and we've enjoyed it tremendously.'

A very colourful character appeared at the reception. He was Cliff S. Emeny.

Cliff came to this country as one of the first fifty volunteers from New Zealand for the R.A.F. in the war. Those first fifty came here for training but within days they were in the air.

Cliff Emeny was then nineteen years of age and is one of the three survivors of the first fifty.

He was late in joining the New Zealand party to come to this country for the celebrations. His invitation went astray and he

Friday, September 24, 1965

CITY PAYS HOMAGE TO THE FEW IN SPLENDID FASHION

THE Guildhall reception celebrating the 25th anniversary of the Battle of Britain was the glittering, unconventional affair that was confidently forecast by its organisers.

After the pomp and ceremony of the reception itself, with a guest list which included Mr. Harold Wilson, Mr. Edward Heath, Gp. Capt. Douglas Bader and no less than seven Marshals of the Royal Air Force, the 1500 men and women settled down to enjoy themselves.

The fortissimo playing of the RAF Band and Orchestra was turned into a quiet background by the animated conversation of a mixture of "scramble eggs" and SAC's.

In the livery suite, the dancing went on at a frenzied pace, and down in the Crypt songs were sung which became pro-

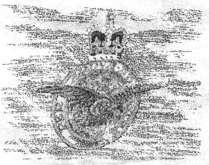

consumed, and 500 bottles of wine were downed in the Crypt.

Surprisingly, only 200 bottles of beer passed through the lips of the notoriously bitter-loving RAF officers and men.

As the Lord Mayor, Sir James Miller, said before leaving the reception: "It's been a wonderful evening, and we've enjoyed it tremendously."

A very colourful character appeared at the reception. He was Cliff S. Emeny.

Cliff came to this country as one of the first fifty volunteers from New Zealand for the R.A.F.

in the war. Those first fifty came here for training but within days they were in the air.

Cliff Emeny was then eighteen years of age and is one of the three survivors of the first fifty.

He was late in joining the New Zealand party to come to this country for the celebrations. His invitation went astray and he never heard about it until around ten days after the party had left for London.

He missed the plane in consequence but Cliff Emeny was not to be denied the trip. He

telephoned from New Zealand to the R.A.F. and to the Town Clerk's Office in the City of London.

That cost him ten pounds but "my oh my", said Cliff, "wasn't it worth it?

"I had a wonderful time and it was marvellous to meet my old war time friends again".

Cliff Emeny joined 264 Squadron at Hornchurch in 1940 as air gunner then radio observer in Beaufighters; then pilot in Mosquito fighter bombers operating over Burma.

There he was shot down and captured by the Japanese. He became doctor by election of the airmen prisoners and eventually broke out and organised the capture of Rangoon with Indian and Burmese troops.

Cliff has been a farmer and contractor and is an executive member of the Constitutional

MAURICE RUBECK took the pictures

never heard about it until around ten days after the party had left for London.

He missed the plane in consequence but Cliff Emeny was not to be denied the trip. He telephoned from New Zealand to the R.A.F. and to the Town Clerk's Office in the City of London.

That cost him ten pounds but ' my oh my' said Cliff, 'wasn't it worth it? I had a wonderful time and it was marvellous to meet my old war time friends again'.

Cliff Emeny joined 264 Squadron at Hornchurch in 1940 as an air gunner then radio observer in Beaufighters; then pilot in Mosquito fighter-bombers operating over Burma.

There he was shot down and captured by the Japanese. He became doctor by election of the airmen prisoners and eventually broke out and organised the capture of Rangoon with Indian and Burmese troops."

Cliff had been a farmer and contractor and is an executive member of the Constitutional Society and Free Enterprise Society of New Zealand. He was in fact the leader of the free trade movement in New Zealand and he conducted his campaigning with no holds barred. If anyone deserved the trip it was Cliff Emeny.

To keep faith with the vow he had made in prison to 'devote his life to studying the causes of war, and defence of human freedom on earth' Cliff became more and more involved in politics. Soon after he and Joan were married and were living in Hamilton he joined a Sunday evening group, which met weekly to discuss the theory of politics and government and from the age of 40, theory turned to practice and he founded The Constitutional Society and Free Enterprise Society of New Zealand. Constitutionally Cliff was concerned with implementing 'binding referenda' so all citizens could be involved in the decision-making processes of Government. It would also 'help to keep politicians honest between elections'. The second plank,

301

'Free Enterprise' covered Free Trade and doing away with as much unnecessary bureaucratic interference as possible. Joan gave her whole-hearted support to all her husband's political efforts. He was a prolific letter writer to the press. Many of his letters were controversial and caused much public comment and debate. Joan rode out each public squall with him.

Besides raising a family of six children Joan was Cliff's partner in two major business ventures. The first was skin care products. This was a successful financial partnership with frequent overseas trips and a good income. It was also beneficial in the treatment of Cliff's skin.

After 10 years in skin care products they discovered the benefits of herbal medicines, which improved Cliff's health immeasurably. Their interest in herbal medicine developed into a natural health care business, which Joan is still involved in to this day.

Cliff died on 4 October 2000. Before his death he had given careful and deliberate thought to the order and arrangement of his service and had personally written the following, which was read by his son-in-law Malcolm Johnstone.

"I would like you to know that I greatly appreciate your coming to this service today. Showing such thoughtful support to Joan and my family. In our twenty plus years living in New Plymouth we have enjoyed meeting many kindly, thoughtful and sociable people...

Here are a few groups I especially would like to thank for the company and pleasure they have given us. Members of the Brevet Club, who did me the much appreciated- honour of making me their patron in recent years. The Air Force Association, members of the Prisoner of War Association, the Reverend Tom Woods, for the thoughtful ideals he conveyed through his services at St Andrews, and the friendly sociable companionship enjoyed from other members of St Andrews' congregation...

Maybe there are here today some of those people who phoned me, about my many letters to the editor over the years. I did appreciate their interest in such matters. Such writings are just part of keeping my WWII Japanese Prisoner of War Solemn vow. 'To devote my life to studying the causes of war, and defence of human freedom on Earth.'

Regretfully I must leave this task unfinished...

Our campaigning has caused Parliament to legislate for a citizens initiated referendum. New Zealand is the only nation in the English speaking world to adopt such legislation. But our Parliament has deprived New Zealand voters of its effectiveness by insisting such referendums are only 'indicative' and not binding on any government to implement.

All New Zealand voters have to do now is to raise a big enough public petition to make Parliament change the word 'indicative' in the citizens initiated referendum bill to 'binding'.

For my last message to my beloved family, I must take you back to the horrors and suffering of being a prisoner of war of the Japanese in Burma, 1944–45. Thrown into an empty cell, severely beaten, bruised and shocked from extremely brutal interrogation, and not even provided with anything to collect essential food and water for survival. The only way to preserve one's will to live was to create a mental vision of a better world – a world worth the struggle to survive. The vision I kept constantly before me was that of being part of a free and happy family and of being married to a sweet, loving young woman and the joy of our young children around us.

Not only was I lucky enough to survive imprisonment, but even far luckier to renew my brief early wartime experience with Joan and her family. Our marriage in March 1946, and our six wonderful children since, has fulfilled that life saving vision of Burma days, to perfection. Sure, there were occasional ups and downs during the last 55 years, but essentially you, my family have always been my greatest joy in life...

When you lived at home, they were wonderful years for Joan and I. When my political battles so often ended in defeat, there was always my family to return to and immerse myself in for recuperation from the struggle for genuine democracy...

Finally, to Joan. Words cannot adequately describe how deeply I appreciated your steadfast, and uncomplaining support for those several times during our married life, that I have felt compelled to sally forth and do battle for the cause of personal freedom and genuine democracy in our beloved country. Using up the family's scarce resources, and often to start from scratch all over again, to reproduce our essential family economic security. I have a feeling that few other women would have been so willingly supportive of my idealistic obsessions as you have been. Though I may rarely have said so, in the words of Roger Whittaker 'I have loved you dearly, more dearly than spoken word can tell'.

I thank you again for all being here today, and for your patience in listening to my last words. Now time has come to leave you all. With best wishes to you all, I contentedly bid you fond farewell.

(Cliff Emeny)

In 1999 Diana Thomasian (wife of Sergeant Karnig Thomasian) wrote an article about the ongoing trauma suffered by the ex-POW and by those closest to him. Cliff never thought of himself as a 'hero' – simply as someone who did his duty and had the good luck to survive the horrors of the war he had been caught up in. If there is another hero in the Emeny family it is without doubt the one of whom Diana Thomasian writes (Joan Emeny), because in their own way the wives of these men were also heroes. Without fully understanding the impact the past was having on their husbands, the wives faced having to deal with the consequences – often daily. Joan, with her indomitable, spirit was one of these women. So let us salute her and all the many, many other POW wives.

"The Battlefront at home for POW wives

'I regret to inform you...'

Those five words started the hearts of hundreds of thousands of women racing throughout the war years. Suddenly from just being a wife, they were POW wives ... worse, they became widows, robbed of their youth, health, family and home. Their men were reported MIA (missing in action) and then POW (prisoner of war).

They did not carry guns; they did not go to war. But these women were just as much an integral part of the war effort as any soldier. They bore the children, and in many instances cared for the extended family. They were tested again and again on their values of loyalty, faith and trust.

What compelled these ex-POW spouses to keep silent about their suffering and sacrifices for decades? Was it the supreme calling of love and the choice to accept the traumas of war on their men, and keep them from suffering any more?

Imagine, if you can, the anguish when letters were returned from strange places, and living daily with the infinitely unknown. Were their husbands or sweethearts, maimed, tortured, starving? Questions, always questions. The news 54 years ago during World War II was not as quick and timely as it was during the Korean, Vietnam and the Gulf wars. Then, the newsreels were a week old at the movies, and the radio commentators were not always up to date.

Among the families of MIA/POWs was an invisible network of communication. The common denominator of anxiety and trauma brought families and people together in neighborhoods, towns, schools, churches, even over a cup of coffee. It was a time for extension of compassion to anyone and everyone.

Then ... seven words: 'It is my pleasure to inform you ...' Those ex-POW wives who were fortunate looked forward with unbelievable joy to seeing their men come home. The widows were already trying to cope with the hand that the cards of war had dealt them. Many evidenced damage to their own psyches, trying not to be haunted by the mental visions of torture and starvation and the finality of death of their loved ones.

Unexplained and not understood, the marks of imprisonment started to emerge into everyday life... the surprise rage, the hurtful outbursts, lack of tolerance and patience, prolonged moments of silence and withdrawal. Then, the unexpected crying, especially at war movies or war documentaries on television. Nightmares, sweats, moans and groans in sleep, tremors – all these were just the beginning,

The wives were now the chauffeurs for countless visits to medical doctors for every ailment in the book: malaria, diarrhoea, limitation of movements, prosthesis, diabetes, frostbite – just about everything. Medicine was administered, favorite foods were prepared, clothes were pressed, shoes were polished and hair was brushed.

Many women will say that it was not until her husband died that she was able to understand his behavior through the discovery of hidden diaries, photos and letters. Then the bitterness and resentment, the fright of her spouse came to light. The family finally understood. For some, years of therapy became a part of life.

Yet though all this trauma, the ex-POW came home, got a job, and reared, sheltered, and protected his family, But the mark and scarring of imprisonment was always present, and the ex-POW wife shared it.

Reunions of the different, military disciplines became a part of yearly vacations. The wives gladly went with their husbands, listened to the same stories and memories over and over again.

The reunions served as a catharsis for the wives as well as the husbands. They listened and shared their experiences, were healed in many respects by the common stories of other wives. As it is with any close-knit group, the death of one of the buddies was felt by all.

As this last Veterans Day of the century approaches, let it be said that one of the many unsung heroines, the ex-POW wife, should be saluted or given a quiet prayer of gratitude.

Omnia amor vincit. Love conquers all."

APPENDIX

Record of Service and Time Chart

(From Service Records and other sources). Unfortunately his log book was lost when he and his wife Joan moved from Stratford to New Plymouth.

EMENY Clifford Stanley (NZ 40204)

Born:	11 January 1920 (Wellington).
Jan 1933	Left School.
1937	Queen Alexandra's Mounted Rifles.
1938	Army School 'Special Reserve Course'.
1939	Worked passage to England on *Port Caroline*.
1939	Returned to New Zealand on *Wellington Star*.
15.1.40	Posted Ground Training School Levin.
9.2.40	Air Observers School Ohakea.
23.3.40	Embarked in SS *Akaroa*.
9.5.40	Uxbridge pending posting.
3.6.40	264 Squadron (Defiants) Duxford.
26.7.40	Awarded air gunner's 'Wing'.
27.7.40	Promoted to Sergeant.
22.8 40	Squadron moved to Hornchurch.
24.8.40	Squadron lost four aircraft in air and two on ground. The CO and his gunner were killed in this action.
26.8.40	Four more aircraft destroyed.
28.8.40	Four aircraft destroyed and three badly damaged.
28.2.40	Remainder of squadron withdrawn to Kirten-on-Lindsey to resume night fighter patrols.
14.2.41	Posted to 255 Squadron (Defiants).

26.6.41	Posted to 409, a Canadian Defiant squadron.
20.8.41	Squadron operational and soon after began conversion to Beaufighters.
10.11.41	Remustered as and Air Observer (Radar).
29.11.41	Commissioned as Pilot Officer.
Jan 1942	Accepted for pilot training.
10.1.42	Posted to No. 13 Initial Training Wing, Torquay. Then to No. 22EFTS, Cambridge for grading course.
Late May	1942 Left for Canada – Empire Air Training Scheme
1.10.42	Promoted Flying Officer
24.12.42	Awarded pilot's 'Wings'.
3.2.43	Embarked Halifax to return to England.
30.4.43	Posted to No. 60 OTU, Grantham for conversion on to Blenheims. Then posted to High Ercall for night intruder course on Mosquito.
18.11.43	Posted to Burma.
29.11.43	Promoted to Flight Lieutenant.
Late Dec 43	Arrived in India.
5.1.44	Joined 27 Squadron at Agartala.
Mar 1944	Transferred 45 Squadron.
April 1944	45 Squadron equipped with Vengeance dive bombers moved to Bangalore to convert to Mosquitos (Emeny joined Squadron at Bangalore).
Sept 1944	Squadron became operational based at Itshar in Burma.
9.11.44	Emeny led a flight of six Mosquitos in a dawn raid on Japanese airfield Meiktila and was shot down. Both Emeny and his navigator Johnny Yanoto survived but were captured by the Japanese and taken 150 miles to the infamous Rangoon prison.

28.4.45	Prisoners took over control of prison when Japs pulled out of Rangoon. Emeny part of first patrol that ventured out of prison. A day later led a party north that took over Mingaladon Airfield.
3.5.45	Landing of British forces in Rangoon.
8.5.45	Emeny reached Calcutta by plane. He weighed six stone 10 pounds.
8.5.45	VE DAY (Victory in Europe).
July 1945	Returned to New Zealand.
14:8:45	VJ Day (Victory in Japan).

New Zealand Post Office Telegrams

"11th May, 1945

Address: F/Lt C.S.Emeny

       Te Kiri

       Taranaki

Further to the information fowarded to you by this Department per telephone, concerning your son, Flight Lieutenant Clifford Stanely Emeny, I have to confirm that information received from the Base Personnel Office, Bombay, states that he has now been liberated from Rangoon, and is now safe and well in Calcutta, India.

On behalf of the Air Board I desire to express my sincere wishes, that this good news will to some extent serve to relieve your natural anxiety, and I am to assure you that immediately any further information is available you will be advised without delay.

Yours faithfully,

T.A.Barrow

Air Secretary"

New Zealand Posts Office Telegraphs

"Address: F/Lt C.S.Emeny
        Te Kiri
        Taranaki

The following message from his Majesty the King has been received for transmission to you.

Message begins. The Queen and I bid you a very warm welcome home. Through all the great trials and sufferings which you have undergone at the hands of the Japanese, you have been constantly in our thoughts. We know from reports we have already received how heavy these sufferings have been. We know also that these have been endured by you with the greatest courage. We mourn with you the death of so many of your gallant comrades. With all our hearts we hope that your return from captivity will bring you and your families a full measure of happiness, which you may long enjoy together.

F. Jones,
Minister of Defence"

BIBLIOGRAPHY

Published Books

Bickers, Richard Townsend. *The Battle of Britain*.
London, UK: Salamander Books, 1990.

Bingham, Victor. *The Bristol Beaufighter*.
Shrewsbury, UK: Airlife Publishing, 1994.

Bowyer, Chaz. *Mosquitos at War*.
Hersham, UK: Ian Allan, 1977.

History of the 20th Century. Introduction by Alan Bulloch.
London, UK: Octopus Books: Phoebus, 1976.

Delve, Ken. *The Source Book of the R.A.F.*
Shrewsbury, UK: Airlife Publishing, 1994.

Green, William. *Famous Fighters of the Second World War*. Illustrated by
G.W. Henmann.
London, UK: McDonald, 1957.

Gunston, Bill. *Night Fighters: A Development and Combat History*. Foreword by
John Cunningham.
Cambridge, UK: Patrick Stephens, 1976.

Hudson, Lionel. *The Rats of Rangoon*.
Barnsley, UK: Leo Cooper, 1987.

Hutching, Megan, ed. *Inside Stories: New Zealand POWs Remember*.
Auckland, NZ: Harper Collins in association with The History Group, Ministry of
Culture and Heritage, 2002.

Janes: All the World's Aircraft.
London, UK: Harper Collins, 1994.

Jefford, C.G. *R.A.F. Squadrons*.
Shrewsbury, UK: Airlife Publishing, 1988.

McGill, David. *POW: The Untold Stories of New Zealanders as Prisoners of War*.
Lower Hutt, NZ: Mills Publications, 1987.

Wright, Michael, Bob Hook, eds. *The World at Arms: The Readers Digest
Illustrated History of World War 2*.
London, UK: Readers Digest Association, 1989.

Willis, G.R.T. *No Hero Just a Survivor*.
Huddersfield, UK: Robert Willis Associates, 1999.

Wynn, Kenneth G. *The Clasp For 'The Few'*.
    Auckland, NZ: Kenneth G. Wynn, 1981.

Ziegler, Philip. *Mountbatten*.
    London, UK: Collins, 1985.

Private Papers

Heaven, Sylvia
Osboldstone, Eric
Thomasian, Karnig and Diana

Royal New Zealand Air Force. Officer's Record of Service:
    CLIFFORD STANLEY EMENY 40204
    15.1.40 – 9.5.46

Index

C

Casablanca Conference 105
Chiang Kai-shek 106
Churchill 48, 106
Cliff Emeny's war service 283
Communism 282
Communist 280

D

Dakota (DC3) 159, 177, 180, 183, 189, 226, 264, 265, 267, 274
DC 4s 106
Defiant 22, 28, 30, 33, 43, 51, 54, 56, 57, 74, 120
De Havilland 181
De Havilland Mosquito 84
de Beaux, Wing Commander/Group Captain Paul 54, 96
Dornier bomber 22, 43
Dowding, Air Marshall Hugh 49, 154
Dunkirk 28

E

Edwards, Flying Officer Craig Howard 217, 284
Edwards, Squadron Leader 180
El Alamein 102
Emeny, Clifford Stanley (NZ 40204) 308
Emeny, Joan (nee McDonell) 296

F

Fighter Night Plan 44
Fleet Air Arm 54

H

Heinkel bomber 30
Hill, Wing Commander 224
Hitler 48
Hornchurch 28
Hudson, Wing Commander Bill 226
Hudson, Wing Commander Lionel 294
Hurricane fighter 32, 46, 74, 119, 218

I

Imphal
Imphala 159, 178
India/ Burma 283

P

P38 Lightning 174
Park, Air Vice Marshall Sir Keith 46, 49, 154
Peterson, Wing Commander 52, 53, 66
Po-2 Soviet biplane 113
Poles 42
Port Caroline 4, 6
POW wives 305

Q

Queen Alexandra's Mounted Rifles Territorial Force 1

R

Radar Operators 57
RAF High Ercall 83
Rangoon 126, 200, 203, 222
Rangoon Prison 201, 212
Rommel 102

S

Skinner, Gene 74
Spitfire 22, 33, 46, 49, 74, 85, 106, 107, 110
Stearman 70
Stilwell, General 106

T

Thazi 198
Thomasian, Staff Sergeant Karnig USAAF 295
Thunderbolt fighter 218
Tiger Moth 63, 70
Typhoon 82

U

Uxbridge 21

V

Very pistol 43
Vickers Vilderbeeste 16
Victoria Cross 119
Victory 281

W

WAAC 102
WAAF 42, 94, 95, 97
Wellingtons 45
Wellington Star 10, 11, 12, 14, 28, 77
White, Group Captain Tiny 73, 74

Y

Yanoto, Johnny 88, 273, 283

Z

Zombie 188